On Cloud Nine®

Nanci Bell
and
Kimberly Tuley

Visualizing and Verbalizing for Math

Illustrations by Phyllis Lindamood.
Editing by Michael Sweeney and Daniel Scott.

Gander Publishing
412 Higuera Street, Suite 200
San Luis Obispo, CA 93401
805-541-5523 • 800-554-1819

13   12   11   10   4   5   6   7

4-100817

ISBN 0-945-856-07-5
ISBN 978-0-945-856-07-8

If I can't picture it
I can't understand it.

Albert Einstein

*This book is for all the eyes looking at us who want to learn
math better...and who just may be the next Copernicus,
Einstein, or Hawking.*

Preface

Mathematics is a language that stretches across all cultures, all ages, all genders. It is a universal tool for problem solving and discovery. We wrote this book with the faces of many children and adults looming large in our hearts and minds. The eyes of the children trying to learn were in our imaginations, and as we wrote, a child came alive—a little girl named Tory that you'll soon know. Tory represents all of our students, young and old alike, as she extends herself one more time to learn something that has been painful for her.

It is our hope that the words in this book create enough imagery for you to be able to help children. Even one.

Nanci Bell and Kimberly Tuley
September 1997

The **Contents**

The Concept

Terror in the One-Room School

It was another sunny California day as I gazed out of my one-room school—just a day to be a fourth grader with the other sixteen children in the school who represented kindergarten through eighth grade. Alone in my grade, I unsuspectingly thought this was going to be a day like any other. I was wrong.

Most days in our little school consisted of me working independently in my workbooks—reading, spelling, math. And I was usually through them early and then got to help some of the other children. Life was good. There was the green chalkboard at the front of the room, the alphabet across the top, the windows on the entire left side of the room where, if one dared, one could stare at the mountains, and the large swing set with the heavy chains waiting for action, and there were desks with lids that squeaked and banged throughout the day as they opened and closed. There was also the teacher's desk which seemed to have a life of its own, sometimes residing at the back, sometimes the front right, or sometimes the front left. When I wasn't in this comfortable setting, I was outside in clean air, playing in the fields surrounding the school, roller skating on the outdoor concrete basketball court, or swinging as high as I could with my best friend, Karen. Yes, day in and day out, life was good—well, mostly good. There were the days the county nurse came and announced your weight in front of the whole class—but that's another story. For the most part, the days rolled by comfortably.

Today, as usual, I came in from recess, cheeks rosy from another swinging session. Skipping to my desk—second from the front on the right—I sat down. Stealing a look out the window, I could see that the chains on my swing were still moving, to and fro just a little. I thought that recess definitely seemed to be getting shorter and shorter.

The class was quieting down, most in their seats, the desks starting to talk. I turned my gaze from the window—it was math time. Desk top squeaking as it opened, I looked inside at the array of materials that represented my academic

3

life and grabbed my math workbook and a pencil. Reluctantly, I shut my desk and opened to the page on "Long Division." My stomach started to feel sort of queasy. Yesterday's page hadn't made much sense to me; it was all about some sort of squiggle like a half moon with a line on top that had numbers outside the moon and numbers under the line, and I was supposed to solve the problem by putting numbers on top of the line.

I read the directions and stared at the example. Nope, nothing there to help me do the pages of problems. I tried again, and still it didn't make any sense to me. What was I supposed to do with all these problems? I just couldn't seem to figure it out. I'd already done the pages on multiplication with ease, why couldn't I get this? I had done simple division, but this new diagram just didn't match anything I knew about previously, nor anything I was apparently going to be able to solve myself. But now what to do? The teacher, Mrs. Brown, was busy with the first grade children, and there was no one else in my grade to ask.

I turned around and asked handsome Damon, sitting behind me, for help. He looked at the problems quickly and said, "Oh, that's easy Nanci, just divide the blah-blah into the blah-blah, and that'll give you blah-blah-blah. And sometimes you may have a remainder, and just put that up there."

Thanking him, I turned around in my seat and stared again at the page of problems. Nothing. Nothing he said made sense to me. How did he know how to do these and I didn't? Yes, he was in fifth grade, but still, why could he understand this and I was lost? What should I do now? Mrs. Brown? Where was she?

Looking around the room, I saw her break from the first and second graders, so I raised my hand. This would solve it, surely. I never ever had to ask her for help with anything. This would fix the problem. She could explain it to me, and I'd have an appetite for lunch in about an hour. Lunch, now that was a pleasant thought, maybe this day was going to be all right after all.

Here she came. Medium length straight black hair, pretty, Mrs. Brown ran a very tight ship in this class; no one crossed her. I myself was always a little reluctant to raise my hand. And, if all that wasn't bad enough, she was the mother of my best friend—and handsome Damon.

"What is it, Nanci? Do you need help?"

"Uh. Yes. I…I…don't understand this page of problems in my math."

She leaned over and looked at the page of division problems and said, "Oh, division. You know about that. I corrected some of the simple division problems further back in your workbook. You did fine. Division is just like multiplication, only it is subtraction."

Subtraction! Addition! That had been multiplication and this was division. What was wrong with Mrs. Brown? Maybe she was not seeing the page well enough. Bad light or something. "No, this isn't subtraction, Mrs. Brown. This is division."

Staring at me, with sort of a funny look on her face, she said, "I know this is division. But it is like subtraction. You are dividing this number here into blah-blah, and then multiplying the two numbers, and then putting that number under this number, and subtracting the two. Make sure you put the number over the second number in the line up here, not the first. Do you understand? Remember, subtract the two numbers and if you have a remainder like it shows in this diagram, then write that with an R in front of it. Do you understand? Now, do the pages. I have to go check some work. Just go ahead and finish these two pages and turn your workbook in, then you can go to the supply closet and get a new reading series…I see you finished the fifth grade books yesterday."

Heart thudding, I heard a small voice coming from me say, "Okay."

She left. I saw her clicking her way up the row of desks.

I stared at the page. I was alone in the world. Damon couldn't help. Not even Mrs. Brown could help. What was I to do now?

Still staring at the page, I finally decided to try again. Let's see, the number out here gets subtracted, no multiplied, no subtracted first. But which numbers are multiplying, and why do you multiply and subtract if this is dividing? If I don't get this I may have to stay in at lunch, and that means missing out on that Ding Dong I traded Karen for at recess. I have to get this.

I stared at the page, but soon it miraculously turned into the chains on the swings as I found myself looking out the window; and then a shadow appeared at my desk. Looking up, I saw Mrs. Brown looking down. Not very happy. "Did you finish those pages, Nanci?"

"Uh. No. No, I didn't...Uh. I don't really understand what I'm supposed to do."

"What do you mean? I just explained it to you. Weren't you paying attention?"

"Yes. I...well, I thought I was."

Damon from behind me thought it best if he helped at this moment, and said, "I explained it to her, also."

"What's wrong today, Nanci? Try to pay attention now. You are dividing this number into this number, and then multiplying the two numbers, and then putting that number under this number, and subtracting the two. Make sure you put the number over the second number in the line up here, not the first... Here, let me do one for you."

My head was swimming with information, but the first problem was that I didn't really get what it meant to divide a number into another number. I really didn't understand it though I had done the simple problems rather easily. So I decided to risk asking her what it meant, since I could tell that nothing was going to make sense to me unless I got that part. Meanwhile, Mrs. Brown had continued her explanation.

"Sixteen divides into forty two times, because if you multiple three times sixteen it gives you a larger number, and you can't have a larger number under blah-blah-blah because it can't be subtracted."

I thought, unbelievably, we are back to subtraction again. Poor Mrs. Brown. Or, perhaps poor me, since she had stopped talking now and was waiting for a response from me.

"Nanci. Go ahead and do it. Multiply sixteen times two, put the two over the zero, put the answer under this number and then subtract. Then, put your remainder up here."

Stomach flip-flopping, heart thudding again, I did what she asked. Easy enough, but why was I doing this? Which number is dividing into which number and why does it matter if the number is larger, and what is the remainder anyhow?

I completed the task, and since she seemed to look pleased with me again, I thought it safe to ask her my basic question. "What does it mean to divide a number into another number? And which is which on this diagram?"

She stared at me. I thought for a moment she didn't feel well. Finally, she leaned down again and looked into my face. "You know what it means to divide a number into another number. You did it a few pages back with this sign when you divided three into six. Remember?"

Now I was really in trouble. I could tell from her voice and her expression. No more questions were going to come out of me...none...not ever.

"Oh, yeah. Now I know."

Still staring at me, eyes squinting a little to be sure, she started to lean over the page to make me do another one without her help, when Sammie across the room screeched and saved me. Mrs. Brown, distracted from me, left my side.

Sitting and looking down at that page, I heard someone in front of me say, "You're stupid." And behind me, Damon snickered and pulled my ponytail.

Head down, I somehow resurrected from memory the steps she had done...and I did them. I did them again and again. I got through the page, hoping I'd multiplied and subtracted when I was supposed to, and then I heard the music of the swinging chains. Looking out the window, I saw that during my duress the wind had whipped up. The chains of my swing were singing, calling to me. I could feel tears coming. I was not stupid. When was lunch, anyhow?

That day passed, and I figured out long division, but the terror I felt with Mrs. Brown leaning over me is embedded in my memory, in detail. I can see nearly every detail of the scene. And yes, I got very good at math. Long division was a small glitch in my learning curve, but it was an important one because it helped me know what children feel like when they can't spell, or can't read, or can't do math—how they hurt inside. Sometimes we as educators, or parents, don't understand students' pain, or their fear of a task or their inadequacy.

Kim and I have written this book for all the children and adults who have ever experienced math-terror, and all the children learning math, so they can know what we know—anyone can learn to think and reason with numbers. It is as simple as learning to visualize numbers and concepts, and applying that mathematical imagery to computation and life.

Imagery: The Sensory-Cognitive Connection for Math

Why can't everyone think with numbers? What cognitive processes do some have that others do not? Some individuals easily understand the concepts underlying math processes. They quickly perform math calculations, mentally or on paper, and have an innate sense of whether or not an answer is correct. Math is their friend, something dependable and logical in the world. But for others math is an illogical enemy, filled with random memorization. It's a dragon rearing its head at inopportune times, ready to embarrass or diminish them in the eyes of others. For them, numbers and calculations can be a vast array of steps to memorize. However, for individuals who "get math," the language of numbers turns into imagery and they "see" mathematical relationships. They use an internal language, with imagery, that lets them calculate and verify mathematics, and see its logic.

Mathematics is cognitive processing, thinking, that requires the dual coding of imagery and language. Imagery is fundamental to the process of thinking with numbers. Albert Einstein, the man who illuminated entire aspects of our universe through the theory of relativity, used imagery as the basis for his mental processing and problem solving. Perhaps he summarized imagery's importance best when he said, "If I can't picture it, I can't understand it." Imaging is the basis for thinking with numbers, their functions, and their logic. Even early thinkers recognized the importance of imagery to math. The Greek philosopher Plato said, "And do you not know also that although they [mathematicians] make use of the visible forms and reason about them, they are thinking not of these, but of the ideals which they resemble; not of the figures which they draw, but of the absolute square and the absolute diameter . . . they are really seeking to behold the things themselves, which can be seen only with the eye of the mind?"

The relationship of imagery to the ability to think is one of the preeminent theories of human cognition, the Dual Coding Theory (DCT). Allan Paivio, a cognitive psychologist and father of DCT, stated this, "Cognition is proportional

9

to the extent that the coding mechanisms of mental representations (imagery) and language are integrated." Research through the 1970s, 1980s and into the 1990s has validated DCT as a model of human cognition and its practical, as well as theoretical, application to the comprehension of language (Bell, 1991). And mathematics is the essence of cognition.

In the January 15, 1880, issue of the journal *Nature*, Francis Galton, a British anthropologist, published a curious little research finding. As part of a general study of mental imagery, Galton had friends and acquaintances fill out a questionnaire asking them to report on whether they could "see" numbers and if so in what way. Some of them could, it seemed, and usually the numbers were arranged along a line, or a series of lines, that got progressively less distinct and sometimes vanished into the mental distance as the numbers got larger. Sometimes the numbers had color or texture. A very visual male philosopher reported that his numbers had a great deal of personality: "9 is a wonderful being of whom I felt almost afraid…, 8, I took for his wife…6, of no particular sex but gentle and straight-forward…" Galton himself considered his results a curiosity—interesting mainly for the extent to which they showed the tendency of mental traits to run in families.

Not until 1967 did another article in *Nature* provide evidence that all of us have a mental number line of sorts, even those of us for whom it may not be vivid. Two Stanford University psychologists, Robert Moyer and Thomas Landauer, measured the time it took a person to choose the concept of "larger" between two single typed numerals by flipping either a left-hand or right-hand switch. They found that the smaller the difference between the concept of two numbers, the longer it took, such as deciding between 6 and 7 as opposed to 1 and 9. This "distance effect" has been verified again and again, and suggests strongly that the brain converts the numbers into analog magnitudes—line segments, for instance—before comparing them. Choosing between two lines is obviously harder the closer in length they are.

Stanislas Dehaene and Laurent Cohen, neurologists in Paris, have been recently researching math and the brain, and in a series of papers have sketched a rough model of how the brain processes numbers and does simple arithmetic through imagery. All of their evidence, mostly done with brain-lesion patients, shows that the "elementary ability to perceive and manipulate numbers is part of our evolutionary heritage—something we're born with." One of their patients showed that the ability to grasp the meaning of numbers, by translating them into an approximate analog representation of quantity, and the ability to calculate precisely were two different processes occurring at least in part in different regions of the brain.

Math is thinking (dual coding) with numbers, imagery, and language; reading/spelling is thinking with letters, imagery, and language. Both processes require the integration of language and imagery to assist in the foundational and application processes. Dual coding in math, just as in reading, requires two aspects of imagery: symbol/numeral imagery (parts/details) and concept imagery (whole/gestalt). Perhaps the two imagery systems do reside in slightly different areas of the brain.

Numeral Imagery

Visualizing numerals is one of the basic cognitive processes necessary to understanding math. For example, we image the numeral "2" for the concept of two. When we see the numeral "3," we know that it represents the concept of three of something—three pennies, three apples, three horses, three dots. If someone gives us two pennies for the numeral three, we have a discrepancy between our numeral-image for three and the reality of three. The first imagery needed for math is the symbolic or numeral imagery that represents the reality of a number concept.

What does numeral imagery look like? Here's one example. Cecil was very good in math, could think with numbers, arrive at answers in his head, and easily mentally check for mathematical discrepancies in finance or life situations. When he was asked how he could do this, he gave an easy, quick answer that related his math ability to imagery. "I just visualize numbers and their relationships, and certain numbers are in certain colors, and the number line in my head goes specific directions." Cecil could visualize both numerals and concepts, both types of imagery, but the most unusual was his color imagery—he had assigned colors to specific numbers!

"What color is the number 14?" he was asked.

His eyes went up, and in all seriousness, he said, "Light blue."

Puzzling. "Well, how about the number 3?"

Cecil, eyes up again, said, "Reddish pink."

"How about the number 88?"

Cecil, smiling, eyes up, said, "That one is kind of a purple."

Thinking he might have made them up on the spot, a check months later revealed the same colors! Though Cecil may have experienced other areas of difficulty in his life, he was a wizard at card games and math. Just as easy as breathing, he could compute math mentally, though he only had a third grade education. He saw his numbers in a certain linear pattern of straight to the left. His son, Rod, who graduated in math from college, had similar imagery for math. Though Rod's numerals weren't in a specific color, his number line had a definite pattern in his head, with turns and twists providing him with an imagery base for the numerals. Asked what he used it for, he said, "I don't know, and I don't know how it got there, but it exists at an unconscious level. It is a representation of number relationships that are a part of my internal math structure." Why some have innate imaging ability, and others do not, indeed may be related to a genetic propensity, just as Galton suspected.

Chronological relationships appear in our mind for a number line, the days of the week, the months in the year. *Imagery—both numeral and concept—is our sensory system's way of making the abstract real.* It is a means to vicariously experience math.

Concept Imagery

While imaging numerals is important to mathematical computation, another aspect of imagery is equally as important: *concept imagery.* Understanding, problem solving, and computing in mathematics requires the ability to process the gestalt (whole)—another form of imagery. Sometimes children or adults can visualize numerals, the parts, but can not bring those parts to a whole; just as they can sometimes visualize words but not bring those words to a whole to form concepts. Mathematical skill requires the ability to get the gestalt, see the big picture, in order to understand the process underlying mathematical logic.

"Concept imagery is the ability to image the gestalt (whole)," Bell (1991). Concept imagery is a primary factor basic to the process involved in oral and written language comprehension, language expression, and critical thinking. It is the sensory information that connects us to language and thought. In

On Memory and Recollection, Aristotle wrote, "It is impossible even to think without a mental picture." And Thomas Aquinas wrote, "Man's mind cannot understand thoughts without images of them."

However, many individuals have weakness in creating mental images and thereby have weakness in reading comprehension, oral language comprehension, expressive language, following directions, and logical thinking. Researchers in reading and imagery have produced direct evidence linking reading and mental imagery as well as studied the relationship of imagery to prior knowledge and thinking processes (Stemmler 1969; Richardson 1969; Paivio 1971, 1986; Marks 1972; Sheehan 1972; Levin 1973, 1981; Pressley 1976; Sadoski 1983; Kosslyn 1983; Tierney and Cunningham 1984; Peters and Levin 1986).

While weakness in imagery may cause problems in reasoning and math, strength in imagery is a foundation for math. Cecil, like many others for whom math is easy, will tell you they calculate math quickly because they "see" relationships. They use an internal imaged number line and integrate numeral and concept imagery for simple and complex problem solving. "Forty-six plus seven is easy because it takes four to get to fifty and that leaves three, so the answer is fifty-three." For them, the language of word problems is easily converted to mathematical solutions.

Whether math skill is a genetic gift or not—and the answer is not the purpose of this book—imagery can be developed and applied to math with the formula: *concrete experiences to imagery to computation*.

On Cloud Nine: Concrete to Imagery to Computation

While imagery is the link to mathematical processing, math's roots are in the realm of the concrete. Numbers can be experienced and the relationship of those numbers can be concretized (made concrete) by using manipulatives. What appears abstract, numbers (squiggles) that work together, can be experienced and imaged to concreteness. Indeed, because of its concrete roots, math can be safer than decoding, spelling, or language comprehension.

The *On Cloud Nine* math program moves through three basic steps to develop mathematical reasoning and computation: (1) manipulatives to experience the realness of math, (2) imagery and language to concretize that realness in the sensory system, and (3) computation to apply math to problem solving.

Concrete
to
Imagery
to
Computation

Concrete experiences, manipulatives, have been used for many years in teaching math (Stern, 1971). However, children and adults have often experienced success with manipulatives, but failure in the world of computation (NCTM, 1989; Moore, 1990; Papert, 1993). They had what has often been described as "application problems."

However, manipulatives can be used to concretize imagery which can then be applied to computation. Imagery is the link. Arnheim (1966) wrote, "Thinking is concerned with the objects and events of the world we know...When the objects are not physically present, they are represented indirectly by what we remember and know about them. In what shape do memory and knowledge deliver the needed facts? In the shape of memory images, we answer most simply. Experiences deposit images." *On Cloud Nine* manipulatives deposit images. They concretize numbers and mathematical concepts, and place that realness into imagery as a base to draw from for computation.

To bring concept and numeral imagery to a conscious level as the missing link in math instruction, *On Cloud Nine* integrates and applies the principles of Bell's programs: *Visualizing and Verbalizing for Language Comprehension and Thinking (V/V)* and *Seeing Stars: Symbol Imagery for Phonemic Awareness, Sight Words, and Spelling (SI)*. As individuals become familiar with the concrete manipulatives, they are *questioned* and *directed* to consciously transfer the experienced to the imaged. They image the concrete and attach language to their imagery. The integration of imagery and language is then applied to computation. They develop the sensory-cognitive processing to understand and use the logic of mathematics in mental and written computation.

The Visualizing and Verbalizing Program First

Throughout these next chapters, numbers are introduced at the concrete level (cubes, number line, and clay), transferred to a visualized level, and finally applied to computation. The visualized level is the sensory-cognitive link to independent, self-correcting, generative math skills, but it is often assumed.

While many students learn math easily, and have the imagery base to process from, there are also many students like Clark. Here is a true story of a boy who had experienced math problems that worsened year after year.

Clark had been taught math with a program that used manipulatives and, in fact, he had progressed well in school in the early years when much of the work could be accomplished with memory rather than interpretation or abstractions. He seemed to understand numbers while experiencing the manipulatives, but had difficulty transferring his thinking to a computation level once the manipulatives were taken away. He was in the eighth grade, performing in the average range in academic areas in school, but with a lot of effort. He had trouble in history, science, and math, though reading and spelling had always been easy for him. It was noted that his performance dropped considerably whenever the subject moved into an abstract or interpretive area. Clark would often ask, "But what do they mean by that?"

In the early years of school, Clark had done well committing the math facts for addition, subtraction, and multiplication to memory. Now, on math homework, he applied those memorized facts and diligently followed the model problem, often arriving at correct answers, but only after a lot of extra effort. On tests, however, Clark would often "mix up his signs." He would add instead of subtract, fail to line up columns when multiplying, and avoid word problems at all costs. His parents frequently found themselves saying to him, "You're a bright boy. If you pay closer attention you can do as well on tests as you do on your homework." Secretly, however, Clark knew he paid even closer attention on tests, but something was wrong. He didn't know what, and he wondered if he really just wasn't very smart.

It wasn't that Clark wasn't smart, it was that he had an undiagnosed sensory-cognitive weakness in *concept imagery*—the ability to create an imaged gestalt. Because of this weakness he often connected to the "parts" of what he read or heard rather than the gestalt or whole. He was unable to answer critical thinking questions for a main idea, conclusion, inference, or prediction because he couldn't process the wholeness of the language, or thoughts, and therefore didn't have a *base* for interpretation. Further, because he was primarily processing bits and pieces, he often felt confused. He asked and reasked the same questions, sometimes with his eyes squinting slightly. People looked at him quizzically when he didn't grasp something, shaking their heads. His ability to think critically was impaired and he was sometimes laughed at because he didn't create or follow logical thoughts. He really didn't know what was wrong with him, and it was especially confusing since he could read and spell words easily. Moreover, Clark's weakness in concept imagery was complicating his life because it was difficult to detect.

Math, in particular, was a haze of abstract parts for him. Although he was able to memorize his math facts, he could never be sure when he should apply a certain function. When he saw the problem 345 x 56, he knew he should multiply, but had no mental estimate of an answer. He tried to remember which step he should apply first, but got the steps for dividing and multiplying mixed up. The world of numbers seemed to be based on confusing, conflicting information that he'd never really understood. He was especially frustrated when he was told, "Clark, you can get this if you just try." People didn't seem to know he was trying as hard as he could.

Finally, one of Clark's teachers referred him to Lindamood-Bell Learning Processes for a diagnostic evaluation to determine what his overall cognitive ability was, and what, if anything, was interfering with his comprehension of abstract material and math. Clark underwent three hours of language processing testing which determined that he had good potential for learning. His scores in oral vocabulary, spelling, word recognition, paragraph reading rate and accuracy, and visual motor processing were within or above the normal range for his age and grade level. However, his performance in reading recall, reading comprehension, following oral directions, oral language comprehension, and math were moderately to significantly *below the normal range* for his age and grade level. His weaknesses stemmed from one primary source.

Clark's difficulty processing information had a definitive cause and label: weak concept imagery. He was relieved. This was the reason some information seemed to pass right through him. This was why he was often confused. This was why he had to read and reread information to understand it. This was why he had difficulty following directions, and why sometimes directions seemed to fly in one ear and out the other. *This was why he had difficulty understanding math concepts.* Not getting the big picture had affected many areas of his life, and it had gotten worse as he got older and the information became denser, more complex, and abstract. Though both disturbed and relieved, his primary question was could something really be done about it?

Clark was enrolled in the V/V program. He attended a Lindamood-Bell Center two hours daily for a few weeks, then over his spring break he attended six hours a day. His ability to visualize and verbalize gestalt images was established.

First, to stimulate and refine his verbalizing, he learned to look at a given picture and describe his images. He attended to detail by using the V/V "structure words" of what, number, color, size, movement, background, etc. And then, as he was able to describe a given picture, he moved to visualizing and verbalizing images in his mind's eye from a single word, then a sentence, and then sentences within a paragraph. At the V/V Sentence by Sentence level, his sensory system began to process gestalts, and as that was developing, the gestalt imaging was applied to higher order thinking skills.

When Clark was able to create images at the Sentence by Sentence level, the *On Cloud Nine* math program was introduced and soon his sessions were split between V/V and *On Cloud Nine*. He not only learned to consciously create concept images when reading and listening to others, but also when turning math equations into meaning. Concept imagery for oral and written language was developing, and he learned to apply that imagery to mathematical concepts and computation. One day, he said, "I don't know why I used to think math was so hard, this is really easy." His cognitive processing was developed. His grades in school improved, he studied less and did better on tests, his language comprehension for lectures improved, he spontaneously began to contribute to conversations, his thinking became surprisingly logical to his parents and friends, and he felt better about himself. The post testing indicated that all of his scores were now at or above his age or grade level, including reading comprehension, following directions, and math.

V/V First

Just as with Clark, it is essential to be certain the sensory-cognitive function of concept imagery is in place with students prior to developing mathematical processing. *On Cloud Nine,* or any math program, may reach a plateau of effectiveness if students have weakness in concept imagery. When *On Cloud Nine* takes students from the concrete to the visualized level and then into computation, the ugly specter of weak gestalt processing may rear its head. To prevent this, you may want to begin the V/V program first. Here's some pacing advice.

Your students should be able to visualize and verbalize into the Sentence by Sentence level of V/V as *On Cloud Nine* is being introduced. Once able to create concept images for a paragraph, students should continue spending a separate amount of time on V/V and *On Cloud Nine.* For example, while students complete the number line and exposure to addition and subtraction math facts, they may be well into Sentence by Sentence with the V/V program. And, by the time they reach place value in math, V/V may have taken them to the Sentence by Sentence with Higher Order Thinking (HOT) and perhaps the Multiple Sentence level. As students progress to carrying and borrowing, multiplication, and division, they also continue to progress in V/V. The V/V time may now be spent mostly on visualizing and verbalizing whole paragraphs or whole pages of material, and by the time the math sessions have reached computing equations with decimals and fractions, the V/V sessions may be overlapping to study skills and content. The two programs merge as students read word problems, create concept images, discover what math facts are stated, and what questions are asked, and solve the problems.

With the sensory-cognitive function of processing imaged numerals and gestalts, students have the underlying ability to learn mathematical concepts and compute mathematical problems mentally and on paper. They can think and reason with numbers. Their imagery is easily accessible for problem solving and interpretation—visible only to themselves.

The Math Ladder

The **Steps** of On Cloud Nine

The Math Ladder

Start: Setting the Climate

Step 1.   Imaging Numerals

Step 2.   Imaging the Number Line

Step 3.   Addition Family Facts

Step 4.   Subtraction Family Facts

Step 5.   Word Problems

Step 6.   Place Value

Step 7.   Jumping

Step 8.   Carrying and Borrowing

Step 9.   Multiplication

Step 10.   Division

Step 11.   Decimals

Step 12.   Fractions

The On Cloud Nine Guide

*O*n *Cloud Nine* stimulates imagery as a foundation for mathematical reasoning and computation from basic number concepts through decimals, fractions, and word problems. It can be used developmentally or remedially, or just to supplement your existing math curriculum. It should be thought of as providing a sensory-cognitive basis for math.

This chapter is a guide to understanding the whole and the parts of this program.

The Whole

On Cloud Nine uses "visualizing and verbalizing" to develop three basic processes leading to mathematical skill: concrete experiences, imagery, and computation. *On Cloud Nine* stimulates the mathematical dual coding of imagery and language—the sensory-cognitive processing with numbers that can be applied to all mathematical learning. The purpose of the program is to make all individuals into "Cecils" who can think with numbers, image relationships, and do mental and written computation. In essence, the purpose is to build a sensory-cognitive mathematical base for life-long success with math and mathematical reasoning.

The Parts

While the whole of *On Cloud Nine* is to develop thinking and reasoning in math, the parts are the steps to arrive at that lofty goal. Each step contains an overview, sample lessons, and a summary. More importantly, each step follows the specific pattern of beginning with concrete experiences, moving to imagery, and ending with application to computation and independence.

It is important to follow each step in order. Previously, your students may have memorized computation steps, but not understood the mathematical principles behind those steps. If they cannot reason with numbers, they may not be able to self-correct or move into complex operations such as decimals, fractions, and algebra. Each step is a foundation for the next step—*a ladder to mathematical independence.*

The On Cloud Nine Math Ladder

The *On Cloud Nine* **math ladder** illustrates climbing from rung to rung, step to step, to develop addition, subtraction, multiplication, division, decimals, fractions, and word problems. Experiencing and imaging numerals, a number line, a base ten system, place value, and concepts for basic mathematical processes builds a mathematical mind capable of climbing any other *extension ladders* such as algebra, geometry, trigonometry, and calculus.

The math ladder also gives students the gestalt of where they are and where they are going. It is a built-in climate. They track their progress as they start each new step, giving them a purpose for interaction and energy.

Tory

This book takes you through the basic steps of *On Cloud Nine* with a girl named Tory. She is in fifth grade, doing well in spelling, has some problems with reading comprehension, and is seriously struggling in math. Every night she pulls and tugs at her hair as she does her math homework. Every day she tells her mom she hates math. Every parent-teacher conference since first grade has involved discussion of Tory's weakness in math. Math is her enemy and despite quite a few years in school and some very good teachers, she is in pain. Terror is growing in her heart as she progresses up the grades where more complex math is expected of her.

Sample Lessons

Each step has a sample lesson to present the teacher-student interaction and each lesson has three parts: (1) The Set, setting the task; (2) Lesson, the interactive lesson; and (3) Lesson Summary, a short, itemized summary.

The language within the lessons can be changed to suit your particular choice or to suit whatever mathematical language is in vogue. For example, you can substitute "adds" for "plus" or "take-away" for "subtraction," etc.

As you read the lessons, note the questioning to stimulate the "hold" aspect of numeral imagery. The following questions directly stimulate students' ability to hold and compare the imagery within equations. "What is the last number you see?" "What is the first number you see?" "What is the sign you see?" "Change the first and the last number around in the equation, and tell me what you see?" Taken from the *Seeing Stars* program, these are important elements in *On Cloud Nine*.

Error Handling: Responding to the Response

All Lindamood-Bell programs use a Socratic teaching approach to develop sensory-cognitive processing. The teacher questions and gets a response; then, to stimulate more thinking, the teacher responds to the response to help the student compare his/her response to the stimulus. This questioning approach develops sensory-cognitive processing in reading, spelling, and math.

While the sample lessons in *On Cloud Nine* demonstrate the questioning and teacher-student interaction, they do not show the student making errors. Here is an error handling frame for math which can be used for any error.

Positive feedback:
   "It was good that you skipped numbers when counting by twos."

Respond to the response:
   "You're showing me that eight is two more than five."

Compare the response to the stimulus:
   "Let's check with these cubes and the number line to see if that matches counting by twos."

Self-corrects:
   "Two more would put me at seven, so I would count like this: five, seven, nine."

Do the Visualizing and Verbalizing Program First

Most students we see at Lindamood-Bell Centers are taken through the V/V program either prior to or in conjunction with *On Cloud Nine*. This establishes concept imagery as a base for math. Unfortunately, you usually can't just *tell* students to image. They need direct stimulation.

Language Concepts Needed

On Cloud Nine consciously uses language and imagery in each step. Students need the following language concepts: forward, backward, up, down, after, before, more, less, whole, and part. A sample lesson is provided to give you suggestions for developing the spatial concepts for younger or language impaired students. Since the V/V program may be done prior to working with students in math, these basic language concepts can be incorporated into the Word Imaging step of V/V.

Visual-Motor Coordination Needed

In developing numeral imagery, students are requested to air-write the numerals they visualize, then write them on paper. This requires eye-hand coordination that may need direct stimulation. We encourage you to integrate a visual-motor program with *On Cloud Nine* if your students have difficulty forming numerals properly.

Practice and Pacing

Each *On Cloud Nine* step has a Practice and Pacing section which takes into consideration five basic concepts to note throughout the program: (1) lesson energy, (2) task levels, (3) overlapping of steps, (4) self-correction and automaticity, and (5) daily stimulation.

These five areas are inherent in every Lindamood-Bell program whether it be the *Lindamood Phoneme Sequencing* (LiPS) Program, the Bell *Visualizing and Verbalizing for Language Comprehension and Thinking* (V/V) program, or the Bell *Seeing Stars: Symbol Imagery for Phonemic Awareness, Sight Words, and Spelling* (SI) program. An interactive program is paced by integrating each step with the other steps, moving toward a goal of automaticity, and keeping positive energy in the learning environment.

Daily Stimulation IS Necessary

Daily stimulation is a primary consideration given to all Lindamood-Bell sensory-cognitive programs. It is a part of our philosophy, our consciousness!

If a student is trying to develop and establish automaticity for a skill, their sensory system needs daily stimulation, not stimulation a few times a week, here or there, hit or miss.

There are primary brain functions related to cognition. We, as educators, must provide a learning environment to stimulate those underlying brain functions. Years of assuming and years of failure for too many students mandates that we analyze and change where needed. One of those changes may be daily, *intensive* sensory-cognitive stimulation. Intensive intervention is four hours a day, five days a week. Research indicates that intensive intervention over a short period of time, six or eight weeks, results in significant gains in sensory-cognitive processing and skill in reading, spelling, and math. Perhaps it is time for a change.

Summary Pages for Each Step

As with the *Visualizing and Verbalizing* and *Seeing Stars* teaching manuals, this manual has a Summary Page at the end of each chapter succinctly summarizing the critical aspects of each *On Cloud Nine* step. First a part of the V/V manual, teachers and parents considered the Summary Pages very helpful. Hence, Summary Pages are included in the Appendix of *On Cloud Nine*, where the whole program can be seen in its entirety for easy implementation. No ear-marking of each chapter will be necessary, just turn to the Appendix for a quick reference of the whole and the parts.

Small Group and Classroom Instruction

Each step of *On Cloud Nine* can be used with small or large groups. The Summary Page includes a few specific suggestions for group practice, but the program is created for either one-to-one or groups. No change is needed in the basic steps.

Math Worksheets

If you are using *On Cloud Nine* in conjunction with another math program, you may already have an ample supply of written problems.

Materials Needed for On Cloud Nine

The following materials are needed for *On Cloud Nine*. They can be purchased in the *On Cloud Nine* Kit or made at home or school.

- Number line that is composed of tracks of ten. Such number lines are usually made from plastic and may be found in teacher-supply stores and catalogs. The track must run from one to one hundred when assembled.

- Linking cubes. Cubes must correspond in size to the number line; each cube takes up one space. At least one hundred cubes are needed in ten different colors—ten in each color.

- 5x8 blank cards. One package.

- White 3x5 blank cards. The cards are for practicing addition, subtraction, multiplication, and division facts, so an ample supply is needed.

- One black medium-point marker. Numeral imagery is enhanced by using distinct dark lines on a light background for teaching numerals.

- Clay. This can be either homemade or store bought.

- Overlays of clear plastic.

Word Problems

Word problems should be included at *each* step of *On Cloud Nine* to reinforce the application of math to the real world.

Terms to Know

The following are a few terms for you to know, but not necessarily teach your students. (We all learned to do math and we probably didn't know the definition of the commutative property.)

Commutative axiom of addition: the function that allows an equation to be reversed while the answer remains the same: $4 + 3 = 7$ and $3 + 4 = 7$.

Commutative axiom of multiplication: the function that allows an equation to be reversed while the product remains the same: 5 x 3 = 15 and 3 x 5 = 15.

Product: another name for the answer in a multiplication equation.

Denominator: In a fraction this is the part that designates how many parts make up the total. It is the bottom number.

Numerator: In a fraction this is the part that designates how many parts of the whole. It is the top number.

Divisor: This is the number by which another number is being divided. It is the number that does the action. Two is the divisor in the problem $8 \div 2$.

Dividend: This is the number which is being divided. Eight is the dividend in the problem eight divided by two.

Associative axiom of addition: that function that allows three numbers to be added in any order without changing the sum: 2 + 5 + 9 can be added (2 + 5) + 9 or 2 + (5 + 9) or (2 + 9) + 5.

Mixed Number: a combination of a whole number with a fraction: $2\frac{1}{3}$ is a mixed number.

Proper Fraction: A fraction in which the numerator is smaller than the denominator designating a number less than a whole: $\frac{2}{3}$ is a proper fraction.

Improper Fraction: A fraction which is equal to, or more than, one whole: $\frac{9}{7}$ is an improper fraction. It is a fraction in which the numerator is as large as, or larger than, the denominator.

And here's the fun part. Look at the definitions for number and numeral. One dictionary says, "Number—a symbol or word, or a group of either of these showing how many or what place in a sequence: 1, 2, 3, 13, 23, 123 are cardinal numbers; 1st, 2nd, 3rd, 4th, 24th are ordinal numbers." And another says, "Number—1: the total of persons, things, or units taken together (the number of people in a room); 2: a distinction of word form to denote reference to one or more than one (a verb agrees in number with its subject); 3: Numeral (the number 5); 4: a particular numeral for telling one person or thing from another (a house number); 5: group, many (a number of presents); 6: one of a series of things (the March *number* of a magazine)." The definition for numeral is a symbol or group of symbols representing a number. Another definition, in a math book, is a "name of a number." Arg. Perhaps a good way to define numeral versus number is this: *number* refers to the concept behind a written representation, and *numeral* refers to the written representation for a concept. Arg, still.

The definitions for numeral and number can be confusing, even to us professionals, let alone a child or student having trouble in math. Hence, we have primarily used the word "number" when working with students. We think that fussing about the two names is a part but not the whole. The whole, or gestalt, of *On Cloud Nine* is to teach individuals to think and reason with numbers…and frankly, if that is intact it doesn't matter what you label them. It is our intention to have language be a link, not a disruption, toward making numbers something that promotes thinking and reasoning.

Setting the Climate

All of us are more willing to do something if we know what we are going to do and why we are going to do it! Setting the climate does just that for students: it explains *what* and *why*, an important point of departure for students who may have experienced difficulty with math or may be just learning math. You need their energy for the learning task at hand, learning that can help them become independent in life, able to get a good job, support a family, make a contribution to improve the world, or just make it through a day of math in a one-room school. Creating images from what is heard, seen, and touched (manipulated) helps students to understand and remember concepts of numbers. Verbalizing those images helps students verify whether their image matches the stimulus. These are first steps in the ladder of learning math.

The what: Students will learn to visualize and verbalize with numbers by (1) experiencing the reality of numbers and math through manipulatives, (2) visualizing and verbalizing that reality, and (3) applying that to computing math mentally and on paper. They will climb the *On Cloud Nine* math ladder.

The why: Students will be able to think and work with numbers from basic math through fractions, or whatever level is appropriate for their age and grade level.

Keep the Climate short and sweet, not long and windy. Here is a sample lesson for introducing *On Cloud Nine*. You met Tory in Chapter 4, but to help your imagery, she is a young girl with a dark complexion and shoulder-length dark hair. Although she gets better than average grades in reading, she experiences terror in math.

SAMPLE LESSON

Setting the Climate

Kim: *"I'm going to teach you to picture math in your imagination, your mind's eye. This will help you think about numbers and math problems." (Draw a head and imagery bubble.)*

Tory: "Hmmm. OK."

Kim: *"First, you'll experience then you'll imagine. Touch these two blocks and then imagine the number two." (Fill in the imagery bubble with the numeral 2.)*

Tory: "Yes, I can picture that."

Kim: *"Great. Tell me what you imaged!"*

Tory: "I saw the number two."

Kim: *"Great, you were seeing and saying. You got information that you put into imagery and then you used words to describe it. That's called visualizing and verbalizing, or seeing and saying." (Draw the word "two" coming out of the mouth.)*

You are ready to climb your math ladder. Up you'll go, one step at a time, until math is easy for you. Here's your own math ladder. (Give her a math ladder to put her name on.)

Each student has his/her own math ladder to "see" and track progress (see the Appendix for a master copy). Setting the climate should take only a few minutes, because discussing a problem won't develop sensory-cognitive processing. Only the actual stimulation will do that. Begin the program!

On Cloud Nine Math Ladder

Student Name: _____

12	Fractions
11	Decimals
10	Division
9	Multiplication
8	Carrying and Borrowing
7	Jumping
6	Place Value
5	Word Problems
4	Subtraction Family Facts
3	Addition Family Facts
2	Imaging the Number Line
1	Imaging Numerals

Summary: Start

Setting the Climate

> **Goal:** To briefly explain to the student(s) what and why.

1. *Say, "I'm going to teach you to see numbers and math in your imagination."*

2. *Say, "It will help you think about and do math."*

3. *Say, "Here's how you can picture that."*

4. *Diagram a head with student seeing and saying.*

5. *Give each student his/her own math ladder.*

6. *Keep the climate presentation succinct and relevant.*

Imaging Numerals

Visualizing and verbalizing stimulation for math begins with establishing the reality of numbers. Just as letters are the foundation of written language, numerals are the foundation of mathematics. Letters can be made real through articulatory and auditory feedback, and placed in imagery for automaticity in reading and spelling; likewise, numerals can be made real through manipulatives and placed in imagery for rapid retrieval and computation in math. Unlike reading and spelling, however, math is always based in the concrete.

While visualizing numerals may seem simple, it is a necessary step, whether your students are beginning to learn math, remediating a weakness, or improving their foundation for math. This step is not to be skipped. Though learned easily and quickly by some students, numeral imagery must not be assumed, as it is an underpinning to mathematical thinking. This is what Cecil did automatically. It was his foundation, enabling him to be quick with mental math and accurate with written math, despite only a few years of formal schooling.

Here is Tory, moving immediately to this from the climate. Her eyes look skeptical. Perhaps the drawing could have been better! Perhaps she heard someone snicker behind her yesterday.

SAMPLE LESSON

The Set

Kim: *"I'm going to show you some math cubes that you can touch and hold, then I'll show you the number that represents those cubes. After I take away the cubes and the number, I want you to tell me the name of the number and write it in the air. This is the first step in helping your brain learn to visualize and verbalize math. (Use the term visualize, image, or picture, depending on the vocabulary level of your student.)*

Tory: "Hmmm. OK."

Lesson

Kim: *"Here are two cubes and here is the number that represents those cubes—two. (Showing two cubes and the Numeral Imagery Card for 2.) If I take this card away, you can still see the number two in your imagination and you know what it represents. Say the number name and write it in the air."*

"Here is the number that represents those cubes—2."

Tory: "Yes, I can picture that. Two." (Tory says and the writes the number 2 in the air.)

"Yes, I can picture that. Two."
Tory says and air-writes the number 2.

Kim: *"Great. Now we'll do some more. Here are some cubes (placing five cubes on the table). Let's count them together and here's the number that represents that many cubes. See it, say it, and write it in the air (taking away the Numeral Imagery Card for 5)."*

"See it, say it, and write it in the air."

Tory: "Five." (Touching the cubes, saying and writing the number 5 in the air.)

Kim: *"Great. We can keep doing that with lots of numbers, we can even get to numbers such as one hundred, and one thousand, but if we do we may run out of these cubes, so we'll have to use some beans!"*

Tory: "Beans?"

Lesson Summary:

Numeral Imagery

1. Teacher shows cubes and student touches them.
2. Teacher shows the corresponding Numeral Imagery Card, then takes it away.
3. Student(s) sees (visualizes), says (verbalizes), and writes the number in the air and on paper.
4. Saying and air-writing should be done simultaneously.
5. Air-writing is large enough to see a "shadow" effect.
6. Begin with zero through ten, and then increase numbers as is appropriate for the age and level of the student(s).

How to Air-write the Numerals

How the student air-writes the numerals is important for establishing numeral imagery. The primary concern for numeral air-writing is that the numbers can't be too large or too small. If the air-writing is too quick, too small, or too large it isn't as likely to "stick" in the mind's eye. The goal is that the numerals are written large enough to leave a shadow effect, a ghostliness, to aid imagery.

Also, it seems preferable that air-writing be written up in the air rather than down. Though writing down may still be helpful, experience with symbol imagery and numeral imagery indicates that having students write up is initially more productive. Be sure to transfer air-writing to paper-writing.

Imaging in Color

Here is where Cecil comes to mind! Now is a good time to do a little bit of numeral imaging in color. Needless to say, we are not trying to duplicate Cecil's colored numbers, but in fact, imaging in color seems to intensify the imagery. And it is fun to do. Instead of imaging black numerals on a white background, try having students see a red numeral, or green, or purple, or let the numeral stay black and put it on a yellow background. By doing some of this, you are more likely to develop the imagery since it often forces imagery to be brought to a conscious level, even for good visualizers. Remember you are not trying to make specific numerals be specific colors, you are just trying to intensify the imaging experience.

Language Concepts Needed

As stated earlier, most Lindamood–Bell math students are taken through the V/V program prior to or in conjunction with *On Cloud Nine*. The purpose of this is to establish concept imagery as a base for math. At that time, specific language concepts for spatial relationships can be established with imagery and language in the Word Imaging step of V/V. Specifically, students need the following language concepts: forward, backward, up, down, after, before, more, less, whole, and part.

While these concepts could have been established with V/V, the following lesson gives you further ideas for stimulation. The teacher begins by modeling the movement and language and having the student copy the action. See, visualize, verbalize and do! Second, the teacher has the student hear, visualize, verbalize, and do! Receive, visualize, verbalize, and do!

SAMPLE LESSON

Developing Language Concepts

The Set

Kim: *"We're going to practice imaging, saying, and doing some words like up, down, forward, backward—just to make sure we can image movement words. They're an important part of the math ladder.*

"We're going to move around this room and imagine and describe everything we do. It's going to be kind of like the game Simon Says. First, I'm going to say something and do it. Then I want you to do the same thing and say what you are doing."

Tory: "That sounds fun!"

Lesson

Kim and Tory stand up, place heels to the wall, and face the same direction.

"We're going to practice imaging, saying, and doing some words like up, down..."

"We're going to move around this room and imagine and describe everything we do."

Teacher says/does—Student says/does:

Kim: *"I go forward."* (Stepping forward while speaking.)

Tory: "I go forward." (Stepping forward while speaking.)

Kim: *"I go back."* (Modeling.)

      Tory repeats words and action.

Kim: *"I put my arm up."* (Modeling.)

      Tory repeats words and action.

Kim: *"I put my arm down."* (Modeling.)

      Tory repeats words and action.

Teacher says—Student visualizes/ verbalizes/does:

Kim: *"Now I'm going to tell you to do something and I want you to picture yourself doing it, say what you're going to do, then DO it. Like this: picture, say, do. Got it?"*

Tory: "I think so."

Kim: *"Go forward. Are you picturing it? Good. Now, tell me what you're going to do and then do it."*

Tory: "I'm going to go forward." (Stepping forward.)

Kim: *"Good. Now, go back. Are you picturing? Good. Now, tell me what you're going to do and then do it."*

Tory: "I'm going to go back." (Stepping back.)

Continue the lesson and then apply the same language concepts to paper. Establish a point and left to right directionality. Ask your student the following questions: What is forward from this point? What is backward?

The Lesson Summary:

Developing Language Concepts

1. Teacher says and models movement—Student(s) says and does.
2. Teacher says—Student(s) visualizes, verbalizes, does.
3. Student(s) applies concepts to paper.

Checkout Activities

The following activities are a method of reinforcing and checking out your students' ability to understand and image both the concept of a number and the symbolic image that represents it.

1. Teacher says a number name, the student(s) shows you the corresponding amount of cubes (manipulatives), says, and air-writes the numeral.

2. Teacher says a number name, the student(s) says and air-writes the numeral.

3. Teacher says a number name, the student(s) says, air-writes, and paper-writes the numeral.

4. Teacher points to a numeral, the student(s) shows you the corresponding amount of cubes, air-writes, and paper writes.

5. Teacher shows specific amount of cubes, the student(s) says number name, air-writes and paper writes the numeral.

Practice and Pacing

Practice the Numeral Imaging step by first showing cubes to represent the reality of a number concept, then showing the Numeral Imagery Card, and finally have students say and air-write the numeral after the stimulus card is taken away. But make an adjustment in the stimulation within a short period of time, sometimes in the same session: only hold up the Numeral Imagery Card or only say the name of the number. In other words, get rid of the cubes representing the reality of the number! In both cases be sure the student is imaging, air-writing, and saying the number name. This increases the imagery stimulation and is completely appropriate if you are sure students have the concept or reality of what a given numeral represents.

This step must not be omitted, but pacing it needs to be consistent with the level of your students. For example, younger children with less experience with numbers may need a considerable amount of stimulation in numeral imagery, as may students with severe weakness in math. However, older students or those with moderate weakness in math may need very little. All sensory-cognitive programs are paced on the basis of the gestalt and the sensory-cognitive needs of individuals. The gestalt lets you pace students on the basis of how this part fits the whole, and the needs and levels of the students.

Good programs have been delivered with overkill at each step because the deliverer didn't have the big picture and understand how the parts (steps) fit the whole. In our reading programs, we have seen teachers have students do pages of phonemic awareness patterns because the patterns were in the manual. But the students were able to do the patterns within the first few minutes of stimulation. The rest of the time was unproductive practice that could have been spent elsewhere to yield faster progress in phonemic awareness and application to written language. Worse than that may be the loss of energy the students probably had for the instruction in general. Pacing appropriately can only be accomplished by keeping the gestalt in mind, where you are in relation to where you're going. When this is known, fussing over irrelevant details or staying too long on irrelevant tasks won't happen.

The next thing to know about pacing is the importance of overlapping steps. Do some practice at this step, and if it seems fairly stable, overlap to the next step while continuing this step—working two steps at the same time. Most important, don't belabor the stimulation. It is definitely better to move too quickly rather than too slowly. Moving too slowly adds the boredom factor and a subsequent loss of lesson energy from both teacher and students. You can always go back and reactivate a step, just don't do so by making it a negative and announcing to the students, "Let's go back and…" Instead, put your pacing decision in a positive with something like, "All these steps are connected so we'll go back and forth a little with each one."

Finally, always explain where your students are in the process of learning, what they are doing, and why. They need the big picture perhaps more than anyone.

Summary

Develop numeral imagery for isolated numerals with all ages of students—no matter their grade or level of math skill—as a base for applying imagery to increasingly more difficult levels of math. The stimulation begins by having the students experience the reality of numbers with cubes and applying that concreteness to the symbolic representation of the number by showing a Numeral Imagery Card. Then the student visualizes, verbalizes, and air-writes the numeral. Once the concrete aspect of the number is established, the stimulation extends to only a Numeral Imagery Card or only the name of the number, with students continuing to visualize, verbalize, air-write, and paper-write.

The goal of *On Cloud Nine* is to concretize math by experiencing the reality of numbers through manipulatives, use imagery to vicariously experience that mathematical reality, and apply the imagery and mathematical understanding to mental and written computation. Beginning mathematical dual coding, visualizing/verbalizing, at this low level step is the first rung of the *On Cloud Nine* math ladder.

Summary: Step 1

Imaging Numerals

Goal: Develop the ability to visualize, verbalize, and air-write numerals, with an understanding of the reality the number represents.

1. Numeral Imagery

a. Teacher shows cubes and student(s) touches them.

b. Teacher shows the corresponding Numeral Imagery Card, then takes it away.

c. Student(s) sees, says, and writes the number(s) in the air and on paper.

d. Saying and air-writing should be done simultaneously.

e. Air-writing is large enough to see a "shadow" effect.

f. Begin with zero through ten, and then increase numbers as is appropriate for the age and level of the student(s).

g. Occasionally image in color as a further means to stimulate numeral imagery.

2. Developing Language Concepts

a. Teacher says and models movement—Student(s) says and does.

b. Teacher says—Student(s) visualizes, verbalizes, does.

c. Student(s) applies concepts to paper.

3. Checkout Activities

a. Teacher says a number name, the student(s) shows the corresponding amount of cubes (manipulatives), says, and air-writes the numeral.

b. Teacher says a number name, the student(s) says and air-writes the numeral.

c. Teacher says a number name, the student(s) says, air-writes, and paper-writes the numeral.

d. Teacher points to a numeral, the student(s) shows the corresponding amount of cubes, air-writes, and paper writes.

e. Teacher shows specific amount of cubes, the student(s) says number name, air-writes and paper-writes the numeral.

4. **Pace by overlapping to the next step while continuing to develop numeral imagery**

Group Instruction

Stimulating numeral imagery for a small group or an entire classroom does not require modification of the step; but it does require group management. Have the group or the class respond as a whole, and then check specific students to be certain they are imaging. Be alert to how individuals within the group are forming numbers when they air-write, and also call on those students with difficulty in math. Have the other students in the group give thumbs up or thumbs down regarding agreement or not, thus helping them stay active rather than passive during the instruction.

Visualizing and Verbalizing the Number Line

Now we arrive at another of Cecil's particularly fascinating mathematical abilities. Remember that along with imaging certain colors for certain numbers, Cecil also had a specific design to the number line he held in his imagination? While his was more or less up and to the right with bends at certain numbers, his son, Rod, had an elaborate figure eight for the first twenty numbers, which continued with elaborate dips and bends at specific numbers. We all have an internal number line, some more vivid than others. Ask yourself to consciously think about your number line. What direction does it go? Does it go straight or does it bend? Do you visualize colors for numbers?

Directly stimulating a visualized/verbalized number line for students is the second step of *On Cloud Nine*, the next step up the math ladder. An imaged number line is important for grasping the gestalt, the parts that make up that gestalt, and the relationship of those parts to the whole. We live in a parts/whole world, and math is no exception. Having an internal number line allows us to mentally calculate life's opportunities such as how many pages left to read, our distance from that weight goal, or how much farther to grandma's house. The number line is an imaged internal mathematical tool that allows us to move forward and backward with numbers, approximate, adjust, estimate, calculate.

While it would be fun to recreate Rod's wild number line for the mind's eye, our number line is constructed from snap-together units of ten, hence, it is in a very straight line that students will take from concrete to imagery. The gestalt of the visualized/verbalized number line is developed first and then the parts, numerals, added to it.

The Gestalt: Concept Imagery for Building, Exploring, and Imaging the Number line

By building a number line from one to a hundred, in units of ten, students feel and touch the concept of the number line. But more importantly, they see the whole, and the relationship of the number 1 to the number 100, 1 to 50, 1 to 10, and 1 to 2, etc. Here is the first development of concept imagery for mathematics.

Students see and learn the sequence and pattern of numbers in our number system. They see what number comes after 5, what number comes before 5. They see what the number 15 has in common with the number 25, the number 35, the number 45; and they see, amazingly enough, how those numbers resemble the first 10 numbers. They touch the number 1, then touch the number 2, then touch the number 100. They notice how some numbers are close together and some are far apart.

They see that snapping together the number line on the floor makes a short line from number 1 to 20. They see, in contrast, how far the number line goes across the room when it builds from number 1 to 100. They see how tall the number line grows if it is turned to a vertical position; how short it is when from number 1 to 30, how tall from 1 to 80, 1 to 100. They can imagine how much taller it would be if it could grow to 200. Would it hit the ceiling? All this provides a base for their imagery system. They can look at the number line from number 1 to 20 and close their eyes to imagine it, then look at it from number 1 to 100 and image it again. They can gesture that imagery from small to large, big to little, short to tall. Building the number line, exploring it, visualizing it, and verbalizing the imagery, creates the gestalt of the 1 to 100 number line.

S A M P L E   L E S S O N

The Concept—Building, Exploring, Imaging the Number line

The Set

Kim: *"Now that you can visualize those numbers so well, we're going to put them on a line so that you can for sure see the big picture of numbers. This is the second step up this math ladder we are climbing! And even if it's easy for you, it's important that you can picture the number line in your imagination."*

Tory: "OK."

Kim: *"Not only that, we get to do this on the floor!"*

| 1 | 2 | 3 | 4 | 5 | 6 | 7 | 8 | 9 | 10 | 11 | 12 | 13 | 14 | 15 | 16 | 17 | 18 | 19 | 20 | • • •

Lesson

"We'll take these little plastic parts and snap them together to make the number line."

Kim: *"We'll take these little plastic parts and snap them together to make the number line. Go ahead and start with the one through ten part, put it on the floor, then snap the next one on, and the next one."*

Tory: "OK." (Snapping the number line together from one through one hundred.)

"Now, let's explore this and visualize it. Touch the number two and the number three."

Kim: *"Great. Now, let's explore this and visualize it. Touch the number two and the number three."*

Tory: "OK. That's easy." (A small finger touches the number 2 and the number 3.)

Kim: *"See how close they are to one another. Now touch the number two again, and then the number fifty-two."*

"Touch the number two again, and then the number fifty-two."

Tory: "OK." (Touching the number 2, then searching and finding the number 52 much farther up the number line.)

Kim: *"Great. Did you notice that you had to go quite a bit farther up the number line to get from two to fifty-two? Right. Now, touch two to one hundred!"*

Tory: "That will be a lot farther!" (Touching the number 2, Tory has to move way up the number line to touch the 100.)

Kim: *"Good job! It's pretty far up there, huh? Now, let's visualize. Close your eyes or don't look at this number line. Imagine yourself touching the two and then touching the three."*

Tory: (Eyes closed.)

Kim: *"Did you imagine it? Show your imaginary number line with your hand, and tell me where you are on the line. Like this...two to three."* (Tory gestures up in the air, a little jump from number 2 to 3—visualizing the relationship of the numbers on the line.)

Tory: "Two to three." (Tory says and moves a little space between the number 2 and the 3 on her imaginary number line.)

Kim: *"Great. Imagine your number line again, and move from the number two to the one hundred! Only do it as far as your arm can reach, you don't have to get up like you did when you touched it on the floor."*

Tory: "Yikes, that will be a lot farther away. Two to a hundred." (Her finger points in the air to her imaginary number line starting way over to the left for the number 2 and going way over to the right for the 100.)

Kim: *"Great. As we experience the number line, your imagery will get stronger and stronger, and we'll do things like touch the number five on your imaginary number line and then touch the fifty, then touch the one hundred."*

"Show your imaginary number line with your hand, and tell me where you are on the line."

"Imagine your number line again, and move from the number two to the one hundred!"

"As we experience the number line, your imagery will get stronger and stronger..."

"Touch the number five on your imaginary number line and then touch the fifty..."

Tory: "I can do that right now. Here's where the five is (hand up, she touches a spot to the left of her body) and here's where the fifty is (her finger touches a spot about in front of her), and here's where the one hundred is (touches a spot to the far right). This is just like the imaging that I did with the numbers by themselves, but now I can put them on a line. It got pretty easy for me fast."

Kim: *"Great! Now, we'll do some more things with this number line. For example, what do you think would happen if we held it going up rather than across the floor?"*

We explored the relationship of holding it up vertically for one through forty, and saw how high it would go if we continued to build it to one hundred, laughing that it would probably crumble like stacked blocks. We continued to practice touching to imagery—she conceptualized the gestalt of the number line, the relationship of the parts to the whole. Her eyes were brightening. Numbers weren't so scary.

The Lesson Summary:

The Concept—Building, Exploring, and Imaging the Number line

1. Student(s) assembles the concrete number line from number one to one hundred.
2. Student(s) explores the gestalt of the number line by comparing and contrasting smaller numbers to larger numbers.
3. Student(s) images and describes (visualizes/verbalizes) the number line and touches imaginary numbers, comparing and contrasting smaller to larger numbers.

The Parts: Numeral Imagery for Exploring and Imaging the Numbers of the Number line

Now that the gestalt of the number line is concretely explored and imaged, the parts can be added on for specific imagery and the number relationships of base ten. Using the plastic cubes that snap together (described in Chapter 4), students put all the cubes on the number line, then learn to count by ones, tens, fives, and twos—beginning with the easiest units to count, then moving from larger chunks to smaller and smaller chunks. This step develops and integrates numeral imagery with concept imagery.

The lesson continues with Tory. Having just explored the gestalt of the number line in the same session, we get out the cubes. After we discuss that they come in different colors for each group of ten, she is ready to put them on our constructed number line.

SAMPLE LESSON

The Parts: Counting on the Concrete Number Line and Discovering Base Ten

The Set

"...we're going to use these cubes to count with a number line, and we'll practice imaging that counting."

Kim: *"Now that you have the number line imaged, we're going to use these cubes to count with a number line, and we'll practice imaging that counting."*

Tory: "OK. These look fun."

Lesson

Kim: *"See how they pull apart and snap back together? See how they are in different colors? How many are in each color?"*

Tory: "Ten." (Counting each cube.)

"Our number system is based on tens. Go ahead and put the cubes on the number line—all the way to one hundred. Keep the colors together."

Kim: *"Right. Our number system is based on tens. Go ahead and put the cubes on the number line—all the way to one hundred. Keep the colors together."*

(With younger students you may begin with less than a hundred, pacing the students according to their level.)

Tory: "There, I've got them all on. That's a lot of cubes!"

Counting by ones:

Kim: *"Right. It takes a lot of parts, numbers, to get to one hundred! Now, I want you to take your finger and touch each cube as you count all the way to one hundred."*

Tory: "OK! One, two, three, four…" (Touching and saying each number on the number line all the way to one hundred.)

Counting by tens:

Kim: *"Good for you. Touch each ten and count up the number line to one hundred. Like this: Ten, twenty, thirty…"* (Touching and saying each number, to get her started.)

Tory: "Ten, twenty, thirty, forty, fifty, sixty, seventy, eighty, ninety, one hundred." (Touching and saying all the way up to the top.)

Kim: *"Yup! That's perfect. Now, touch the ten, then touch the fifty. (Tory touches the 10, then the 50, on the number line.) Now, let's use your imaged number line instead of this one. Don't look at ours, and count by tens all the way up."*

Tory: "Easy. I can still imagine my number line. Ten, twenty, thirty…" (Touching and saying her imaginary number line from left to right.)

"Now, I want you to take your finger and touch *each* cube as you count all the way to one hundred."

"Touch each ten and count up the number line to one hundred. Like this: Ten, twenty, thirty…"

Counting by fives:

Kim: *"Great again! Now, use our number line again and touch and count by fives. Like this. Five, ten, fifteen, twenty...(demonstrating a few). Be sure the number you are saying is matching where your finger is pointing."*

"Now, use our number line again and touch and count by fives. Like this. Five, ten, fifteen, twenty..."

Tory: "Easy. Five, ten, fifteen, twenty, twenty-five, thirty, thirty-five, forty, forty-five..." (Touching and saying each number, counting and moving her body up the number line.)

Kim: *"Yup. Did you notice that your last number was five way down here, and it is another five way up here? Only now it moves five at a time within a ten."*

Tory: "Yeah, there's a pattern...hmmm...ends with a five, lands on the ten, ends with a five, lands on a ten."

Kim: *"That's right. Let's try counting by tens again, but this time let's start with the number three."*

"Let's try counting by tens again, but this time let's start with the number three."

Tory: "Three, thirteen, twenty-three, thirty-three...it did it again! Wow, I didn't really think about that before."

"Our number system is a series of tens repeated."

Kim: *"Our number system is a series of tens repeated. We only have ten squiggles we call numbers, so once we use them up we have to start combining those same numbers to show a different number, but we always go in the same order. It's a called a base ten system. Once you know about these tens down here, it is the same tens all the way up to a hundred, and even past a hundred. If we had another number line we could go to two hundred!"*

"It's called a base ten system."

Tory: "Wow, that would go way out the door!"

Kim: *"Right. The numbers would grow by tens. One hundred one, one hundred two, and then up to one hundred ten, and it can keep going up like this, one hundred twenty, one hundred thirty, etc."*

"Let's practice imaging some more. This time use the number line in your imagination and count by fives."

Tory: *"I can picture that."*

Kim: *"Of course you can! In fact, let's practice imaging some more. This time use the number line in your imagination and count by fives."*

The Lesson Summary:

The Parts—Counting on the Concrete Number line and Discovering Base Ten

1. Student(s) assembles the concrete number line.
2. Student(s) touches and counts by ones, ten, fives, and twos (odd and even) on the *concrete* number line.
3. Student(s) touches/gestures and counts by ones, tens, fives, and twos on an *imaged* number line.
4. Student(s) discovers base ten.
5. Student(s) counts, varying the starting number, to discover the pattern.

Tory touched and counted by fives, her hand in the air, touching, visualizing, and verbalizing her imaged number line. She was definitely beginning to image a number line, the gestalt and the parts. Whether she had this imaged prior to our session, who knows, but we do know *this stimulation brought imagery to a conscious level*—a level we can use to further develop her math skills. She is going to climb to the top of the ladder, and we're going to help her.

We repeated the same experience for counting by twos. The next day we rebuilt the number line, experienced the numbers concretely, then moved the stimulation to imagery and language (visualizing and verbalizing), only we focused more on counting by twos.

Counting By Twos

Once students have the gestalt and parts of the number line, it is helpful to have them grasp the concept of neighbors to be flexible going up and down the number line and counting by twos. The following lesson continues with Tory using both the concrete and imaged number line.

> ┌─────────────────────────────────────┐
> │ S A M P L E   L E S S O N │
> └─────────────────────────────────────┘

Make It Even and Up-and-Down the Number line

The Set

Kim: *"Let's keep giving our imagination more information about numbers, especially the idea of counting by twos. Usually when we think of counting by twos we think of two, four, six, eight. Right?"*

Tory: "Right. Just like we did on the number line and on my imaginary number line."

Kim: *"Exactly: Let's look at that in a different way, without the number line. We're going to use cubes to SEE the concept of counting by twos and making it even."*

Tory: "Hmmm. Making it even? OK."

Lesson

Kim: *"Let's make stairs out of these cubes. We'll make ten stairs from one to ten. Like this. Here's one cube, here's two cubes, here's three cubes. See how it makes stair steps."*

Tory: "Yeah. That's kind of neat."

Kim: *"It is. As the stairs went up, how many cubes at a time did we put on each stair?"*

"Let's keep giving our imagination more information about numbers, especially the idea of counting by twos."

"Let's make stairs out of these cubes. We'll make ten stairs from one to ten."

"This time visualize yourself doing that, just like we did with the number line."

"Instead of counting one at a time, let's count two at a time."

Tory: "One. One each time." (Exploring the cubes and verifying that it went up one each time.)

Kim: *"Right. That's just like counting one at a time. One, two, three, four…(touching each stair and going up.) You do it."*

Tory: "One, two, three, four, five, six…" (Touching each stair step and saying each number.)

Kim: *"Great. This time visualize yourself doing that, just like we did with the number line."*

Tory: "That's no problem. I can easily imagine those stairs, one, two, three…" (Small finger going up the stairs.)

Kim: *"Great. Instead of counting one at a time, let's count two at a time. And let's use the cubes first. Begin with the one cube. Place two cubes on it. Are you EVEN with the next number, or did you skip it?"*

Tory: "I had to skip over one stair. Because I went up by two rather than just one."

Kim: *"Yes, you skipped up two and your cubes are even with the next stair. Check to see if that always works…if you begin with the three and place a two cube on the three, you aren't even with the four, but you are even with the five."*

Tory: "Right. Easy. When I placed two cubes on, I went over a stair and was even with the next stair."

Kim: *"That's right. It has to be. You just learned something important about math—it always has to do the same thing. It always plays fair. Unlike reading and spelling words. Once you understand math, it always does the same thing. And pretty much it does it with the same ten numbers!"*

Tory: "That's not how I used to think about math. I always thought that math was really confusing because it was always different. But this makes it seem like math is really pretty easy once you get it."

Kim: *"Right. Now, let's look at that on the number line. Count two at a time, but start with the number one."*

Tory: "OK. I go over the number two to three, over the four to five, over the six to seven, over the eight to nine...I get this...eleven, thirteen, fifteen, seventeen, nineteen, twenty-one, twenty-three, twenty-five..." (Touching and saying.)

Kim: *"Right. That's good, and you kept your finger on the number line matching what you were saying. This time I'm going to have you move all around the number line. Put your finger on the twelve. Count forward by ones until I say stop. OK, stop."* (Stopping her on 23.)

Tory: "Easy." (Easily counting forward by ones and stopping on 23.)

Kim: *"Great. Do more counting, only use your visualized number line. Start with twelve and stop on seventeen."*

Tory: "Easy. I can picture it. Twelve, thirteen..."

"You just learned something important about math—it always has to do the same thing. It always plays fair."

"Count two at a time, but start with the number one."

"Do more counting, only use your visualized number line. Start with twelve and stop on seventeen."

Kim: *"Stop! (Stopping her at number 17.) Check your visualized number line against ours. Are you matching? Touch the number you are on. Now count back by twos with our number line until I say stop again. Touch and say each number."*

> "Check your visualized number line against ours. Are you matching?"

Tory: "Seventeen, fifteen, thirteen, eleven, nine, seven, five…"

Kim: *"Stop! Great. Now we can go up and down like that by ones or twos, or even fives or tens. Let's do some more. Sometimes we'll use the number line in front of us and sometimes we'll use our imagined one. The good thing about the one in our head is that it is always with us! Always!"*

> "Sometimes we'll use the number line in front of us and sometimes we'll use our imagined one."

Tory and Kim counted forward by ones. Then by fives. Sometimes Tory touched and said the numbers using the concrete number line, sometimes she touched and said them using her imagined number line. By the time these sessions were through Tory was easily able to image relationships on the number line, parts and whole. Sometimes a practice lesson with the number line was only with her imaged number line, and the concrete one stayed in the box.

While the number line was stabilizing, she overlapped to the next step on the math ladder: Addition Facts. She was doing more than one step of *On Cloud Nine* at a time. Perfect pacing.

Lesson Summary:

Make It Even and Up-and-Down the Number line

1. Student(s) uses cubes vertically to show stairs as numbers increase from one to ten.
2. Teacher questions to explore and verify concept of cubes increasing by one.
3. Student(s) visualizes the cubes increasing by one.
4. Student(s) discovers increasing by two.
5. Student(s) explores the make-it-even concept on the concrete number line.
6. Student(s) images the make-it-even concept on the imaged number line.
7. Student(s) counts *up and down* the concrete and imaged number line using finger to point to placement of numbers.

Practice and Pacing: Overlap between Steps!

As stated earlier, it is very important to overlap steps when pacing a sensory-cognitive program such as *On Cloud Nine*. While Tory is beginning to image the number line and demonstrate that she is beginning to understand the parts/whole relationship of numbers, she should be overlapped to the next step. In fact, she may be doing two or three steps of *On Cloud Nine* at the same time. This keeps the lesson energy and lets her see, and track, that she is moving forward—up the math ladder.

Though overlapping is important to pacing, here are the basic understandings your students should have prior to the overlap to the next step of addition facts to ten. They should be (1) familiar with the number line through one hundred, (2) able to count by ones and twos on a concrete number line to ten, (3) able to move about as directed on a concrete number line to ten, and (4) able to visualize a number line to ten.

The question of mastery is often asked of us. Our usual answer is that mastery implies automaticity, which could take quite a long time to establish, so for pacing *On Cloud Nine* think that a step is *nearly* mastered when students demonstrate about eighty percent accuracy, and self-correct the other twenty percent. While this doesn't equate to mastery, it is enough to let you comfortably move forward and still know that you'll provide some further practice with a step.

We strongly encourage stimulation on a daily basis, a minimum of twenty minutes a day.

Summary

The number line is discovered, explored, and established for students, first for the gestalt and then for the parts. The stimulation begins with the concrete number line—it can be seen and touched, put together and taken apart. As the concrete gestalt is establishing, the parts are discovered. Interlocking cubes are placed and counted to establish a sense of numbers progressing in linear fashion, the patterns of numbers noted, a base ten established. As the concreteness is explored, it is transferred to imagery, dual coded, to be used as a base for further developing math skills.

Students move around by ones, tens, fives, and twos with manipulatives on the concrete number line and in their mind with an imaged number line. They discover it is just as easy to move forward and back on a visualized number line as a concrete number line. They image a number line, focus on the beginning, and see the numbers one through ten, move toward the end and see the numbers seventy through one hundred. They place their mental finger (their awareness) on a number to designate a starting place, and move up and down by ones, tens, fives, and twos. They discover that their imaged number line is something they carry with them everywhere, and that it is flexible—it can expand and contract.

Concept and numeral imagery are establishing as a part of students' sensory systems, an internal reference. The third step on the math ladder is developing.

Summary: Step 2

Imaging the Number Line

> **Goal:** To establish an imaged number line for both the gestalt and parts of number relationships.

1. The Concept—Building, Exploring, and Imaging the Number Line

   a. Student(s) assembles the concrete number line from number one to one hundred.

   b. Student(s) explores the gestalt of the number line by comparing and contrasting smaller numbers with larger numbers on the concrete and imaged number line.

2. The Parts—Counting on the Concrete Number Line and Discovering Base Ten

   a. Student(s) touches and counts by ones, tens, fives, and twos (odd and even) on the concrete number line.

   b. Student(s) touches/gestures and counts by ones, tens, fives, and twos on imaged number line.

   c. Student(s) discovers base ten.

   d. Student(s) counts, varying the starting number, to discover the base ten pattern.

3. Make It Even and Up-and-Down the Number Line

   a. Student(s) uses cubes vertically to show stairs as numbers increase from one to ten.

   b. Teacher questions to help student(s) explore and verify concept of stairs increasing by one.

   c. Student(s) visualizes the stairs increasing by one.

   d. Student(s) discovers the make-it-even concept on the concrete number line.

   e. Student(s) images the make-it-even concept on the imaged number line.

f. Student(s) counts up and down the concrete and the imaged number line using finger to point to placement of numbers.

Group Instruction

An imaged number line can be established with groups of students; however, the questioning and exploring requires group management and control. Using the thumbs-up or thumbs-down response from the group while a specific child is responding is a simple method of keeping students actively involved in the questioning. If working with an entire class, numerous concrete number lines can be placed around the room with two to four students working each number line and responding to the stimulation. Each student in the class can visualize his or her own number line for that aspect of the stimulation. Be sure to spot check specific individuals for imagery.

The Addition Family Facts

The top of the math ladder is still very far away, but we're making progress as we move into the next step of establishing a base for math: addition facts for ten—and on through the twenties. These facts are used throughout our lives and must be imaged, internalized, for automatic access and reference. And they are dependable—unlike reading and spelling!

Have you ever tried to spell a word, even a word you know you know, but could only come up with a variety of phonetic representations? When I, Nanci Bell, wrote the book *Seeing Stars*, I told a little story about the day I went to leave a note for my plumber and found that the word "fossit" had mysteriously vanished from my spelling lexicon. No matter how many ways I spelled it, with my three children in the background clambering and fighting in a familiar pre-school routine, I couldn't land on the right representation: fossit, fausit, phawcet, phossit, fossat, fossut, or even phawsit...all *looked* wrong, but the right way was lost somewhere in my head. Even the dictionary didn't help, until fortunately the word decided to fly to me again, "faucet"—and life progressed as usual. At that moment, spelling wasn't my friend, it was holding me up, slowing me down with too many possibilities, perhaps even contributing to the ensuing argument about who got the last cookie for their lunch. Math wouldn't have done that to me!

In contrast, number facts are friendly. Three plus two will never be anything but five. Never. There aren't other possibilities. The consistency and dependability of math is probably responsible for the phrase, "You can count on me." And numbers are something you can count on. There are only so many numbers to ten, and there are only so many combinations of numbers that make up ten. Once the finite possibilities for math are imaged and placed in memory, the world of numbers begins to take on a constancy and dependability that can be counted on.

On Cloud Nine discovers, reinforces, practices, and memorizes the addition facts of ten by (1) using manipulatives to make the facts for each number real, (2) putting that realness into imagery for automatic use, and (3) transferring the imagery to mental and print computation. This step has the student(s) do the following.

- Discover the concept of addition and number family facts with the Addition Family Fact Sheets.

- Reinforce with cubes to experience the relationships within the *number family.*

- Use the *concrete number line*, with cubes, to experience specific facts.

- Use an *imaged number line* to image specific facts.

- Use Family Fact Cards to place specific facts in memory.

Tory is ready to experience math facts of ten, and place them in her imagery system for instant retrieval with the *On Cloud Nine* Family Fact Sheets.

SAMPLE   LESSON

Discovering the Family Facts with the Family Fact Sheets

The Set

Kim: *"I want you to discover with the cubes some of the math facts. We'll call them families, because each number has a family of number facts. You may already know some of these, but I want you to be able to visualize them and think with them."*

Tory: "Families of numbers? Hmmm."

"Every number has
a family of facts that
are special only to
that number."

Family Fact Sheet for number 1:

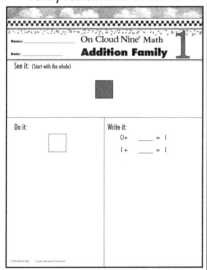

Lesson

Kim: *"Right. Every number has a family of facts that are special only to that number. Let me show you what I mean. We will start with the family of the number one, the math facts for number one. Here's a Family Fact Sheet to help us know who is in the family of number one.*

"We'll put cubes here to know which number we are working on. If we're working on the number one, how many cubes will go on the top of the sheet? Pick any color cube you want. We'll call that cube our goal for the family."

Tory: "Just one cube. I pick yellow for my goal color."

Kim: *"Right. One cube for the number one. Now, let's go to the Do It part of our sheet and discover the facts in the family of one. For example, if you have nothing in your hand, zero, how many more will you need to make the family of one or to match your goal?"*

Tory: "If I have nothing, I will need one more to get to one." (Putting a cube on the Do It part of the sheet.)

Kim: *"Right. If you start with nothing, or zero, you have to get one cube to make the family of one. So, we could say that zero plus one equals one. Right?"*

Tory: "Right."

Kim: *"Start with that cube on the Do It part of your sheet. (Tory points on the sheet.) Now how many do you need to make one?"*

Tory: "Zero. (Sort of snorting...) I can't put

anything more. If I do, I'll have more than one!"

Kim: *"Right. So, we could say that one plus zero equals one."*

Tory: "Okay."

Kim: *"Let's write down what we discovered so far. You say it to me and I'll write. You said we started with nothing and then needed one more to get to one. I'll write that down. You talk me through it. How do I write nothing?"*

Tory: "Zero."

Kim: *"Right. (Writing 0 on the sheet.) Now you said we need one more so we write that with a plus sign, like this. That means we have added."* (Writing 0 + 1.)

Tory: "Right. I knew that."

Kim: *"I know you knew but we're just climbing up that math ladder and we don't want to skip a step and then not make it to the top! So, we're going to take each step even if we only talk about it quickly. Now let's be sure we have the whole equation."*

Tory: "Zero plus one equals one." (Kim writing 0 + 1 = 1 as Tory verbalized.)

Kim: *"Exactly. Now let's write the other numbers in the family of one."*

Tory: "One plus zero equals one." (Kim writing 1 + 0 = 1 as Tory verbalized.)

Kim: *"Perfect. That's the family of one, and there can't be any other numbers in that family. Watch. Could these numbers be in the family of one? Zero plus two (showing nothing in her*

"Let's write down what we discovered so far."

"Zero plus one equals one."

"One plus zero equals one."

hand and then putting two cubes in it)? Could zero plus two be in the family of one?"

Tory: "No! That's two!"

Kim: "Right! How about zero plus four? Could those numbers be in the family of one?"

Tory: "No! Those numbers don't make up one!"

Kim: "Exactly. Math facts will be your friends, Tory, because they always stay the same. They won't change on you. Once you know them, have them imaged, they'll always be the same. Now you have a family sheet for the number one."

The lesson continued…

Kim: "I knew this would be easy for you, now let's discover a few more families. Let's do the family of two. Put your goal cubes up there so we know which family we're in, and now let's start with nothing, zero, on the sheet. How many more will you need to make two?"

Tory: "Two! (Getting two cubes.)"

Kim: "Great. Tell me what to write down for our first equation."

Tory: "Zero plus two equals two."

Kim: "Perfect. This time let's start with two cubes on the sheet. How many more do you need to make two?"

Tory: "Zero!"

Kim: "Right. Notice it is the same two numbers that make two and it doesn't matter what order we put them in! Here's zero in my hand (holding nothing in the left hand) and here's two in my other hand (holding two cubes in

"That's the family of one, and there can't be any other numbers in that family."

"Let's do the family of two."

"Put your goal cubes up there so we know which family we're in."

"Start with nothing on the sheet. How many more will you need to make two?"

"This time let's start with two cubes on the sheet. How many more do you need to make two?"

"Now for the facts of three. You talk me through it this time."

the right hand). It doesn't matter which hand comes first (crossing the hands), it will still make two. Let's find more in the family of two. Usually we discover them from zero to one, etc., but I skipped ahead just to show that."

The lesson continued. They started the threes:

Kim: *"Now for the facts of three. You talk me through it this time."*

Tory: "OK. I put three red cubes for my goal. If I have zero, I need three to equal three. (Putting three green cubes on the dotted squares on the Do It part of the sheet.) If I start with one (taking the three green cubes off the dotted squares and putting one green cube back), I need to add two to equal three. (Putting two yellow cubes on the dotted squares. The Do It part of the sheet has one green and two yellows.) If I have two, I need..."

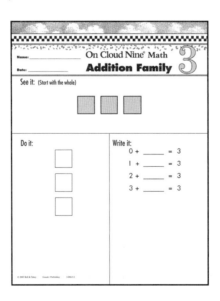

The Family of 2:	The Family of 3:	The Family of 4:
0 + 2 = 2	0 + 3 = 3	0 + 4 = 4
1 + 1 = 2	1 + 2 = 3	1 + 3 = 4
2 + 0 = 2	2 + 1 = 3	2 + 2 = 4
	3 + 0 = 3	3 + 1 = 4
		4 + 0 = 4

The Family of 5:	The Family of 6:	The Family of 7:
0 + 5 = 5	0 + 6 = 6	0 + 7 = 7
1 + 4 = 5	1 + 5 = 6	1 + 6 = 7
2 + 3 = 5	2 + 4 = 6	2 + 5 = 7
3 + 2 = 5	3 + 3 = 6	3 + 4 = 7
4 + 1 = 5	4 + 2 = 6	4 + 3 = 7
5 + 0 = 5	5 + 1 = 6	5 + 2 = 7
	6 + 0 = 6	6 + 1 = 7
		7 + 0 = 7

The Family of 8:	The Family of 9:	The Family of 10:
0 + 8 = 8	0 + 9 = 9	0 + 10 = 10
1 + 7 = 8	1 + 8 = 9	1 + 9 = 10
2 + 6 = 8	2 + 7 = 9	2 + 8 = 10
3 + 5 = 8	3 + 6 = 9	3 + 7 = 10
4 + 4 = 8	4 + 5 = 9	4 + 6 = 10
5 + 3 = 8	5 + 4 = 9	5 + 5 = 10
6 + 2 = 8	6 + 3 = 9	6 + 4 = 10
7 + 1 = 8	7 + 2 = 9	7 + 3 = 10
8 + 0 = 8	8 + 1 = 9	8 + 2 = 10
	9 + 0 = 9	9 + 1 = 10
		10 + 0 = 10

Lesson Summary:

Discovering the Family Facts with the Family Fact Sheets

1. Student(s) places goal cube(s) on the Family Fact Sheet.
2. Student(s) discovers, with cubes in hands or on the sheet, the facts within the number *family*.
3. Teacher/student(s) writes the facts for each family as student(s) verbalizes.
4. Student(s) always begins and ends with the zero.
5. Student(s) and teacher discuss numbers increasing and decreasing on either side of the sign.
6. Teacher/student(s) dialogue and actions:

    — Teacher says, "If you have *zero*, how many more do you need to get to _____?"

    — Teacher or student(s) places one cube and teacher says, "If you have *one*, how many more do you need to get to _____?"

    — Teacher or student(s) places two cubes and teacher says, "If you have *two*, how many more do you need to get to _____?"

Discovering the math families with the Family Fact Sheets should be paced according to the needs of your students. For example, if the students are beginners or severely impaired in math, it is preferable to do only a few of the families, but at least do enough to show contrast in the numbers. We usually do the zero, one, two, and three sheets in the first session. Then reinforce those and add a few more in the next session.

Having discovered the facts for a few families, Tory was ready to begin imaging the equations and using Family Fact Cards. In fact, she might have imaged the relationships at the time of discovery. Here she is learning how to use the Family Fact Cards to image (and memorize) the facts.

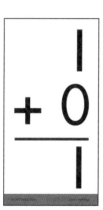

S A M P L E   L E S S O N

Using Family Fact Cards to Visualize and Verbalize the Facts

The Set

Kim: *"Now that you have discovered the family facts, let's put them into imagery to help you remember them. I'll show you a Family Fact Card for you to visualize, then I'll take it away and you tell me what you saw."*

Tory: "OK. That should be pretty easy. I can visualize numbers now. Um, I've had flash cards before. Are these like them?"

Kim: *"I bet you have, and yes these are similar, only this time we're going to use them to help you visualize, so we're going to call them Family Fact Cards rather than flash cards. For example, I'll hold the card up and after I take it away you say and write in the air."*

Tory: "Oh…"

Lesson

Kim: *"Let's do the family of one. (Holding up the 1 + 0 = 1 card for about three seconds, and then taking it away.) Now, let's visualize that as we say it. Like this. (Air-writing while verbalizing.) One plus zero equals one. Now you do that."*

Tory: "One plus zero equals one." (Air-writing each part of the equation: numbers and signs.)

Kim: *"Great. Now, with the cards let's do the whole family of one. Here's another fact in the family*

of one. *(Holding up 0 + 1 = 1 for a few seconds and then taking it away.) Visualize it and verbalize it as you write.*"

Tory: "That's easy. Zero plus one equals one (air-writing and verbalizing)…and one plus zero equals one (air-writing and verbalizing). I did the whole family!"

Kim: *"Right. Let's continue visualizing and verbalizing more family facts. Try this one."*

Lesson Summary:

Using Family Fact Cards to Visualize and Verbalize the Addition Facts

1. Teacher holds up a Family Fact Card for a few seconds.
2. Student(s) images and air-writes the numbers and signs.
3. Teacher questions for specific numbers or signs in the equation.

The lessons overlapped with Tory discovering families, using her Family Fact Sheet; talking Kim through the facts of the family, and then imaging from the Family Fact Cards. By the next few sessions, Tory had discovered the facts of one through ten. She had practiced imaging each family from the Family

Fact Cards, after discovering it with manipulatives. Then she imaged the other families previously discovered and imaged. Soon she had worked on all the Family Fact Cards, and having walked up the math ladder step by step, she knew nearly all her facts. Here is a lesson in practicing numeral imagery for the addition facts.

SAMPLE LESSON

Practicing with the Family Fact Cards

The Set

"I'll show you this card and then I'll take it away…"

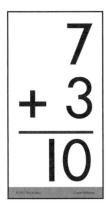

Kim: *"We've discovered the families and their facts. Today we'll just practice imaging and remembering them. I'll check your imagery by asking you for specific numbers. I suppose you've figured out by now that imaging helps you remember."*

Tory: "Yeah, it really does. I can just see the answers in my head…my imagination. It really helps."

Lesson

"I can see it in my imagination. Seven plus three equals ten."

Kim: *"I'll show you this card and then I'll take it away…then you say and write the whole equation in the air. Ready! Here's your first one. (Holding up the card: 7 + 3 = 10.)*

Tory: "Easy. I can see it in my imagination. Seven plus three equals ten." (Saying and air-writing numbers and signs.)

"Right. Now, what is the second number you saw?"

Kim: *"Right. Now, what is the second number you saw?"*

Tory: "Hmmm. (Sort of whispering to herself, her hand up and writing the equation.) Three."

"What is the last number you saw?"

"Seven plus what number equals ten? Can you see it in your imagery, and tell me the number?"

"Write it on paper for me."

"Let's do some more imaging of family facts."

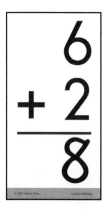

Kim:	*"Right again. What is the last number you saw?"*
Tory:	"Easy. The ten."
Kim:	*"Right again. So if I said seven plus three equals…what is the answer you would see in your head and say to me?"*
Tory:	"Ten!"
Kim:	*"Perfect. Seven plus what number equals ten? Can you see it in your imagery, and tell me the number?"*
Tory:	"Easy again. It is the three. Seven plus three equals ten. I can see the number three."
Kim:	*"Perfect again. Write the equation on paper for me. And we'll do some more.*
Tory:	"This is really helping me remember those facts." (Writing the equation on a piece of paper.)
Kim:	*"Great. Now, here's some more fun stuff to do. If you know that seven plus three equals ten, then you also know what three plus seven equals. Right?"*
Tory:	"Sure. That's ten too. We checked that with those cubes a while back. It didn't matter what hand I had it in, the numbers in the family had to stay the same. And I can see it in my imagination. Seven and three are part of the ten family and it doesn't matter which order they come in."
Kim:	*"That's exactly right. Let's do some more imaging of family facts. (Holding up the 6 + 2 = 8 card for a few seconds and taking*

"OK. Tell me what you saw."	*it away.) OK. Tell me what you saw."*
	Tory: "Easy, easy. That was six plus two equals eight."
"What was the first number you saw?"	**Kim:** *"Yup. What was the first number you saw?"*
	Tory: "The six!"
	Kim: *"Yup. What was the sign you saw telling you what to do with the six?"*
"What was the sign you saw?"	**Tory:** "Easy. It was the plus sign telling me to add the six to the two."
	Kim: *"Right. What was the last number you saw?"*
	Tory: "The eight."
"What was the last number you saw?"	**Kim:** *"Change the first two numbers around in your picture and tell me what you see."*
	Tory: "Well, now it would have to be two plus six…equals eight."
	Kim: *"Perfect. Six and two are part of the eight family and…"*
"Change the first two numbers around in your picture and tell me what you see."	**Tory:** "And it doesn't matter which one goes first or last, just like we did in my hand."
	Kim: *"Exactly."*

Lesson Summary:

Practicing with the Family Fact Cards

1. Teacher holds up a Family Fact Card for a few seconds.
2. Student(s) images and air-writes the numbers and signs.
3. Teacher questions for specific numbers or signs in the equation.
4. Student(s) begins to visualize and verbalize without air-writing.

Practicing

The goal is to develop automaticity with the math facts, and while imagery is the means to do that, it requires practice to reinforce both concept and numeral imagery. Continuing to use manipulatives reinforces both aspects of imagery, concretizing as well as reinforcing.

Here are some practice activities with the cubes, number line (concrete and imaged), and numeral imagery to develop visualizing and verbalizing automaticity:

- Imagery and cubes alone
- Imagery and cubes on the concrete number line
- Imagery and NO cubes on the concrete number line
- Imaged number line alone
- Imagery and doubling
- Imagery with Family Fact Cards always

Here is Tory, ready for some reinforcement and practice activities. She has discovered the families and learned to image the facts, but these need reinforcement to establish the reality of math. She'll begin by talking through the addition facts for each number using the cubes without the Family Fact Cards.

SAMPLE LESSON

Imagery and Cubes Alone

The Set

Kim: *"Now we are going to practice the addition facts with imagery and just the cubes. Let's start with the family of four. Even though I know you are learning to image the facts in this family, we're going to get to know the family better!"*

Tory: "OK."

Lesson

Kim: *"Talk me through all the facts of four—begin with zero, nothing. Put a stack of four cubes on the table. We'll match the stack on the table with cubes in your hand. For example, there's nothing in your hand and you want to get to four. So go get some cubes to match the ones on the table. Be sure your movements with the cubes match what you're telling me."*

Tory: "OK. If I begin with nothing, I need four cubes (placing a stack of four cubes in her hand) to make the four family."

Kim: *"Great. This time start with one."*

Tory: "OK. If I start with one (moving one cube off), that means I need these three to get four (placing three on the one). Now, I have four again."

Kim: *"Right. You've got four again. So, one plus three equals four. Each time, tell me what the fact is. This time start with two."*

Tory: "If I begin with two (placing two in one hand), then I will need these other two to get four (putting the two cubes with other two cubes). Two plus two equals four."

Kim: *"Great again. You've got four cubes again. Now begin with three."*

Tory: "If I begin with three (placing three in her hand), then I just need this one to get four (placing the one with the three). Three plus one equals four."

Kim: *"Perfect. You've got four cubes again, now*

> *begin with four. How many more will you need?"*

Tory: "Hah! If I begin with all four, I don't need any more!" (Holding up her hand with all four cubes in it.)

Kim: *"Just like what we wrote on this Family Fact Sheet (showing the sheet for the family of four), the numbers get smaller on one side and bigger on the other, but no matter what you do those numbers are in the family of four! Visualize that and talk me through what you picture, but I'll make it easier for you—you don't have to write it in the air this time!"*

Tory: "Zero plus four equals four (starting to air-write and then stopping herself)."

Kim: *"Exactly right. Do the rest of them.*

Tory: "One plus three equals four." (Eyes up, but not air-writing, just verbalizing.)

Lesson Summary:

Imagery and Cubes Alone

1. Student(s) places a set of cubes on the table for a specific number.
2. Teacher requests student(s) to start with a specific number of cubes in hand and get remaining cubes to match a specific number.
3. Student(s) demonstrates the facts of a specific number with cubes in hand.
4. Student(s) verbalizes while experiencing each equation.
5. Student(s) visualizes and verbalizes the facts, sometimes air-writing, sometimes not.

Practice continues with the number line and cubes. The following lesson may be done on the same day the students discovered the families and learned to image the facts. These are reinforcement activities that show relationships with numbers and it is often wise to do them the first time the family is discovered, as well as for general practice. Also, remember to *only* do this practice for the families your students have previously discovered and imaged.

> # SAMPLE   LESSON

Imagery and the Number Line with Cubes

The Set

Kim: *"Let's practice those family facts and that imaging some more. This time let's use the number line and the cubes."*

Tory: "OK. (Putting the number line together, ready to go!)

Lesson

"Visualize three plus two, and then show it on the number line with the cubes."

Kim: *"Here we go. I'll give you an equation, you visualize it, and then use the cubes on the number line to show it. Visualize three plus two, and then show it on the number line with the cubes."*

Tory: "Three (getting and putting three cubes on the number line) plus two (getting and putting two cubes on the number line) makes five! Easy."

Kim: *"It sure does. Now, say and write that in the air."*

Tory: "Three plus two equals five." (Air-writing the numerals/signs.)

Kim *"Great! Now take those off and do three plus seven. Visualize it, then put the cubes*

79

> *on the number line as you tell me what you are doing."*

Tory: "Three (getting and putting three cubes on the number line) plus seven (getting and putting seven cubes on the number line) makes ten!"

Kim: *"It sure does. Now say and write that in the air again."*

Tory: "Three plus seven equals ten." (Air-writing the numerals/signs.)

Lesson Summary:

Imagery and the Number Line with Cubes

1. Teacher gives student(s) an equation verbally.
2. Student(s) uses the cubes on the concrete number line to experience the equation.
3. Student(s) visualizes and verbalizes the equation, *sometimes* air-writing.

Tory experienced and imaged, and when her responses were quite automatic, the lesson was extended to the number line without the cubes in preparation for only the imaged number line. For example, if the equation was 4 + 2, Tory placed her finger on the number four and then moved forward two spaces. Once experienced, it was visualized and verbalized. Here it is.

SAMPLE LESSON

Imagery and the Number Line without Cubes
The Set

Kim: *"You're doing great using the cubes and the number line, so now let's practice with just the number line and your finger! This will continue to help you visualize these facts so they can for sure be your friends."*

Tory: "They're starting to be my friends now."

Lesson

Kim: *"Point to the number four. How many does it take to get to six?"*

Tory: "I need to move up two spaces to get to six (moving her finger as she verbalizes)."

Kim: *"Good. Say that equation to me and write it in the air."*

Tory: "Four plus two equals six (air-writing)."

Kim: *"Great. And if you have three, how many spaces do you need to move to get to six?"*

Tory: "I need to move up three spaces to get to six (moving her finger)."

Kim: *"Great again. Now, visualize and verbalize, but this time you don't have to write it in the air. Just tell me what you picture."*

Tory: "Three plus three equals six." (Eyes up, visualizing and verbalizing, but not air-writing.)

"Point to the number four. How many does it take to get to six?"

"I need to move up two spaces to get to six."

"Good. Say that equation to me and write it in the air."

The Lesson Summary:

Imagery and the Number Line without Cubes

1. Student(s) points to starting number on the concrete number line.
2. Teacher has student(s) add a number to the starting number, using the number line but no cubes.
3. Student(s) visualizes and verbalizes the equation, sometimes air-writing, giving the answer.

Tory is ready to practice the imaged number line and these facts. Again, the practice lessons can be combined and used all in one day. Tory's imagery is getting good, she is quickly moving her finger up, and it's time to apply the reality of math to her internal number line. Now she'll visualize, verbalize, and gesture the addition facts on her imaged number line.

SAMPLE LESSON

Facts and the Imaged Number Line

The Set

Kim: *"Adding on the number line is getting easy for you, so now let's just visualize the number line and do the same thing with adding numbers. But, instead of touching your finger on a number line in front of you, I want you to touch your finger on the number line in your imagination."*

Tory: "Easy."

Lesson

Kim: *"Imagine your number line from one to ten. Show me where the one is. Now show me the ten. Good. How about the three? OK. You have your imaged number line set. Here's your equation. Four plus three. Where is your starting point? Put your finger there."*

Tory: "My starting point is four so I have my finger here. I go up three more to seven."

Kim: *"That's good. I like how you verbalized as you were pointing. Visualize and verbalize the whole thing to me, but you don't have to write the numbers in the air, just touch the spot on your imaginary number line and tell me what you saw."*

> "...instead of touching your finger on a number line in front of you, I want you to touch your finger on the number line in your imagination."

82

Tory: "Three plus four is seven." (Verbalizing and touching her imaginary number line.)

Kim: *"Perfect. Show me four plus five."*

Lesson Summary:

Facts and the Imaged Number Line

1. Student(s) imagines own number line.
2. Student(s) points to starting number, designated by teacher, on imaged number line.
3. Teacher has student add a number to the starting number.
4. Student(s) visualizes and verbalizes the equation, moving finger on imaged number line.
5. Student(s) visualizes and verbalizes the equation again, sometimes air-writing, giving the answer.

While it is great that Tory can image and use numbers, one of the best tools of math that she should experience is the concept of doubling, and doubling plus one. As with all of *On Cloud Nine*, she will first experience doubling with manipulatives, then visualize and verbalize, and then apply the concepts to paper computation.

SAMPLE LESSON

Experiencing and Imaging the Doubles
The Set

Kim: *"I can't wait to show you this! It is one of the most helpful things you can use in math. It's called doubling. And you can even use it to help you with subtraction. Get out those cubes."*

Tory: "I hate subtraction (getting out the cubes and sort of mumbling). I don't do very well in it."

Kim: *"Well, that will soon change. But for right now we're going to learn the doubles. And just like the rest of the math facts, these will be your friends. Let's meet the doubles!"*

Lesson

Kim: *"Show me one cube."*

Tory: "OK." (Placing one cube on the table.)

Kim: *"Good. Now, get out one more cube and place it right next to that one."*

Tory: "OK." (Placing a new cube on the table, right next to the first one.)

Kim: *"Good. Touch each cube, and tell me what you have, like this. One plus one equals…"*

Tory: "One plus one equals two!" (Saying and touching each cube.)

"Start with two blocks on the table and then get two more."

Kim: *"Right. We doubled the one. In other words, we did the one two times. That's called doubling. Let's double the number two. Start with two blocks on the table and then get two more."*

Tory: "OK." (Placing a stack of two cubes and then another stack of two cubes right next to it.)

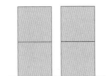

Kim: *"Perfect. You doubled the two. So, talk me through what you have now. Say and touch those blocks. Two and two makes…"*

"Perfect. You doubled the two. So, talk me through what you have now. Say and touch those blocks. Two and two makes…"

Tory: "Two plus two makes four."

Kim: *"Great. Now, let's image that just like we did the others. Say and write it in the air."*

Tory: "Two plus two equals four." (Saying and air-writing.)

Kim: *"Great again. This time start with three. Double three using the cubes first, then visualizing and verbalizing. We'll put these on cards for you to learn and make these instant or automatic, just like we did the Family Fact Cards."*

Lesson Summary:

Experiencing and Imaging the Doubles

1. Student(s) uses cubes to experience the concept of doubling a number.
2. Student(s) verbalizes the equation.
3. Student(s) visualizes and verbalizes the equation, air-writing.
4. Student(s) sees the cubes increasing by two, one on each side.
5. Student(s) uses Doubles Cards to visualize and verbalize, committing the doubles to memory.

Tory experienced doubling with cubes standing side by side to "see" them double, then she applied that reality to imagery, but she also saw the cubes increase by two, one on each side, as the numbers increased. For example, for three plus three, she experienced three stacked cubes standing next to three stacked cubes, and when the number increased to four plus four, she saw that one block had to be added to each stack of cubes, so the answer increased by two! Numbers were becoming her friends—friends she could count on.

The doubles were learned and here she is doubling plus one.

SAMPLE   LESSON

Doubles Plus One

The Set

Kim: *"Now we're going to use the doubles to help us get answers easily in math. It's a trick a lot of people use."*

Tory: "Cool! A trick."

Lesson

Kim: *"Here we go. Show me two cubes. Good. Now, show me a another set of two."*

Tory: "Here they are on the table." (Placing two stacks of two cubes.)

Kim: *"Good. What is two plus two?"*

Tory: "Easy. Four. Two plus two is four."

Kim: *"Right. Keep those cubes out there and show me two plus three. How many more cubes do you have to put on?"*

Tory: "One. Oh. I get it! I have to put on one more cube. So, two plus two is four, and two plus three has to be five!"

Kim: *"That's exactly right. How many did you go up?"*

Tory: "I went up one more. So, if two plus two was four, two plus three had to be five. One more up."

Kim: *"Exactly. Let's do some more. You know what four plus four is, right?"*

Tory: "Eight! Four plus four is eight."

Kim: *"Right. Show me that with cubes."*

Tory: "OK. There." (Placing two stacks of four cubes on the table.)

Kim: *"If you know that four plus four is eight, you also know that four plus five makes what? Show me with the cubes."*

"If you know that four plus four is eight, you also know that four plus five makes what? Show me with the cubes."

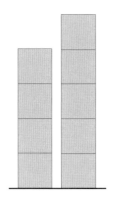

Tory: "Four plus five has to make nine. I have to put one more cube on. So, it has to be nine! I used to hear some of the other kids in school talk like that, but I never really knew what they meant. They'd say things to me like, Tory, four plus five is easy because you know what four plus four is. But I never really knew what they were talking about!"

Kim: *"Now you do! Let's practice visualizing that also. You won't even have to write in the air, just tell me what you see—visualize it and verbalize it on the visualized number line! Start with the one we just did. Four plus four, and go up one."*

Tory: "Four plus four is eight, so four plus five is nine (eyes up, imaging as she talked)."

Tory experienced and visualized and then practiced doubling plus one on paper with a variety of written problems.

The Lesson Summary:

Doubles Plus One

1. Student(s) experiences doubling with cubes.
2. Student(s) experiences doubling *plus one* with the cubes.
3. Student(s) visualizes and verbalizes the equation.
4. Student(s) computes written problems.

Flash Cards as "Imagery Cards"

Math facts rest in imagery for us, and when they disappear it is just as unpleasant as when spelling disappears! Not being able to retrieve a math fact can be just as frustrating as trying to leave a note for a plumber. For us adults, the addition facts are usually intact, even with the onset of old age. But this is not always the case for children. So, reinforcement with flash cards is a tried and true stand-by in math, but one that now needs to be consciously brought to an imaged level. There are several ways to practice math facts with "imagery cards." One is what Tory did previously, where a Family Fact Card with the math fact equation was held up, then taken away. She visualized and verbalized what she saw, and told specific number placement. Another is to put the equation on the front of a card and the answer on the back. Another is similar, but puts the facts in a triangle that can also be used when we get to subtraction. We use Cloud Triangle Cards.

For the first way described above, show the Family Fact Card with the whole number fact equation and have students visualize and verbalize what they see. For the second, show an imagery card that only has the facts on the front and the answer on the back. This method is good for testing imagery and automaticity. Categorize the cards into groups of fast, medium, and slow (which can often be named according to fast, medium, and slow animals or vehicles, such as rockets, dogs, and snails). The cards can be kept for each student, similar to sight word practice in reading, in a personalized card-recipe box.

The Cloud Triangle Cards have the facts of the family but not a sign, thus the cards can be used for both adding and subtracting. If only using for adding, then always cover the largest number when you ask the question. With each

number of the equation in a separate corner of the Cloud Triangle Card, cover one number. Here's an example. Hold up the card with the numerals 2, 3, and 5. Cover the five and ask the student what the answer would be if you add the two numbers uncovered. These cards can be used to practice both addition and subtraction.

Facts from Eleven through Twenty

Once students have learned the facts through ten, and can image those relationships and numbers, they need to image and memorize the facts from eleven through twenty. This can be overlapped with the "jumping" step of *On Cloud Nine* or taught now after experiencing and learning the doubles. Either way, students must learn the facts for eleven through twenty, and they must know them as automatically as they know the facts from one to ten.

Approach learning the eleven—twenty facts using the doubles. Begin with five plus five, and move to six plus five, then seven plus five, then eight plus five, etc. Do this exploration with the cubes and number line, just as you did with the facts of ten and below. After experience with manipulatives, use Family Fact Cards and have students image them just as you did with the facts of ten and below. Use the same procedure of experience with the concrete, visualizing and verbalizing, and then application to written computation.

Once subtraction is introduced, there is an easy way to teach the nines. Use the tens and have students subtract one—adding imagery. For example, thinking with tens, students can easily add nine plus six, by first adding ten plus six and taking one away. They can experience this on the number line with and without the cubes, then with imagery and language, and finally on cards.

Practicing Visualizing and Verbalizing with the Math Ball

The Math Ball game is another way to get visualizing and verbalizing into the practice of math facts. Use a small ball or bean bag for the activity, and set which number is in the game. For example, if the student and teacher are working on facts for the family of eight, the teacher begins the game by tossing the ball to the student and saying a number, "two." The student catches the ball and tosses back to teacher saying "six," the number needed to get to eight. This activity stimulates visualizing and verbalizing, gets students active, and can easily be done with groups or even whole classrooms (if you've got the courage…or the control).

S A M P L E   L E S S O N

The Math Ball Game

The Set

Kim: *"Let's play a game to help us visualize and verbalize the math facts. Let's start with the family of eight. I'll say a number as I pass the ball, you pass it back to me and say the number I need to get to eight. For example, if I throw you a four you would throw me back another four.*

Tory: "Fun!"

Lesson

Kim: *"Ready. We're doing the family of eight. Here's a six (saying and tossing the ball). Catch it and throw back the ball, telling me the number we need to get to eight if we are at six!"*

Tory: "Two." (Throwing back the ball.)

Kim: *"That's right. Try to be as quick as you can. Here's the three. If we're working on the family of eight, what number do you have to throw back to me?"* (Throwing the ball to Tory.)

Tory: "Five back to you."

Kim: *"Great. Here comes a one."* (Throwing the ball.)

Tory: (Throwing it back.) "Seven back to you."

> **Lesson Summary:**
>
> *Math Ball Game*
>
> 1. Teacher throws the ball, saying one number in a designated number family.
> 2. Student(s) catches and throws/says the appropriate number back to the teacher.
> 3. May be played as a game with one or more students.
> 4. If working on the family of five, teacher says, "Here comes one," throwing the ball. Catching the ball and throwing it back, the student says, "Four back to you."
> 5. Visualizing and verbalizing are unconsciously stimulated.

Pencil and Paper Tasks

Application to print computation is usually done at the end of each lesson, rather than waiting for a separate lesson. Apply math while it has just been experienced and imaged. Students should follow these steps for computation: (1) check the sign, (2) visualize what the sign tells you to do, (3) verbalize the equation, and (4) do! Check, visualize, verbalize, and do! If need be, have the student use a concrete or visualized number line to locate a starting point, then verbalize the direction indicated by the sign.

Pacing and Practice

As with all of *On Cloud Nine* steps, overlapping is the key to maintaining lesson energy and joy in learning. But overlapping also helps climb the math ladder because one process supports another. Your goal is automaticity in imaging addition facts, but long before that you will probably overlap to subtraction. Look for the following: (1) the ability to answer addition facts to ten with about 80% accuracy, (2) the ability to independently prove facts with cubes and the number line, and (3) the ability to consistently and accurately visualize the number line to ten.

Summary

Both concept and numeral imagery are the bases for understanding and memorizing the addition math facts for ten. With the reality of math cubes and the number line, base ten is discovered, experienced, visualized, and verbalized. The dual coding of imagery and language are brought to a conscious level with numerous practice exercises, focusing on the formula of concrete to imagery to computation. Every exercise is followed by paper and pencil activities for the application of dual coding to written math computation.

As students learn and memorize the number families for addition, the instruction overlaps to subtraction, the next chapter. Math is slowly becoming Tory's friend, and she is soon to conquer subtraction.

Summary:
Step 3

Addition Family Facts

> **Goal:** To develop the dual coding of imagery and language to a conscious level for understanding and memorizing the addition facts from one through ten and twenty.

1. Discovering the Family Facts with the Family Fact Sheets

  a. Student(s) places a goal cube on the Family Fact Sheet.

  b. Student(s) discovers, with cubes in hands or on the card, the facts within the number *family*.

  c. Teacher writes the facts for each family as student(s) verbalizes.

  d. Student(s) begins and ends with the zero.

  e. Teacher and student(s) discuss numbers increasing and decreasing on either side of the sign.

  f. Teacher/student(s) dialogue and actions:

  — Teacher says, "If you have *zero*, how many more do you need to get to _____?"

  — Teacher or student(s) places one cube and teacher says, "If you have *one*, how many more do you need to get to _____?"

  — Teacher or student(s) places two cubes and says, "If you have *two*, how many more do you need to get to _____?"

2. Using Family Fact Cards to Visualize and Verbalize Addition Facts

  a. Teacher holds up a Family Fact Card for a few seconds.

  b. Student(s) images and air-writes the numbers and signs.

  c. Teacher questions for specific numbers or signs in the equation.

  d. Student(s) begins to visualize and verbalize without air-writing.

3. **Practice Activities**

a. Imagery and Cubes Alone:

   1. Student(s) places a set of cubes on the table for a specific number.

   2. Teacher requests the student(s) to start with a specific number of cubes in hand and get remaining cubes to match a specific number.

   3. Student(s) demonstrates the facts of a specific number with cubes in hand.

   4. Student(s) verbalizes while experiencing each equation.

   5. Student(s) visualizes and verbalizes the facts, sometimes air-writing, sometimes not.

b. Imagery and the Concrete Number Line with Cubes:

   1. Teacher gives student(s) an equation verbally.

   2. Student(s) uses the cubes on the concrete number line to experience the equation.

   3. Student(s) visualizes and verbalizes the equation, *sometimes* air-writing.

c. Imagery and the Number Line *without* Cubes:

   1. Student(s) points to starting number designated by teacher.

   2. Teacher has student(s) add a number to the starting number.

   3. Student(s) visualizes and verbalizes the equation, sometimes air-writing, giving the answer.

d. Addition Facts and the Imaged Number Line:

   1. Student(s) imagines own number line.

   2. Student(s) points to starting number, designated by teacher, on imaged number line.

   3. Teacher has student(s) add a number to the starting number.

   4. Student(s) visualizes and verbalizes the equation, moving finger on imaged number line.

   5. Student(s) visualizes and verbalizes the equation again, sometimes air-writing, giving the answer.

e. Experiencing and Imaging the Doubles:

   1. Student(s) uses cubes to experience the concept of doubling

a number.

2. Student(s) verbalizes the equation.

3. Student(s) visualizes and verbalizes the equation, air-writing.

4. Student(s) sees the cubes increasing by two, one on each side.

5. Student(s) uses Doubles Cards to visualize and verbalize, committing the doubles to memory.

f. Doubles Plus One:

1. Student(s) experiences doubling with cubes.

2. Student(s) experiences doubling *plus one* with the cubes.

3. Student(s) visualizes and verbalizes the equation.

4. Student(s) computes written problems.

g. Imagery Cards and Written Computation Always!

4. Teaching Up to Twenty

a. Teach the facts from eleven through twenty with the same procedures of manipulatives, imagery, and imagery cards for memory. Use "doubles plus or minus one" and the tens for the nine combinations.

5. Math Ball Game

a. Teacher throws the math ball, saying one number in a designated number family.

b. Student(s) catches and throws/says the appropriate number back to the teacher.

c. May be played as a game with one or more students.

d. If working on the family of five, teacher says, "Here comes one," throwing the ball. Catching the ball and throwing it back, student says, "Four back to you."

e. Visualizing and verbalizing are unconsciously stimulated.

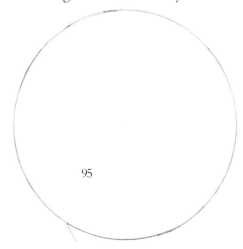

Group Instruction

As with all Lindamood-Bell programs, and all *On Cloud Nine* steps, group instruction is primarily an issue of group management and control because all of the activities can be used with large and small groups. Felt boards, chalk boards, and overhead projectors can be used to introduce number families to groups with one student setting the family, another student talking through the facts, another writing the facts, and the group or class writing in the air. The Family Fact Cards can be practiced with a group or whole class. Once the card is shown and taken away, all students can air-write, and specific students can respond to specific questions such as, "What is the second number you saw?" The Math Ball game can be played with an imaginary ball.

The Subtraction Family Facts

Tory skipped into the room for her lesson, happy, ready to work on addition facts and imaging—something she was now doing very easily. Her eyes were bright. Then she heard the news. Today she would begin subtraction. Suddenly she was quiet, and in a small voice said, "I'm not good in subtraction." Terror was in the air.

Tory would soon learn that being good in addition means being good in subtraction. They are twins that belong to the same family of tens, only one walks forward and one walks backward. Just as there are only so many facts for adding numbers together to equal ten, there are also only so many facts for subtracting numbers from ten. Adding and subtracting facts are in the same *family*.

In this step, students experience the subtraction facts for each number from one through ten. As they did for addition, they place those facts into memory through imagery, and then compute with pencil and paper. The concrete number line is now familiar, as is moving both up and down on it. The language of subtraction is brought to a conscious, experienced level for students. As with addition, *On Cloud Nine* approaches subtraction from first the gestalt and then the parts: concept imagery to numeral imagery. This step has the students do the following:

- Discover the concept and number family facts with the Subtraction Family Fact Sheets.
- Reinforce with cubes to experience the relationship within the *number family.*
- Use the *concrete number line*, with cubes, to experience specific facts.
- Use an *imaged number line* to image specific facts.
- Use Family Fact Cards to place specific facts in imagery and memory.

Having experienced the concept of base ten, it is important to be sure Tory grasps the concept of "subtraction," then she can begin the process of discovering the subtraction facts. Here she is facing subtraction. Eyes large, breathing quiet.

> **" ...if we are subtracting and getting less, would we go up or down the number line?"**

S A M P L E   L E S S O N

Discovering the Family Facts of Subtraction with the Family Fact Sheets

The Set

Kim: *"We've been working on addition and moving up the number line, and imaging those family facts. Right?"*

Tory: "Right…"

Kim: *"Right. When we used the number line to add, were we going up the number line or down it?"*

Tory: "Up it. Because we were adding, getting more."

Kim: *"Exactly. When you add you get more. What do you do when you subtract? Sometimes called take-away. Do you get more or less when you take-away?"*

Tory: "Less."

Kim: *"So, if we are subtracting and getting less, would we go up or down the number line?"*

Tory: "Down. That's easy to think about. So, our numbers will get smaller."

Kim: *"Right. Good thinking. Have you heard some other words we use for subtraction?"*

Tory: "Minus and take away."

Kim: *"Right. Let's discover why. Put five cubes*

on your number line. (Tory put cubes on the concrete number line.) Good. Now subtract two from your five. (Tory took two cubes away.) Did you put two more on or take two away?"

Tory: "I took two away. So it's called take-away because I take stuff away."

Kim: *"Right. If I asked you what is five minus two here's what you would do (demonstrating removing two cubes). If I said what is two less than five, here's what you would do (demonstrating removing two cubes)."*

Tory: "So, for subtraction we can say subtract, take-away, minus, or less than."

Kim: *"Right. For adding we can say addition, plus, more than. Those are just words that mean the same thing, telling us the same thing to do. Now, let's discover the subtraction facts.*

Tory: "...OK."

Kim: *"Guess what? They live in the same family as the addition facts. Subtraction is like the twin to addition. One goes up, the other goes down. We'll use our Family Fact Sheets, but in a little different way."*

Tory: "Subtraction goes down, huh. Do they really live in the same family?"

Lesson

Kim: *"Yup. And that makes these facts easy. Let's discover it. This time on our Family Fact Sheet, I want you to begin with ten cubes (a ten stack). If you take zero of those away, how many do you have left?"*

"Subtraction is like the twin to addition. One goes up, the other goes down."

"This time on our Family Fact Sheet, I want you to begin with ten cubes (a ten-stack). If you take zero away, how many do you have left?"

Tory: "I begin with ten and take zero of them away, I have ten left. Same." (Taking no cubes away.)

Kim: *"How would you say that as an equation? Ten take away zero equals…"*

Tory: "Ten take away zero equals ten."

Kim: *"Great. How would you write it?"*

Tory: "Ten minus zero equals ten (writing 10 – 0 = 10 on a piece of paper)."

Kim: *"Perfect. You already know that when you take away an amount we use the minus sign. Now, show me all of the remaining subtraction facts from ten. Be sure to verbalize what you're doing with the cubes as you move them."*

Tory: "This time I begin with ten, but break off only one cube, leaving me nine."

Kim: *"Right. Say that in an equation."*

Tory: "Ten minus one equals nine."

Kim: *"Perfect. Now, write that."*

Tory: "Ten minus one equals nine." (Writing 10 – 1 = 9.)

Tory experienced, verbalized, and wrote all the facts of ten.

Kim: *"Notice how I can check my subtraction facts with addition. Let's hold a stack of ten cubes and take four away. I'm left with six. If I add the six back to the four, I get ten. You try it. Here's a ten-stack. Take seven away. What are you left with?"*

Tory: "If I take seven away from ten I have three."

"How would you say that as an equation? Ten take away zero equals…"

Tory experienced, verbalized, and wrote all the facts of ten.

100

Kim: *"Good! Now, what will happen if you add that three back to the seven?"*

Tory: "I'll have ten! Seven plus three is ten. That's part of the family of ten. So, by adding I can tell whether my subtraction is correct."

Kim: *"Right. They're all in the same family. Look over here at the side of the card. There are your addition facts. Just go in reverse—instead of left to right, go right to left and there they are. There's that family you learned!"*

Tory: "Holy moly!"

Kim: *"It's fun, huh! Now let's finish our subtraction facts from one to nine. Be sure to verbalize what you're doing as you move the cubes."*

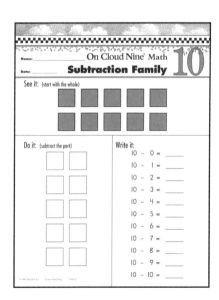

Lesson Summary:

Discovering the Family Facts for Subtraction with the Family Fact Sheets

1. Student(s) explores concept and language for subtraction.
2. Student(s) discovers with cubes, beginning with ten, the facts within each number family.
3. Student(s) verbalizes and writes the equation.
4. Student(s) discovers that adding and subtracting are twins in the same family.
5. Student(s) discovers that adding the family facts can check subtraction.
6. Teacher/student dialogue:

   "If I begin with _____ and take _____ of them away, I have _____ left."

   "If I take what I have left and add it to the number I took away, I will get what I started with."

Having discovered the family facts for subtraction, Tory visualized and verbalized the facts from the Family Fact Cards, just as she did with addition. Understanding the gestalt, she was ready to place the parts in imaged memory.

SAMPLE LESSON

Family Fact Cards to Visualize and Verbalize Subtraction Facts

The Set

"I'll show you a Family Fact Card to visualize, then I'll take it away and you tell me what you saw."

Kim: *"Now that you have discovered the family facts, let's put them into imagery to help you remember them. Just like we did for addition. I'll show you a Family Fact Card to visualize, then I'll take it away and you tell me what you saw."*

Tory: *"OK. That should be pretty easy."*

$$\begin{array}{r} 5 \\ -\ 3 \\ \hline 2 \end{array}$$

"What is the second number you saw?"

"What if I said to you five minus what number equals two? Can you see it in your imagery, and tell me the number?"

Lesson

Kim: *"I'll show you this card and then I'll take it away…and you say and write in the air the whole equation. Ready! Here's your first one."* (Holding up the card: 5 - 3 = 2.)

Tory: "Easy. I can see it in my imagination. Five minus three equals two." (Saying and air-writing numbers and signs.)

Kim: *"Right. What is the second number you saw?"*

Tory: "OK. We did this with addition. Three."

Kim: *"Right again. What is the last number you saw?"*

Tory: "Easy. The two."

Kim: *"Right again. So, if I said five minus three equals…what number would you see in your imagination and say to me?"*

Tory: "Two!"

Kim: *"Perfect. What if I said to you five minus what number equals two? Can you see it in your imagery, and tell me the number?"*

Tory: "Easy again. It is the three. I can see the whole equation."

Kim: *"Perfect again. Write it on paper for me. And we'll do some more."*

Tory: "OK." (Writing 5 - 3 = 2.)

Kim: *"Great. Now, here's some more fun stuff to do. If you know that five minus three equals two, then you also know what five minus two equals. Right?"*

$$\begin{array}{r} 6 \\ -\ 2 \\ \hline 4 \end{array}$$

"What was the sign you saw telling you what to do with the six?"

"What was the last number you saw?"

"Change the last two numbers around..."

Tory: "Sure. That's three. Just like with adding. It doesn't matter what order we place them, because three and two are part of the five family!"

Kim: *"That's exactly right. Let's do some more imaging of family facts. (Holding up the 6 - 2 = 4 card for a few seconds and taking it away.) OK. Tell me what you saw."*

Tory: "I have it. That was six minus two equals four."

Kim: *"Yup. What was the first number you saw?"*

Tory: "The six!"

Kim: *"Yup. What was the sign you saw telling you what to do with the six?"*

Tory: "It was the minus sign telling me to take away two from the six."

Kim: *"Right. What was the last number you saw?"*

Tory: "The four."

Kim: *"Change the last two numbers around in your picture and tell me what you see."*

Tory: "Hmmm. I can see that. It would have to be six minus four equals two. Same family!"

Kim: *"Exactly. Let's image some more."*

Lesson Summary:

Family Fact Cards to Visualize and Verbalize Subtraction Facts

1. Teacher holds up a Subtraction Family Fact Card for a few seconds.
2. Student(s) images and air-writes the numbers and signs.
3. Teacher questions for specific numbers or signs in the equation.
4. Student(s) visualizes and verbalizes, with and without air-writing.

Practicing

The goal of automaticity with the subtraction facts requires practiced imagery, while continuing concrete reinforcement. So, just as with addition, practice comes in the form of visualizing and verbalizing with cubes, the concrete number line, the imaged number line, imagery cards, and print computation. Remember, you can overlap between addition and subtraction at any level, but the prerequisite is accuracy and confidence in the corresponding addition facts. Competency in the family facts for addition enables the family facts for subtraction to be learned with ease and comfort.

Here is Tory experiencing each of the subtraction facts using the cubes and then the number line and cubes. She verbalizes as she moves the cubes and begins by choosing the number of cubes to correspond with the number she will practice.

S A M P L E   L E S S O N

Imagery and Cubes for Subtraction

The Set

Kim: *"Let's practice the subtraction facts with imagery and the cubes, just like we did addition. Let's get to know the family of four better!"*

Tory: "OK."

Lesson

Kim: *"If we're going to practice the subtraction facts of four, how many cubes will you need on the table?"*

Tory: "A stack of four cubes." (Placing a stack of four cubes, vertically, on the table.)

Kim: *"Right, there's four, now take zero away, and how many will you have left?*

Tory: "Four...of course!"

Kim: *"Right. Now, take you four, and this time take away one... and how many do you have left?*

Tory: "Three. Easy." (Taking away one cube.)

Kim: *"Great. Talk me through each of the facts, beginning with four again. Be sure your movements with the cubes match what you are telling me."*

"Be sure your movements with the cubes match what you are telling me."

Tory: "OK, here's four and if I take two away (placing four on table and taking two away), I have two. If I start with four again and take three away, I have one. And, if I start with four and take all four away, I none!"

"OK, here's four and if I take two away (placing four on table and taking two away), I have two."

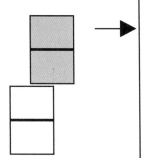

Kim: *"Just like what we wrote on the Family Fact Sheet (showing the sheet for the family of four), the numbers get smaller and bigger, but no matter what you do those numbers are in the family of four!*

Tory: "Yup!"

Kim: *"Let's practice the imaging now. Visualize the subtraction facts from four and talk me through what you picture, but you don't have* *to write it in the air, just tell me what you are picturing."*

Tory: "Four minus zero equals four, four minus one equals…" (Eyes up, gesturing images, but not air-writing.)

The Lesson Summary:

Imagery and Cubes for Subtraction

1. Student(s) places a set of cubes on the table for a specific number.
2. Student(s) demonstrates subtracting zero from the number first, then moving sequentially until subtracting the number itself.
3. Student(s) verbalizes as experiencing each equation.
4. Student(s) visualizes and verbalizes the facts, sometimes air-writing, sometimes not.

With the cubes illustrating the decreasing aspect of subtraction, Tory is ready to place them on the concrete number line, just as she did with addition.

SAMPLE LESSON

Imagery and the Number Line with Cubes for Subtraction

The Set

Kim: *"Let's practice the family facts and imaging some more. This time let's use the number line and the cubes. Set up the number line and get out the cubes."*

Tory: "OK." (Putting the number line together.)

Lesson

Kim: *"Here we go. I'll give you an equation, you*

"I'll give you an equation, you visualize it, and then use the cubes on the number line to show it."

visualize it, and then use the cubes on the number line to show it. Visualize three minus two, and then show it on the number line with the cubes."

Tory: "Three (getting and putting three cubes on the number line) minus two (taking two cubes off the number line) makes one! Easy."

Kim: *"Yup. Say and write that in the air."*

Tory: "Three minus two equals one (air-writing the numerals and signs).

"Say and write that in the air."

Kim: *"Great! Now, take those cubes off and show me four minus two with different cubes. Visualize it, then put the cubes on the number line as you tell me what you are doing."*

Tory: "Four (getting and putting four cubes on the number line) minus two (taking two cubes off the number line) makes two."

Kim: *"It sure does. Say and write that in the air again."*

Tory: "Four minus two equals two." (Air-writing the numerals and signs.)

Kim: *"Right, and what does two plus two make?"*

Tory: "Four! Two and two are part of the four family and I can add and subtract with those same numbers. You're right. Adding and subtracting really do belong in the same family."

Lesson Summary:

Imagery and the Number Line with Cubes for Subtraction

1. Teacher gives student(s) an equation verbally.
2. Student(s) uses the cubes on the concrete number line to experience the equation.
3. Student(s) visualizes and verbalizes the equation, *sometimes* air-writing.

Now that Tory can use the cubes for subtraction on the concrete number line, it is time to experience the number line without the cubes in preparation for the imaged number line. She will point with her finger to show going down the number line for subtraction.

S A M P L E   L E S S O N

Imagery and the Number Line without Cubes for Subtraction

The Set

Kim: *"You're doing well using the cubes and the number line. Let's try practicing the subtraction facts with just the number line. By gesturing and using the number line, your math "pictures" will get more solid and concrete. That will make your math facts even faster!"*

Lesson

Kim: *"Point to the four. Good. If you have four, how many spaces do you go back to get to two?"*

Tory: "I need to move back two spaces to get to two." (Moving finger *down* two spaces to the number 2).

Kim: *"Good. And if you have four, how many*

"Point to the four...How many spaces do you go back to get to two?"

> *spaces do you go back to get to one?"*

Tory: "I need to move back three spaces to get to one." (Moving finger *down* the number line).

Kim: *"Great. When you are subtracting, are you going up or down on the number line?"*

Tory: "Down."

Lesson Summary:

Imagery and the Number Line without Cubes for Subtraction

1. Student(s) points to starting number designated by teacher.
2. Student(s) subtracts a number from the starting number and gestures distance and direction.
3. Student(s) visualizes and verbalizes the equation, sometimes air-writing.
4. Student(s) notes that subtraction is going *down* the concrete number line.

Tory can conceptualize the meaning of subtraction (the gestalt) and is imaging the facts. Now it is time to apply this to her imaged number line. This stimulation not only reinforces her imagery, but also prepares her for mental addition and subtraction beyond the base ten. Here is Tory continuing to climb the math ladder, solidifying each step.

SAMPLE LESSON

Subtraction Facts and the Imaged Number Line

The Set

Kim: *"Subtracting on the number line is easy for you, so now let's just visualize the number line and do the same thing. But, instead of*

"...instead of touching your finger on a number line in front of you, touch your finger on your imaginary number line."

touching your finger on a number line in front of you, touch your finger on your imaginary number line. We're working that imagery part of your brain, you know!"

Tory: "I know."

Lesson

Kim: *"Imagine your number line from one to ten. Here's your equation. Six minus three. Where is your starting point? Put your finger there."*

Tory: "My starting point is six so I have my finger here. I go down three more to three."

Kim: *"Perfect. You verbalized as you were pointing. Now, visualize and verbalize the whole equation, but you don't have to write the numbers in the air. Just touch the spot on your imaginary number line and tell me what you see."*

"Six minus three. Where is your starting point? Put your finger there."

Tory: "Six subtract three is three." (Verbalizing and touching her imaginary number line.)

Kim: *"Perfect. Show me five minus three."*

Tory: "Hmmm. That's easy. It's two. But, you know what? I noticed that it had to be two because five is one less than six."

Kim: *"Great! You're beginning to think with numbers. Good for you!"*

Lesson Summary:

Subtraction Facts and the Imaged Number Line

1. Student(s) imagines own number line.
2. Student(s) points to starting number, designated by teacher, on imaged number line.
3. Student(s) subtracts a number from the starting number.
4. Student(s) visualizes and verbalizes the equation, moving finger on imaged number line.
5. Student(s) visualizes and verbalizes the equation again, *sometimes* air-writing.

Imagery Cards for Subtraction

As with addition, flash cards effectively reinforce the facts and place them in imagery for memory. Also, as with addition, use a Family Fact Card with the entire equation and a card with the answer on the back. The Family Fact Card can be specifically used for placing the equation in imagery and asking for specific numerals to be visualized and verbalized after the card is taken away, or the entire equation can be requested. (See the sample lesson on Family Fact Cards presented in Chapter Seven on addition.) At this level, students may need to air-write some equations and just verbalize others. Do the latter if you feel confident of students' imagery.

The card without the answer can be used to test the answer and storage/ retrieval of the equation. As with addition, sort the cards into fast, medium, and slow, and place in a personalized card box if working one-on-one or in small groups.

It is with subtraction that the Cloud Triangle Card becomes very effective in practicing addition and subtraction together. Some facts of the family are on the card, but without a sign. The equation and answer are in the three corners of the triangle. Cover the answer and turn the other numbers in each corner into an equation. The Cloud Triangle Card for 6, 2, 8 can be used for addition and subtraction and read as: "Six plus blank equals eight," or "Eight minus blank equals six," etc.

A. Family Fact Card with whole equation:

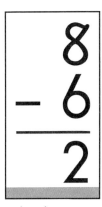

B. Card with equation on front and answer on back:

8-6=	2

C. Cloud Triangle Card:

Pencil and Paper Tasks

Climbing this far up the math ladder now requires that we give attention to the mathematical sign, since now students have learned to do at least two mathematical tasks: adding and subtracting. Attending to the sign is an important aspect of math and one that has caused many students frustration on tests. Be sure to reinforce attending to the sign and have students practice written computation with both addition and subtraction mixed together on the paper.

Here are the steps we suggested for written computation, in case they slipped away from you the way "faucit" does on some mornings: (1) check the sign, (2) visualize what the sign tells you to do, (3) verbalize the equation, and (4) do! Check, visualize, verbalize, and do! The preliminary steps—those followed *before* the equation is solved—can be placed on a card for students to follow.

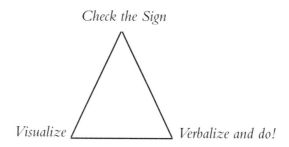

Your error handling for pencil and paper tasks must respond to the response, as we discussed in Chapter Four. It is important not to simply mark the student's paper with a red (-) minus or (+) plus! Circle an answer that needs to be corrected and follow the same outline: (1) give positive feedback, (2) respond to the response, (3) compare the response to the stimulus, and (4) question for self-correction.

Pacing and Practice

Throughout the *On Cloud Nine* program, overlapping steps is the key to pacing. Practicing addition and subtraction are the perfect twins for the practice task. You might teach the addition facts up to five and then overlap to the same in subtraction, depending on the age and level of your students. Before moving to the next step of *On Cloud Nine*, look for the following: (1) the ability to answer subtraction facts to ten with about 80% accuracy, (2) the ability to independently prove facts with cubes and the number line, and (3) the ability to consistently and accurately work with both addition and subtraction facts. Note that the activities for addition are applicable to practicing subtraction.

Summary

Subtraction in real life begins with more and ends with less. Subtraction on a number line starts with a number and moves backward, down the line. Subtraction is a direction that results in an amount. If you are working on a horizontal number line subtraction moves to the left. If you are working on a vertical number line subtraction moves down. By the time this step is completed, your students have the gestalt of subtraction as well as the parts. They have the concept of minus. They have stored, and can retrieve, the subtraction facts for one through twenty. Imagery is a key ingredient in the movement up the math ladder, and every activity has developed it, both for concepts and numbers. Every lesson has been completed with written computation. Mental and written math are established.

Tory is ready to move up one more rung on the ladder.

Summary: Step 4

Subtraction Family Facts

Goal: To develop the dual coding of imagery and language to a conscious level for understanding and memorizing the subtraction facts from one through ten.

1. **Discovering the Family Facts with the Family Fact Sheets**

a. Student(s) explores concept and language for subtraction.

b. Student(s) discovers with cubes, beginning with ten, the facts within the number *family*.

c. Student(s) verbalizes and writes the equation.

d. Student(s) discovers that adding and subtracting are twins in the same family.

e. Student(s) discovers that adding the family facts can check subtraction.

f. Teacher/student(s) dialogue:

— Teacher says, "If I begin with _____ and take all of them away, I have _____ left."

— Teacher says, "If I take what I have left and add it to the number I took away, I will get what I started with."

2. **Using Family Fact Cards to Visualize and Verbalize Subtraction Facts**

a. Teacher holds up a Family Fact Card for a few seconds.

b. Student(s) images and air-writes the numbers and signs.

c. Teacher questions for specific numbers or signs in the equation.

d. Student(s) begins to visualize and verbalize without air-writing.

3. Practice Activities

a. Imagery and Cubes Alone:

   1. Student(s) places a set of cubes on the table for a specific number.

   2. Student(s) demonstrates subtracting zero from the number first, then moving sequentially until subtracting the number itself.

   3. Student(s) verbalizes while experiencing each equation.

   4. Student(s) visualizes and verbalizes the facts, sometimes air-writing, sometimes not.

b. Imagery and the Concrete Number Line with Cubes:

   1. Teacher gives student(s) an equation verbally.

   2. Student(s) uses the cubes on the concrete number line to experience the equation.

   3. Student(s) visualizes and verbalizes the equation, *sometimes* air-writing.

c. Imagery and the Number Line *without* Cubes:

   1. Student(s) points to starting number designated by teacher.

   2. Student(s) subtracts a number from the starting number, and gestures distance and direction.

   3. Student(s) visualizes and verbalizes the equation, sometimes air-writing, giving the answer.

   4. Student(s) notes that subtraction is going *down* the concrete number line.

d. Subtraction Facts and the Imaged Number Line:

   1. Student(s) images own number line.

   2. Student(s) points to starting number, designated by teacher, on imaged number line.

   3. Student(s) subtracts a number from the starting number.

   4. Student(s) visualizes and verbalizes the equation, moving finger to imaged number line.

   5. Student(s) visualizes and verbalizes the equation again, sometimes air-writing.

e. Imagery Cards and Written Computation Always!

Group Instruction

Small or large groups can do the subtraction steps for *On Cloud Nine*, just as they did for addition. Felt boards, chalk boards, and overhead projectors enable you to present the concepts to large groups. The imagery activities can be done by all students at the same time, with specific questions asked of specific students. Again, remember that having students give thumbs up or down gives them a physical means of responding without having to speak.

Word Problems Made Easy

This chapter describes a process for teaching one of the most terrifying aspects of math: *word problems*. While the chapter is coming after subtraction, it could be placed lower or higher on the math ladder. Word problems should be a part of each *On Cloud Nine* step. When students have learned to add, they should also do word problems using addition. When they have learned to subtract, they should do word problems using subtraction and addition. When they have learned to multiply, they should do problems using multiplication, addition, and subtraction. The goal with word problems is to teach students to translate language into mathematical solutions.

Solving word problems requires thinking with both concept and numeral imagery. It requires mathematical cognition and that requires imagery. Concept imagery lets students decide, "this part requires the function of addition" or "this part requires the function of multiplying fractions."

On Cloud Nine's word problem steps are applicable for solving word problems from simple addition and subtraction to more advanced processes.

1. *Read or listen to the whole problem:*

   Students read all the language, the *whole problem*, to know where the problem is heading. If they start solving the problem too soon, they may have an answer, but not the one the problem requests.

2. *Visualize and verbalize the gestalt:*

   Students consciously create images to match the words, then verbalize their imagery. The images are created for the gestalt or the main points of the passage, and should be just enough to match without extra detail. Depending on the level of language processing of the students, the paragraph may be read in its entirety or sentence by sentence. This is the V/V program directly applied to word problems in mathematics.

3. *List the math facts that are known:*

   Students list the math facts that are definite on the left side of the paper under the heading, "What I know." They need not be concerned about whether the facts are relevant—they just need to list them.

4. *List what needs to be known:*

   Students list the question(s) the problem asks on the right side of the paper.

5. *State the problem in sentence form:*

   Students state the problem in their own words, orally or in writing.

6. *Convert the sentence to numbers and solve:*

   Students cross out the words as they convert them to numbers presented from the problem. This calls attention to which words turn into which functions. For example, the words "more" and "joined" turn into addition when converted to an equation.

7. *Verify that all parts of "Need to Know" were answered:*

   Students cross out on the right side of the paper each item they have answered.

The following is a lesson with Tory so you can see and experience the ease of this process.

> ### SAMPLE LESSON
>
> #### *Word Problems with Addition and Subtraction*
>
> #### The Set
>
> Kim: *"Now we're going to work on word problems. You will be reading a story with me that asks you to solve a math problem. There is a step-*

"The first step is to read the problem, visualize it, and verbalize it to me."

by-step process I want you to follow. The first step is to read the problem, visualize it, and verbalize it to me."

Jon and Matt went to the Farmer's Market on Thursday night to buy fruit, vegetables, and flowers. They were under strict orders from their mother to get only these things. As they walked through the market, they saw a juggler twirling 7 milk bottles through the air. They also saw a face painter with 12 children lined up waiting. Matt bought 1 bunch of daisies, a jar of honey, and a bag of spinach greens. Jon bought a box of strawberries, an order of beef ribs, a bag of oranges, and a bag of turnips. How many items did Jon and Matt buy all together? How many of these items did their mom want them to get? How many items were not on their mom's list?

Tory: "OK, I've read it. Those boys were bad."

The Lesson

Kim: *"Good. Now I want you to tell me what you visualized. Be very specific about the main points and tell me enough so I can get a picture in my mind from your words."*

Tory: "Well, for Matt and Jon I see these two brothers, about ten and eleven years old. They pass the juggler and the face painter. The juggler is wearing bright colors and he has seven white milk bottles he is tossing in the air and catching. The face painter is a man with paint all around him and a lot of children lined up, waiting for him."

Some students, especially younger ones, may need to read only one or two sentences at a time and then create their images. This would be the Sentence by Sentence step of V/V.

Kim: *"You're giving me some really good descriptions of your images. Then what happens in your picture?"*

Tory: "I see one of the boys buying a bunch of yellow daisies, a jar of honey, and leaves of spinach greens. Then I see the other boy with a box of strawberries, a bag of oranges, and some white turnips. He gets some beef ribs and eats them."

Kim: *"Good. The next step is to take out a piece of paper and draw a line down the middle. On the left side put the heading: What I Know.*

Tory: "OK." (Listing all the details.)

Kim: *"Good. Now, on the right side, put the heading: What I Need to Know. Then list the questions that belong under that heading."*

Tory: "OK." (Listing the questions asked.)

Kim: *"Good. Now, decide which items you don't need in order to answer the Need to Know questions and cross them out."*

Tory: "Easy." (Comparing, then crossing off.)

"On the left side put the heading: What I Know."

"On the right side, put the heading: What I Need to Know."

"...decide which items you don't need in order to answer the Need to Know questions and cross them out."

What I Know	What I Need to Know
~~1 juggler~~ ~~7 milk bottles~~ ~~1 face painter~~ ~~12 kids waiting~~ 1 bunch of daisies 1 jar of honey 1 bag of spinach 1 box of strawberries 1 bag of oranges 1 bag of turnips 1 order of beef ribs	How many things did they buy? How many of those things were they supposed to buy? How many were not on mom's list?

"Now, put the problem in sentence form."

Kim: *"Now, put the problem in sentence form. What I mean by sentence form is just tell me what it asked you to do."*

Tory: "Well, first it asks how many things they bought. So I guess I have to count them."

Kim: *"That's right. Do you need to add or subtract to do this problem?"*

Tory: "I add them all together. So that's one plus one plus one plus one plus one plus one equals seven things."

Kim: *"Right. You answered the first question. What's next?"*

Tory: "It asks how many of those things were on their mom's list. So, Mom asked for only fruits, vegetables, and flowers and I'll add those things together."

Kim: *"Is there a way you could use subtraction in this problem?"*

Tory: "Hmmm. I guess I could take the things they weren't suppose to buy away. There were two things they weren't supposed to buy so seven minus two equals five."

"Check to see if you answered everything asked on the right side?"

Kim: *"Check to see if you answered everything asked on the right side?"*

Kim: *"You just did that perfectly. If you follow those same steps with all word problems, it will be easier to see what you are supposed to do."*

Tory: "Can I draw pictures too?"

Kim: *"Yes, if you make them quickly and it helps you to hold your picture in your mind."*

The following error handling lesson is included at this point to demonstrate how to question students to help them compare their response to the stimulus. This lesson occurred much later in the work with Tory.

S A M P L E   L E S S O N

Error Handling for Word Problems

Kim: *"Let's do a word problem. Get your checklist out so you can follow the process."*

A gaggle of geese are heading south for the winter. Two of the geese, Henry and Mertyl, stop off in Washington state and like it so much they decide to stay. Their best friends, Tom and Lucy, miss them so much that they circle back and join Henry and Mertyl in Washington. Mertyl's 3 sisters and their husbands also cut their journey short and join them. If they began their trip with 26 geese, how many geese stop in Washington state? How many are still flying south?

Tory: "OK, I've read it. I don't think real geese have names like that, but I think I can figure it out."

Kim: *"Great, what do you need to do first?"*

Tory: "I need to read it, make pictures in my head, and tell you what I see. Then I need to write down the stuff I know."

Kim: *"You're right, so go ahead."*

Tory: "What's a gaggle?"

Kim: *"A gaggle is like a flock of birds. With geese, a flock is called a gaggle."*

Tory: "I see these geese flying in the sky. They're heading south so I kind of see them moving down on a map. Then different geese are leaving and landing in Washington state. Lots of trees and green, I've been there. First I see two geese land. Then, their two friends land. Then three lady geese and their husbands land. Now, there's a bunch on the ground and some in the air. Whew. I need to start my list because there are a lot of details."

Kim: *"Right. You are efficient with your images."*

Tory: "Okay. Now, I need to say the problem in a sentence."

Kim: *"Yes."*

Tory: "The first question asks how many geese landed in Washington. So, I add all those numbers together: two plus two plus three plus three equals ten."

Kim: *"Right. State the next question."*

Tory: "How many are still flying south. Hmmm. I guess I add them all together."

Kim: *"If you add them all together, does that mean the gaggle is going to get bigger or smaller?"*

Tory: "When I add, my number gets bigger."

Kim: *"Right. Let's see if that matches your picture. When they flew away did you see the gaggle of geese get bigger or smaller?"*

Tory: "It got smaller. So I'm subtracting. Twenty-six geese started, ten landed in Washington, so twenty-six minus ten equals sixteen."

Kim: *"Good thinking. Now, check on your sheet to see if you answered everything asked on the right side?"*

With the frame for the word problem process established, here is one more example of a word problem lesson, only this time Tory is doing more complex translating from language to mathematical equations. Again, this lesson occurred much later in the work with Tory, but it is shown here as an example of more complex word problem processing.

SAMPLE LESSON

Word Problems with Adding, Subtracting, and Multiplying

The Set

Kim: *"Go ahead and visualize and verbalize the problem through. Be sure to read all of it."*

Jenny is preparing for a class field day. Her class is planning to go whale watching on the ocean. She's very excited about this. Her teacher told them they needed to bring a warm coat, shoes with rubber soles, and a warm hat. She also suggested they bring binoculars to see the whales in the distance. Finally, the field day arrived. Jenny saw 5 full grown blue whales off to the west. She was able to see twice as many porpoises as whales when she looked through her binoculars. Half of the porpoises were very small and looked like babies. How many whales did Jenny see? How many porpoises? How many porpoise babies?

The Lesson

Tory: "Here's what I visualized. I see this girl about thirteen years old. She's in her room and packing for the next day. I see her gathering warm things. Then she's out on the ocean in a large boat surrounded by lots of kids her age. She's holding her binoculars and looking out. She sees whales and porpoises."

Kim: *"Good. What's the next step?"*

Tory: "I need to list the facts I know and those I need to know." (She writes.)

Tory: "There, I think that's everything but I know now which items don't matter. I'll cross them off.

Kim: *"Good. Then state the question."*

Tory: "I cross off the coat, hat, rubber shoes, and binoculars because they aren't necessary to the questions of how many whales. I'm going to start with the whales because it gave me that one. Then I know there are two times as many porpoises as whales so I can figure that. Once I know how many porpoises, I divide that number in half to get the number of babies."

Kim: *"Very good. You weren't thrown off by those other numbers stated in the problem."*

Tory: "Now, I can solve. There are five whales. Two times five equals ten, so there are ten porpoises, and ten divided by two equals five, so there are five babies."

Kim: *"What is your final step?"*

Tory: "I need to verify that I answered what I need to know. Hmmm. Yes, I answered how many whales. Yes, I answered how many porpoises and also how many baby porpoises. I guess I'm done with that one."

Lesson Summary:

Word Problem Process

1. Student(s) reads or listens to the problem.
2. Student(s) visualizes and verbalizes the gestalt.
3. Student(s) lists "What I Know" on the left side.
4. Student(s) lists "What I Need to Know" on the right side.
5. Student(s) states problem in sentence form, either orally or in writing.
6. Student(s) converts the sentence to an equation and solves.
7. Student(s) verifies that all parts of "What I Need to Know" were answered.

Practice and Pacing

As stated at the beginning of this chapter, word problems can be introduced at the early steps of the *On Cloud Nine* math ladder, and then become a part of each rung. Both processes of imagery—concept and numeral—are being developed and reinforced when students think and solve with word problems. As each new rung on the ladder is learned, the mathematical computation skills should be applied to translating language to mathematical problem solving.

As with all tasks, the process of problem solving from language should be practiced continually rather than assumed. Students need repetitive stimulation to be certain a process is automatic. However, they don't need it as often once the process has reached a level of automaticity. Your gauge for this is how well they can verbalize their processing, the speed of their thinking, and how well they self-correct. Remember, independent mathematical thinking, just as in reading, requires the ability to self-correct, which requires the ability to monitor, which requires sensory-input.

Sensory Input

for

Monitoring

for

Self-correction

for

Independence

Summary

The V/V program develops the concept imagery base for grasping the gestalt of the language in the word problem. It enables a translating of the whole to the necessary parts for placing words into mathematical equations.

With the sensory-cognitive base of concept imagery, *On Cloud Nine* gives students a step-by-step process as a tool for translating language to mathematical equations. The steps can be applied to all levels of word problems, transforming foe to friend.

Let's resume the work with Tory who, when we left her in subtraction, had only done a few simple word problems for addition and subtraction. She is ready to continue her climb up the math ladder, and get into place value.

Summary: Step 5

Word Problems

> **Goal:** To be able to reason with language and math by using concept and numeral imagery to translate language into mathematical equations.

Students do the following steps to translate language to mathematical equations.

1. *Read or listen to the whole problem:*

Students read all the language, the whole problem, to know where the problem is heading. If they start solving the problem too soon, they may have an answer, but not the one the problem requests.

2. *Visualize and verbalize the gestalt:*

Students create images to match the words, then verbalize their imagery. The images are for the gestalt or the main points of the passage, and should be just enough to match without extra detail. Depending on the level of language processing of the students, the paragraph may be read in its entirety or sentence by sentence. This is the V/V program now being directly applied to word problems in math.

3. *List the math facts that are known:*

Students list the math facts that are definite on the left side of the paper under the heading, "What I Know." They need not be concerned about whether the facts are relevant—they just need to list them.

4. *List what needs to be known:*

Students list the question(s) the problem asks on the right side of the paper: "What I Need to Know."

5. *State the problem in sentence form:*

Students state the problem in their own words, orally or in writing.

6. *Convert the sentence to numbers and solve:*

Students cross out the words as they convert them to numbers. This calls attention to which words turn into which functions. For example, the words "more" and "joined" turn into addition when converted to an equation.

7. *Verify that all parts of "What I Need to Know" were answered:*

Students cross out on the right side of the paper each item they have answered.

Group Instruction

Teaching word problems to groups follows the same frame as with the one-to-one interaction presented here, but group management techniques of thumbs-up or –down are needed to keep all students involved. The concept of teams can also be helpful with groups, especially classrooms. For example, have the group begin by sharing and discussing concept images for the word problem. Perhaps begin with one student reading aloud and others describing imagery toward a shared gestalt. Have another listing the facts that are known, and another listing the facts that need to be known. Solutions can be discussed between teams and agreed upon. It is also fun to have students write word problems to match a given equation, or make a collection of word problems from events happening in their lives. This stimulates problem solving.

Place Value for the Big Picture

Place value may seem like just a term we teach students, but in reality it is a means of using base ten in our number system. It allows us to count with more than our fingers. Without place value, we would have to use our fingers and toes and the fingers and toes of others, or beans and rocks, in order to count beyond ten! We have assigned value to places of numbers as a means of representing increased value.

Back when cavemen counted with their fingers, they were stuck when they needed numbers beyond their ten hairy digits. Place value is simply a way to continue counting into infinity in writing while making use of the same ten digits. Discover and establish place value with your students by doing the following.

- Manipulate stacks of ten with cubes and imagery.
- Use cubes and the concrete number line to discover place value.
- Write numbers to represent place value.

Tory is ready to discover, understand, and image place value. She is experienced with the number line, both concrete and imaged. She can move up and down by ones, twos, fives, and tens. She can start at any number and count forward or back with a block of ten. She's ready to conceptualize and implement place value, and move one more step up the math ladder.

SAMPLE LESSON

Discovering Place Value

The Set

Kim: *"You can go up and down the number line with tens. We're going to learn why we write numbers the way we do. This is called place value, the next step on your math ladder."*

Tory: "I think I already know how to write numbers, but I'm not sure why they're written the way they are."

Lesson

Kim: *"Exactly. And it is important to know why they are written because we can use it to help us do math. Get out the number line and cubes again, please. First, show me a stack of ten cubes. (Tory does.) Now, show me a one cube. (Tory does.) Now, show me two ten-stacks of cubes." (Tory does.)*

Tory: "That's easy."

Kim: *"I know. I was just making sure that was really strong so we could make this step of the math ladder easy for you. To answer the why of how numbers are written, we need to start by writing some numbers down. I just want you to say them as I write them (writing 62, 38, 27, 45). We call the right column of numbers (pointing to the ones column) the ones. Let's find out why."*

Tory: "I've heard that before but I didn't really know what it meant."

Kim: *"To discover why, I want you to use your number line and cubes. I'll hand you some cubes and you put them on the number line and write the number down on paper in a column."*

Tory: "OK."

Kim: *"First, we'll start with zero. Can I show you zero cubes?"*

ONES
0
1
2
3
4
5
6
7
8
9

tens | ones

1 | **0**

Tory: "No, because that means we have none."

Kim: *"Right. So write down a zero first. (Tory does.) Here's one cube. Where do you put it on the number line and how do you write it? How about two cubes?" (They continue through the number nine with Tory placing cubes and writing the number).*

Kim: *"What happens when I show you ten cubes? Can I have a ten-stack on my number line?"*

Tory: "Yes."

Kim: *"Can I write just one number symbol to show ten or do I have to reuse two of the numbers?"*

Tory: "To write ten, you have to reuse the zero and the one."

Kim: *"Good. And if I use two number symbols, how many columns do I have?"*

Tory: "We have two columns."

Kim: *"Right. If I write the number ten, I have to reuse the number one and the zero. So, I need a new column. This is called the tens column or the tens place. It is the place value for ten."*

Tory: "Oh. I think I have it."

Kim: *"Any number in the tens column has a value of at least one stack of ten cubes. If I have two in my tens column, that's worth two stacks of ten cubes, and we can say its place has a value of two tens. Put two ten-stacks on the number line and tell me what number we have for that."*

Tory: "Two ten-stacks gives us twenty." (Writing it down).

tens | ones

2 | 0

"We have two tens and zero ones."

tens | ones

2 | 3

Kim: *"How many tens do we have? How many ones do we have?"*

Tory: "We have two tens and zero ones."

Kim: *"Right. With the number line and cubes show me two tens and three ones."*

Tory: "Two ten-stacks gives me the number twenty and with three one cubes it gives me the number twenty-three. I write a number two in my tens column and a number three in the ones column on my paper. It matches!"

Note: When discovering place value, an effective way to visualize the difference between tens and ones is to keep the ten cubes linked as ten-stacks, but leave the one-cubes separate.

| 1 | 2 | 3 | 4 | 5 | 6 | 7 | 8 | 9 | 10 | 11 | 12 | 13 | 14 | 15 | 16 | 17 | 18 | 19 | 20 | 21 | 22 | 23 |

"If you have six ten-stacks and four one-cubes, what does that look like on your number line and how would you write it in your columns?"

Continue to explore with cubes, number line, and paper until your student has a solid understanding.

Kim: *"Now, I want you to do some thinking without the cubes on your (concrete) number line. If you have six ten-stacks and four one-cubes, what does that look like on your number line and how would you write it in your columns?"*

Tory: "I skip up six tens to number sixty and add four more ones to get me to number sixty-four. To write it down, I'd put the number six in the tens column and the number four in the ones column."

Kim: *"That's good. The tens place has a value of six*

tens and the ones place has a value of four ones. This time let's use your imaged number line and do it from the other direction. I'll give you the number, you show it on your visualized number line and write it. The number is forty-seven."

"This time let's use your imaged number line and do it from the other direction. I'll give you the number, you show it on your visualized number line and write it."

Tory: "The number gives it away. It tells me there will be four ten-stacks on my number line and seven more (gesturing the spot on her imaged number line), so number four in the tens place and number seven in the ones. This isn't so hard after all."

Lesson Summary:

Discovering Place Value

1. Student(s) discovers the ones column using the cubes and number line, writing the numerals on paper.
2. Student(s) discovers that ten is reusing symbols, thus discovering the tens column or tens place.
3. Student(s) shows on the number line various combinations of ten-stacks and ones-cubes left over, saying and writing columns of ones and tens.
4. Student(s) uses concrete number line without cubes, saying and writing columns of ones/tens.
5. Student(s) uses imaged number line, saying and writing columns of ones/tens.

With ones and tens learned, the stimulation expands the concept of place value into the hundreds column, then thousands, ten-thousands, etc. Continuing to first explore with the number line and cubes through one hundred, the process establishes the reality of place value and extends that reality to imagery. Too many cubes and too long a number line would be needed beyond a hundred, which is precisely why place value was developed in the first place!

SAMPLE LESSON

Discovering Hundreds, Thousands, Ten Thousands

The Set

Kim: *"You understand ones and tens with no problem. Let's keep going, because our numbers go higher than our number line. Right?"*

Tory: "Right. We can have really big numbers, too big to fit in this room or even in this building."

Lesson

Kim: *"That's true. Let's find out about their place value. What if we have nine ten-stacks and nine ones? What does that look like? Put those on the number line, or just use your finger."*

Tory: "I'll just use my finger, it's easier. I go up nine tens to number ninety and nine more is number ninety-nine."

Kim: *"Right. If you add one more cube, what does it look like on the number line? How many tens will you have?"*

Tory: "It's the number one hundred. I have ten of the ten-stacks. That's one hundred."

Kim: *"Right. Remember what happened before when we moved from nine to ten and reused the numbers one and zero?"*

Tory: "We needed a new column, the tens column."

Kim: *"Exactly! What column do you suppose comes after the tens column? You actually already told me the answer when you told me what came after number ninety-nine."*

Tory: "The hundreds column."

Kim: *"Yes, good. Lets write that out."*

Tory: "I see one block of one hundred, so I have one in my hundreds column, zero in my tens, and zero in my ones."

Kim: *"Let's do another number, but not use the (concrete) number line, just visualize it and talk me through your images. What would one hundred, two tens, and four ones look like on your imaginary number line and on paper?"*

Tory: "Hmmm. That's really pretty easy (touching her imaged number line). One hundred, twenty, and four. It would be written like this." (Writing 124 in the columns.)

Kim: *"Right. Tell me what you have here."*

Tory: "One hundred, two tens, and four ones. That makes number one hundred twenty-four. And guess what? I can still see it on my number line."

Kim: *"Great. Let's do some more of those in a little bit, but what about this number in the columns (writing 999)? What will happen if you add one more in the ones column?"*

Tory: "Hmmm. I add one to nine making it a ten, so that makes a zero there…Oh, and

"I see one block of one hundred, so I have one in my hundreds column, zero in my tens, and zero in my ones."

"What would one hundred, two tens, and four ones look like on your imaginary number line and on paper?"

the next one would be a zero too, and the next one, so it would look like this (writing 1000). That's one thousand! Right?"

Kim: *"It certainly is! Still using those tens, aren't we, and what if I wrote this number in your columns (writing 1001), what would you have?"*

Tory: "Easy. I would have one thousand one."

Kim: *"Right. What if I wrote this (writing 1451 in the columns)?"*

Tory: "I would have one thousand, four hundreds, five tens, and one one."

Kim: *"What if I told you to add a ten on to it? Visualize what that would make the answer be."*

Tory: "Adding a ten is easy. The number would have to be one thousand four hundred sixty-one."

Kim: *"What about adding two hundreds on that?"*

Tory: "Easy. The number would have to be one thousand six hundred sixty-one."

Kim: *"Exactly. Can't be anything else. And we can keep going. Like this. If you have nine thousand nine hundred ninety-nine and add a little one to it, guess what you'll get!"*

Tory continued to experience and image place value, grasping it quickly.

"What if I told you to add a ten on to it? Visualize what that would make the answer be."

Lesson Summary:

Discovering Hundreds, Thousands, Ten Thousands

1. Student(s) shows nine ten-stacks and nine one-cubes.
2. Teacher asks student(s) to add one more, showing how to write in columns for hundreds.
3. Student(s) writes the number and verbalizes each column.
4. Student(s) uses the *imaged* number line, saying and writing columns of ones through thousands (and beyond if desired).
5. Teacher writes numbers, student verbalizes their place value.
6. Student(s) adds small chunks of tens, hundreds, thousands to *see* relationships.

Practicing and Pacing

Practicing place value begins with manipulatives and extends to imagery, both using columns of written numbers. You say a number and students verbalize, showing tens and ones with cubes on the number line, then writing the numbers. For example, "I'm going to say a number and I want you to use the cubes and number line to show me that number. Make sure you tell me what you're thinking, and then write it down. Let's try forty-six." Or, have students convert cubes on the number line to a number, then verbalize and write the number. For example, "I'm going to put the cubes on the number line and I want you to tell me how many tens and how many ones. Then write the number, and tell me the number."

The final practice needs to land in imagery. You call out the number written in the tens and the number in the ones. Students verbalize the image and write the number. For example, "Now I want you to use your visualized number line and I'm going to tell you the number in each place value. You're going to tell me what you see and write it on paper."

When to move? The answer for place value is when they have it. Meanwhile, you have been overlapping steps, so while you are working on place value, you can be stabilizing and reinforcing previous steps.

Summary

Understanding place value means having access to infinite numbers while still only using the numerals zero through nine. Students can now understand and image that concept. Higher numbers have concrete meaning, and the way has been paved for carrying and borrowing. Tory's eyes are getting brighter day by day.

Summary:
Step 6

Place Value

> **Goal:** To develop a concrete and imaged understanding of place value in our base-ten number system.

1. Discovering Place Value

   a. Student(s) discovers the ones column using the cubes and number line, writing the numerals on paper.

   b. Student(s) discovers that ten is reusing symbols, thus discovering tens column or tens place.

   c. Student(s) shows on the number line various combinations of ten-stacks and cubes left over, saying and writing columns of ones/tens.

   d. Student(s) uses concrete number line without cubes, saying and writing columns of ones/tens.

   e. Student(s) uses imaged number line, saying and writing columns of ones/tens.

2. Discovering Hundreds, Thousands, Ten Thousands

   a. Student(s) shows nine ten-stacks and nine one-cubes.

   b. Teacher asks student(s) to add one more, showing how to write in columns for hundreds.

   c. Student(s) writes the number and verbalizes each column.

   d. Student(s) uses *imaged* number line, saying and writing columns of ones through thousands (and beyond if desired).

   e. Teacher writes numbers, student verbalizes their place value.

   f. Student(s) add chunks of tens, hundreds, thousands to *see* relationships.

3. Be Sure Place Value is Established in Imagery

   a. Teacher calls out a number and student(s) verbalizes where it is on own imaged number line, then writes it down.

Group Instruction

As with all steps in *On Cloud Nine*, the stimulation can easily be extended to small or large groups. It is helpful to have a group or class create a running number line that is placed along one or two walls. The numbers can be shades of a single color (such as blue) and shaded in increments of ten, going as high as you choose. If the number line goes past the first one hundred, the next one hundred can be shades of a different color, in increments of ten. This way a teacher can call out a number such as one hundred forty-five and students can take turns pointing, visualizing, verbalizing, and writing.

Jumping with the Tens for Mental Adding and Subtracting

Now for Cecil's other math skills: quick and accurate mental adding and subtracting! With the imaged number line and place value established, students have the sensory-cognitive foundation to develop mental mathematics. This step of *On Cloud Nine* brings the imaged number line to a *conscious* level for addition and subtraction beyond the tens, using the basic family facts of ten.

Jumping up takes us forward to the nearest ten when we're adding; jumping back takes us back to the nearest ten when we're subtracting. Because our number system is based on a series of tens repeated an infinite number of times, counting within each ten becomes predictable. The goal is to use the tens for mental adding and subtracting by reaching the ten and then verifying how many ones are *over* or *under* that ten. In mental adding the remaining numbers are added over the ten, in mental subtracting the remaining numbers are subtracted under the ten. Here's the process for learning this.

- Jump up and down on the concrete number line *with* and *without* cubes.
- Jump up and down with imagery.

Cecil's mind did this jumping and use of tens *automatically*. Tory will *learn* to do it automatically. Her family facts for both adding and subtracting are fast and accurate, thus computing the facts with any ten will be easy. Here she is discovering the concept of using the family facts to ten for mental addition and subtraction.

SAMPLE LESSON

Jumping on the Number Line to the Nearest Ten with Cubes

The Set

Kim: *"Your family facts to ten are excellent, for both adding and subtracting. I'm going to show you how to use those facts to add and subtract even big numbers! It's called jumping—like jumping up the number line or jumping down the number line."*

Tory: "Big numbers?"

Lesson

Kim: *"Yup! Get out the number line and let's go. (Tory set up the concrete number line.) I want you to add seven plus five. So, start with a stack of seven cubes."*

Tory: "OK. (Placing the seven cubes on the number line.)

Kim: *"Good. Now, instead of just counting up five more, get five more cubes but don't just put them on the number line yet. Instead, let's use our family facts."*

Tory: "OK…" (Small voice. Holding the stack of five cubes in her hand.)

Kim: *"You're at the seven, how many more will you need to jump up to ten?"*

Tory: "Three."

Kim: *"Right, put those on the number line, and now how many do you have left that will go over the top of ten?"*

"It's called jumping—like jumping up or down the number line."

"Let's use our facts to ten."

"Add seven plus five."

"You're at the seven, how many more will you need to jump up to ten?"

"How many do you have left that will go over the top of ten?"

146

Tory: "Two."

Kim: *"Right. And you know from place value that one ten and two ones gives you what number?"*

Tory: "Twelve!"

Kim: *"Great. So, let's review how we got that. If I'm at the number seven and I want to add five, it takes three to jump up to ten. Since I started with five, but used three of them, that leaves me two left over the top. So, ten plus two and the answer is twelve."*

Tory: "I think I understand. But I need to do it some more."

Kim: *"Right. And I'm going to give you a script to follow. Use this to talk your way through it: If I have seven it takes three to jump up to ten. I have two left over so that gives me twelve. You do it."*

Tory: "If I have seven it takes…hmmm…three to jump up to ten…and I was adding the five…so I have two left over the top of ten…and that gives me twelve."

"Let's try eight plus five."

Kim: *"Perfect. Now, let's try eight plus five. Use the number line and cubes."*

Tory: "OK. If I have eight (placing the eight cubes on the number line)…it takes two to jump up to the ten (placing the two cubes on the number line)…I have three left over so the answer is one ten and three ones…thirteen. I did it. I think I get it."

Kim: *"That's good. You did a nice job of using your math facts, and when you are adding you have to jump up to the ten. This time try twenty-eight plus four."*

Tory: "That problem is too hard for jumping! The numbers are too big!"

Kim: *"Just try it. Get twenty-eight cubes and put them on the number line."*

Tory: "OK." (Getting two ten-stacks and eight one-cubes, and putting them on.)

Kim: *"Instead of jumping up to the first ten, now you have to jump up to the next ten. Look at your number line. Which ten is forward from your starting point, the twenty or the thirty?"*

Tory: "The number thirty. The thirty is next. So, if I begin with the number twenty-eight, it takes two to jump up to the next ten, the number thirty. Wait. (Placing the two cubes on the number line) That leaves me two over the top of the ten. The answer is thirty-two!"

Kim: *"Great. Let's do some more. Jump with these numbers: thirty-nine plus five."*

Tory continued to practice jumping up and verbalizing with the cubes on the number line, using the dialogue. She added numbers all the way up to the top of the number line, and got fairly comfortable with the concept of jumping up to the next ten. It was now time to show her how she could jump down for subtraction. The twin.

"This time try twenty-eight plus four."

"Get twenty-eight cubes and put them on the number line."

"Instead of jumping up to the first ten, now you have to jump up to the next ten."

"If I begin with the number twenty-eight, it takes two to jump up to the next ten and that leaves me two over the top. The answer is thirty-two."

"If you are subtracting, what direction will you have to jump? Up or down?"

Kim: *"Let's try jumping to the ten with subtraction. It's the same, but you change direction on your number line. If you are subtracting, what direction will you have to jump? Up or down?"*

Tory: "Down."

Kim: *"Right. Here's your equation: fourteen minus six."*

"Here's your equation: fourteen minus six."

Tory: "OK. I begin with fourteen cubes (placing fourteen cubes on the number line). My next ten is down to the number ten! So, I take off four to get to the ten, and that leaves me two more to take off, so two less than ten is eight. Right?"

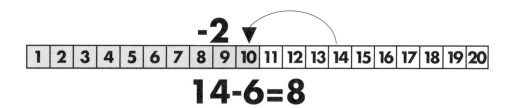

$$14-6=8$$

Kim: *"Exactly. Let's do another one where we subtract and jump down to the next ten. You're getting this. How about the equation thirty-two minus three? Show me with the cubes and talk me through jumping down. What's the next ten?"*

"Show me with the cubes and talk me through jumping down. What's the next ten?"

Tory: "Thirty. (Placing the cubes on the number line.) And I want to subtract three. Two gets me to the thirty and I have to take one more away, so the answer is twenty-nine! I am getting this. Let's do some more."

Kim: *"Just what I was thinking, Howard…er, Tory. That's an old family joke, I'll tell you sometime. Meanwhile, let's do some more. How about forty-four minus six?"*

Tory: "I can do that!" (Eyes bright.)

Lesson Summary:

Jumping on the Number Line to the Next Ten with Cubes

1. Student(s) uses the concrete number line and cubes.
2. Teacher gives the addition or subtraction problem orally or in writing.
3. Student(s) discovers jumping *up* to the next ten with the cubes and number line for addition.
4. Student(s) verbalizes with sample dialogue while jumping *up* from one to a hundred.
5. Student(s) begins subtraction and jumping *down* when jumping up begins to stabilize.

Tory can now think with tens and is using her math facts to jump up and down to the next ten, for addition and subtraction respectively. Using the jumping from ten to ten utilizes the number line through directionality. Once students have mastered the "jump" with the concrete number line and cubes, transition them to using the concrete number line without the cubes.

Here is Tory using the concrete number line without the cubes in preparation for the next step of an imaged number line and mental addition and subtraction. Notice she's walking back and forth with addition and subtraction in the same lesson. Good pacing.

$$\boxed{\text{S A M P L E } \qquad \text{L E S S O N}}$$

Concrete Number Line without Cubes

The Set

Kim: *"Let's work some more on jumping up and down for adding and subtracting on the number line, but this time we won't use the cubes. We'll use the spaces on the number line instead."*

Tory: "OK. I can do that. It took a lot of time to get the cubes when we did equations with higher numbers. This will be faster."

Lesson

Kim: *"That's right. Here's your equation: Four plus seven. Use your finger on the number line instead of the cubes as your starting place. And use the language to help you remember the steps."*

Tory: "I put my finger on the number seven and it takes three to jump up to ten. I have one left over and that gives me eleven."

Kim: *You got the answer and you're correct that four plus seven gets you the same place as seven plus four! If you think of each equation as a sentence telling you what to do, did the way you verbalized match the way the equation read?"*

Tory: "No, it doesn't match, but it was easier my way because the seven was closer to the nearest ten."

Kim: *"Good thinking. I'm glad to see you're flexible with numbers, and I want you to be able to get the answer either way. So, this time walk*

"Use your finger on the number line instead of the cubes as your starting place."

"...use the language to help you remember the steps."

"Four plus seven."

"I put my finger on the number seven and it takes three to jump up to ten. I have one left over and that gives me eleven."

151

me through the way the equation reads."

Tory: "OK. I put my finger on the number four, I know it takes six to jump up to the ten so I jump my finger to ten. I've used six from seven so I have one left over the top of the ten putting me at eleven."

Kim: *"That's really good. It's nice to see you can figure it out beginning with the number four or the seven. How about this problem: twenty-five minus eight."*

"How about this problem: twenty-five minus eight."

Tory: "I put my finger on the number twenty-five. I have eight to take away, so I jump down five to get me to twenty, and that leaves me three more to take away. I stop at the number seventeen."

"I put my finger on the number twenty-five."

"I have eight to take away, so I jump down five to get me to twenty..."

Kim: *"Perfect. You're definitely getting this. See how those family facts helped you quickly think with numbers. Now let's do a few more, and pretty soon we won't need this number line, instead we'll use the one in our imagination."*

"...and that leaves me three more to take away. I stop at the number seventeen."

Tory: "OK." (Eyes sort of squinting in thought.)

Kim: *"Do this problem: seventy-two minus four."*

Tory: "Easy. And, it doesn't matter if the numbers are big or small, I just use the tens!"

Kim: *"I was just going to say that."*

Lesson Summary:

Concrete Number Line without Cubes

1. Student(s) uses the concrete number line and finger, without cubes.
2. Teacher gives the addition or subtraction problem orally or in writing.
3. Student(s) jumps *up* or *down* to the next ten, verbalizing action and concept of what is left over.

The jumping up and down stimulation on the number line should continue long enough for students to grasp the concept and do the action; but very soon the stimulation should overlap to mental addition and subtraction using imagery. Tory is ready for that now. In fact, it is a continuation of the lesson above.

SAMPLE LESSON

Jumping Up and Down with Imagery
The Set

> "This number line would be hard to carry around with you and set up everywhere, so let's put it away and use your imaginary one."

Kim: *"You're ready to use your own number line in your head. The one that's with you all the time! This number line would be hard to carry around with you and set up everywhere, so let's put it away and use your imaginary one."*

Tory: "OK. I think I can do it. I see my number line really easily now."

Kim: *"Great. And do you also see your family facts? We've been practicing them with the imagery cards. Can you image those too?"*

Tory: "Oh, yeah. Really easily."

Lesson

Kim: *"Here we go. Do this problem: twenty-seven plus six. Are you going to jump up or down to a ten?"*

Tory: "Up because I'm adding. I'm at twenty-seven and it takes three to get to thirty, and that leaves me three over the top, so the answer is thirty-three. That was pretty easy. I could see the number line in my imagination and I know that three from six leaves three, and three added to thirty makes thirty-three! Wow!"

Kim: *"I'm so proud of you, Tory. That's exactly the way I want you to think with numbers. Let's do some more. In fact, we'll do lots of this until you can do it automatically without a lot of effort, just the way you can walk without a lot of effort."*

Tory: "OK. That wasn't too hard. Give me another one!"

Kim: *"Do eighty-four minus five. Before you start, tell me whether you are going to jump up or down?"*

Tory: "Down because you said minus, didn't you?"

Kim: *"That I did! Go. Eighty-four minus five is what?"*

Tory: "That one is so easy. Four takes me down to the eighty, and one more off takes me down to the seventy-nine."

Kim: *"Absolutely right! I'm so impressed with you. Now, do the problem: twenty-seven minus nine."*

"Do this problem: twenty-seven plus six. Are you going to jump up or down to a ten?"

"I could see the number line in my imagination and I know that three from six leaves three, and three added to thirty makes thirty-three!"

"Do eighty-four minus five. Before you start, tell me whether you are going to jump up or down?"

"That one is so easy. Four takes me down to the eighty, and one more takes me down to the seventy-nine."

Tory: "It takes seven to get down to the twenty, and two more off makes the answer eighteen."

Kim: *"You're exactly right. Here's another way to think about that. The problem says to take away nine from twenty-seven. And the number nine is one less than ten. If I start at the number twenty-seven and jump back ten that gives me seventeen and since nine isn't quite ten I go up one to eighteen."*

Tory: "Cool! That is easier! I want to try one."

Kim: *"OK. Try forty-six minus nine."*

Tory: "I start at number forty-six and jump back ten to thirty-six and then up one to thirty-seven. So forty-six minus nine is thirty-seven."

Kim: *"You are genuinely understanding our system of tens. Good for you. Let's do some more: ninety-eight plus four."*

Tory: "Hmmm. I think that's easy, but it's not on the number line we used to set up. I think it's like this. It takes two to get to one hundred, and then I have two left over. The answer is the number one hundred two. Right?"

Kim: *"Exactly. It can't be anything else! And it doesn't matter if we are using the tens below the hundred, or above. It will always be the same. Watch. The problem of one hundred eight plus four is easy. It takes two to jump up to one hundred ten, and two left over…"*

Tory: "The answer has to be one hundred twelve!"

Kim: *"Exactly. And you're ready for the next step*

up our math ladder—carrying and borrowing. It's really easy, because it also has to do with our tens."

Lesson Summary:

Jumping Up and Down with Imagery

1. Student(s) uses imaged number line and imaged number facts.
2. Teacher gives the addition or subtraction problem orally or in writing.
3. Student(s) *mentally* jumps up or down with imagery for nearest ten and with imagery for the facts, always verbalizing.
4. Teacher introduces the use of nine as ten less one.

Estimating

Estimating is an important concept in math, and one we use in our daily lives. Looking at that clock or watch, "How long till lunch?" is the frequent cry at school—and at many meetings! In fact, many very important meetings have been stopped mid-speech when the clock struck twelve noon. While estimating the seat-time required to make it till lunch has saved many of us from unwanted and undesirable outbursts, estimating can also save us from paying too much, or adding an extra zero on a math test that will surely get us a frown and a snicker from a classmate—striking that feeling of terror in a heart. Consequently, it is good to practice estimating.

Have students form a rough estimate with concrete manipulatives and/or imagery by checking the sign, visualizing and verbalizing the possible answer, then comparing the estimated answer with the actual answer. Follow these steps.

- Student(s) estimates by checking sign and creating an image.
- Student(s) computes and compares.

Practice and Pacing

While overlapping is the key to climbing up the math ladder, the key to mental addition and subtraction with imagery is to practice a little bit each day—and it takes no paper, no pencils, nothing but imagery. Spend only as much time using the manipulatives as you need to and get to the imagery. But, if confusion surfaces because you have moved too quickly to imagery, then simply get out the concrete number line and the cubes so students can experience and see the concept of jumping up and down to the next ten. Also, monitor your students' automaticity with the family facts through ten. If students are still not automatic, it will slow the process of jumping. While slow is all right, a lack of automaticity gives you diagnostic information about pacing: spend more time imaging the facts while continuing this step.

Pacing is essentially a diagnostic chess game. Keep the whole in mind, and analyze the parts. You can do it. You can do anything.

Summary

Learning to do mental math with addition and subtraction is a gift, and one you just gave your students. This gift can be with them always, in school, in social situations, in stores, in meetings. Their minds can think quickly with numbers.

With the imaged number line and family facts brought to a *conscious* level for application to mental addition and subtraction, students are continuing to build a sensory-cognitive base for math. They are climbing up the math ladder, one step at a time, consciously developing imagery as a base, and tracking their progress. Next comes carrying and borrowing, an easy concept on the math ladder because it also uses the concept of tens. By now your students can conceptualize tens and are ready for more information about math. Also, by now your students are getting the idea that math is really pretty friendly because it is consistent.

Summary: Step 7

Jumping

> **Goal:** To develop imagery for mental addition and subtraction using the base ten and number facts.

1. **Jumping on the Number Line to the Nearest Ten with Cubes**

   a. Student(s) uses the concrete number line and cubes.

   b. Teacher gives the addition or subtraction problem orally or in writing.

   c. Student(s) discovers jumping *up* to the nearest ten with the cubes and number line for addition.

   d. Student(s) verbalizes with sample dialogue while jumping *up* from one to a hundred.

   e. Student(s) begins subtraction and jumping *down* when jumping up begins to stabilize.

2. **Concrete Number Line Without Cubes**

   a. Student(s) uses the concrete number line and finger, without cubes.

   b. Teacher gives the addition or subtraction problem orally or in writing.

   c. Student(s) jumps *up* or *down* to the nearest ten, verbalizing action and concept of what is left over.

3. **Jumping Up and Down with Imagery**

   a. Student(s) uses imaged number line and imaged number facts.

   b. Teacher gives the addition or subtraction problem orally or in writing.

   c. Student(s) *mentally* jumps up or down with imagery for nearest ten and with imagery for facts, always verbalizing.

   d. Teacher introduces the use of nine as ten less one.

e. Student(s) dialogue:

Dialogue for addition:
— Student(s) says, "If I have _____, it takes _____ to get to ten. I have _____ left over to add. That gives me _____."

Dialogue for subtraction:
— Student(s) says, "If I have _____, I take _____ away to get to ten. I have _____ left over to take away. That gives me _____."

4. *Estimate:*

Student(s) estimates by checking the sign, creating an image, and comparing and computing.

5. *Use the Nine:*

Student(s) uses the number nine as one less than ten for addition or subtraction.

Group Instruction

Jumping up and down the number line can be a fun activity for a classroom or group because you can increase the size of the number line and let them actually experience jumping up and down, sort of like the Twister game from years ago. Or, you can let them see the number line on a chalkboard or an overhead projector. Call on specific students or have them work in teams to give answers using their concrete or imaged number lines.

As always, there is no change in the steps of interaction. We always look at a large or small group as one sensory system in front of us, and just adjust our language and attention to more than one person at a time. You know the students that need this the most. Call on them and help their sensory sytem image and process. Respond to their response and the lessons will be positive. Your behavior in valuing your students' responses sets the example for the rest of the class. They may begin to interact with one another in the positive, supportive manner that you modeled.

13

Carry it Over and Borrow it Back

Students can sometimes get by with basic adding and subtracting, especially when they still have enough fingers to get the answer; but they may come up against a wall when moved into carrying and borrowing. Eyes blinking, little frowns on little faces, they are often baffled about the concept of carrying and borrowing, and end up following a pattern they don't understand. If the steps of their math ladder are not strong, as they try to climb to the top with each step getting more difficult and building on the previous step, they may fail. They may find multiplication and division difficult to understand and compute, and fractions and percentages a complete mystery. Math may soon become an enemy.

That will not happen to Tory. Each step of her math ladder to this point is strong and sturdy with imagery for concepts and computation. She has the foundation for carrying and borrowing: *she understands place value and the use of tens*. She has experienced, imaged, and computed that the ones place (column) can hold only the numbers 0 through 9 in written form. She knows that if the number increases to over nine ones, a stack of ten cubes is then "carried over" to the tens place where it will now live. She knows that if the tens place contains nine tens and then one more ten is added, this stack of ten tens is then "carried over" to the hundreds column. And so on.

She is ready to experience, image, and compute carrying—when she has *too much in a column*. She is also ready to experience, image, and compute borrowing—when she has *too little in a column*. Simple, really.

The goal of this step is to teach the concept of carrying and borrowing, including how to compute problems on paper. The number line, tens, place value, and jumping were established in previous steps as bases for this computation.

Here are the steps. Remember, your students must understand place value and the tens to be successful with carrying and borrowing.

- Use the Place Value Card and cubes to teach the concept of carrying and borrowing.
- Verbalize and practice written addition for carrying.
- Verbalize and practice written subtraction, using *borrow, cross,* and *write.*
- If necessary, explore understanding and imagery of place value, jumping up/down with tens, and the concept of addition and subtraction with the cubes and the concrete number line.

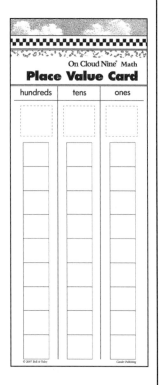

SAMPLE LESSON

Seeing the Concept of Carrying with the Place Value Card

The Set

Kim: *"You already know about place value and jumping with tens, so you are ready for two important steps on your math ladder: carrying and borrowing. We'll use a Place Value Card and our cubes to see and understand it. (Getting out a Place Value Card.) We'll start with carrying, first."*

Tory: "Hmmm. A card with a bunch of squares!"

Lesson

Kim: *"Right. Count the squares."*

Tory: "Nine squares in each row, and…Oh, this says ones, tens, and hundreds. Oh, this is our place value. Right."

Kim: *"Right. Why are there only nine places in the ones?"*

Tory: "Because when we get to ten, we have to move to the tens column and that makes one in the tens and zero in the ones."

Kim: *"Exactly. What we do is carry over to the next column. That's called carrying. Let's try carrying when we add these two numbers: seven plus five."*

Tory: "I can do that with jumping."

Kim: *"I know, but let's use the cubes and the place value card to get you ready for bigger numbers. Seven cubes adding five more (getting a stack of seven and five). Seven cubes will fit in the column, but five more won't fit. I can get three of them on there, just like jumping, but the last one goes on that dotted square to tell me we have one ten. So, I have to carry one whole ten over and trade it in. A cube on the dotted square means one ten is carried to the next column."*

Tory: "Right. And that leaves you two more cubes in the ones. The answer is twelve."

Kim: *"Yes. It's easy. The dotted square tells you to carry and trade in. You do one, and talk to me about what you are doing. Here it is: eight plus six."*

Tory: "Well, I have eight cubes (placing them on the card) and I add six more, but only two more go on, and one is in the dotted square telling me to carry them over to the tens and trade them in for this cube, which represents ten ones. And I have four ones left. I have one ten and four ones, so my answer is fourteen. Easy."

Kim: *"Let's do hundreds. (Placing one hundred, seven tens, and nine ones on the card). Figure out what number this is and then add fifty-three to it. Get cubes for five tens and three*

"Seven cubes adding five more." (Getting a stack of seven and five.)

"Seven cubes will fit in the column, but five more won't fit."

"I can get three of them on there, just like jumping, but the last one goes on that dotted square to tell me we have one ten."

"So, I have to carry one whole ten over and trade in. "

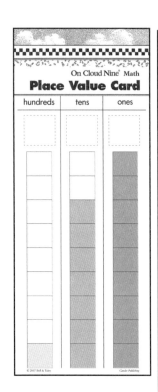

"Always start with
the ones."

"Carrying is just carrying
numbers over to the next
place value."

ones." (The problem is 179 + 53.)

Tory: "OK. It is one hundred seventy-nine and I'm adding fifty-three to it. (Getting a stack of five cubes for the fifty, and a stack of three for the ones.) Do I just place them on?"

Kim: *"Get ready to add by doing this first. Stack the three ones where it says ones, and the five tens where it says tens (showing how to stack the cubes vertically). Now, you're ready to add. Always start with the ones."* (Tory stacked three ones and five tens at the bottom of the card.)

Tory: "I add the three ones, but there's too many, so I carry one ten over to the tens (placing a cube in the tens and taking other ones cubes off) and then I have two ones left (putting two cubes in the ones column)."

Kim: *"Great. Now, add the tens. You've got more cubes stacked at the bottom that you have to add."*

Tory: "Now, I have to add these five tens to these eight tens, but they aren't going to fit either, so now I have to carry again because I have ten tens (placing a cube in the hundreds and taking the other tens off). Now I have two hundreds, three tens, and two ones."

Kim: *"Right. And what is that number?"*

Tory: "Two hundred thirty-two. I had to carry twice."

Kim: *"Yup. And you might have to carry three times if we were adding into the thousands and*

"I'll show you how to do it on paper, because you can't carry this card around with you all your life!"

you had too many hundreds. Carrying is just carrying numbers over to the next place value. Let's do some more. Then I'll show you how to do it on paper, because you can't carry this card around with you all your life!"

Lesson Summary:

Seeing the Concept of Carrying with Place Value Card

1. Student(s) verbalizes a number on the Place Value Card.
2. Student(s) experiences the concept of carrying with the cubes and Place Value Card.
3. Student(s) use the dotted square for the tenth cube as an indication that a ten is carried over.
4. Teacher sets up a number on the Place Value Card, giving the student(s) a number to add to it.
5. Student(s) uses cubes to see the concept of carrying, from tens, hundreds, and thousands.
6. Student(s) always verbalizes thinking and actions.

Having seen and understood the principle of carrying, Tory practiced a few more, and then moved to carrying on paper. For awhile, each lesson was prefaced with the Place Value Card and cubes, until it was evident she could talk herself through the process with ease. Carrying on paper now had a conceptual base, and the only thing new was how to write it on paper. This will now be easy. Remember, problems with carrying are not caused by the written aspect of the problem, they are caused by the conceptual aspect of the problem—not understanding the basis for doing the written tasks.

S A M P L E   L E S S O N

Carrying on Paper

The Set

Kim: *"Now, we're going to add and carry numbers on paper. It's a lot quicker to add numbers on paper than with the Place Value Card and cubes! Instead of using cubes, you can put a little number sort of over the top of the column to show you have carried."*

Tory: "Yeah. I've had some of this in math, but I never really understood why I did it. Now I think I know. But show me anyhow."

Lesson

Kim: *"Here's how you do it. If you have seven in your ones column and add six more ones, how much do you have? You can use the cubes and number line if you need to, or the Place Value Card, or your jumping up to get the answer."* (Writing the equation 7 + 6 in a column on paper.)

Tory: "I already know that six plus seven is thirteen. I have that imaged now from those cards. Or, I could use jumping. Both are faster than getting out the cubes and all that. The answer is thirteen."

Kim: *"Right. How do you write that on paper? Tell me your thinking."*

Tory: "I write it as one ten in my tens column with three ones in the ones column (writing the number 13 on the paper)."

Sidebar text (left margin):

"Instead of using cubes, you can put a little number over the top of the column to show you have carried."

"If you have seven in your ones column and add six more ones, how much do you have?"

$$\begin{array}{r} 7 \\ +6 \\ \hline 13 \end{array}$$

"How do you write that on paper? Tell me your thinking."

Kim: *"Right. You carried a ten over. Now let's do a bigger number on paper, so I can show you about putting the little number at the top of the column so you don't forget to add it!"*

Kim: *"Here's another problem (writing 28 + 5 on paper). Start with the ones and tell me your thinking as you go. If you need to check your thinking, you can always use the cubes and number line, or the Place Value Card. But by now you probably can do it quicker than any of those. Go!"*

Tory: "That's really pretty easy. Eight and five are…(retrieving her number facts or jumping)…thirteen, so I write the three in the ones and carry one ten to the tens."

Kim: *"And, so you won't forget to add that one ten in the tens, put a little number one over the top of the column, like this (placing a little one over the tens column)."*

Tory: "OK. Here's the little one at the top because I carried a ten over! Now, I add the tens column and that makes three, so the answer is thirty-three!"

Kim: *"Exactly. It can't be anything else. We can count on numbers, right?*

Tory: "Right" (Giggling).

Kim: *"You've got this. Let's do some more, even bigger numbers. Like this: (writing 35 + 26). Talk me through it so I know you are visualizing and understanding what you are doing."*

Tory: "Hmmm. Well, it looks hard, but maybe it isn't. I start with the ones, and add five

"So you won't forget to add that one ten in the tens, put a little number one over the top of the column."

$$
\begin{array}{r}
{\scriptstyle 1} \\
\mathbf{28} \\
\mathbf{+5} \\
\hline
\mathbf{33}
\end{array}
$$

1
35
+26
61

"You can even do it
with larger numbers.
Talk me through it."

1
96
+36
132

plus six. I know that because of what we did before in visualizing those facts, but if I didn't I could use jumping to the ten or doubling plus one. Anyhow, five plus six is eleven. I put the one in the ones column, carry the ten to the tens. One plus three is four plus two is six. The answer is sixty-one. Pretty easy, really."

Kim: *"Right. You can even do it with larger numbers. Like this: (writing 96 + 36). Talk me through it."*

Tory: "OK. Six plus six is twelve. Two goes in the ones, one in the tens, so I put the little one at the top of the column, and one plus nine is ten, plus three is thirteen. Do I just write it down?"

Kim: *"Yes. But do you really have thirteen?"*

Tory: "Yes. Oh. Wait. I have three tens and one hundred!"

Kim: *"Exactly. Just like on the Place Value Card. Let's do a few more of those."*

Tory talked her way through a few more. She experienced carrying into the tens, hundreds and even thousands. Then she experienced a column of three numbers.

Kim: *"You're doing great with these. Add up this column of numbers: (writing 28 + 38 + 16)."*

Tory: "Hmmm. OK. Eight plus eight is sixteen, and six more would be twenty-two. (Using jumping, eyes up, she visualized sixteen plus six, whispering.) Four to twenty, two left, twenty-two. Two ones, and I carry two tens, so I put a little two

```
  2
 28
 38
+16
 82
```

"Two ones, and I carry two tens, so I put a little two at the top."

at the top. I can't forget those! Two plus two is four, plus three is seven and seven plus one is eight. I have eight tens. So the answer is eighty-two."

Kim: *"You've got it! By Jove, I think you've got it! Now, we're going to do a bunch of problems on paper with carrying. You can talk me through a few and then do the rest by yourself—just to practice this new step on your math ladder, and get it really strong in your brain."*

Lesson Summary:

Carrying on Paper

1. Teacher sets the task as carrying on paper rather than with cubes and cards.
2. Student(s) represents a number above ten on paper, verbalizing the relationship of ones, tens, hundreds, etc.
3. Teacher presents a written addition problem well beyond the tens, in a column.
4. Student(s) always starts the computation with the ones.
5. Student(s) computes the ones, recognizing the need for carrying when *over nine in the column*, and placing a little numeral in the tens column so as not to forget that ten was carried.
6. Student(s) adds the remaining column.
7. Student(s) repeats the process for adding larger numbers and carrying into the hundreds and thousands.
8. Student(s) repeats the process with a series of numbers in columns.
9. Student(s) always verbalizes thinking and actions.
10. Teacher always provides lots of daily practice on paper after discussing the process.
11. If necessary, student(s) may use number line and cubes, or Place Value Card, to demonstrate problem and place value.

Borrowing

With carrying understood, your students are ready to see and understand the concept of borrowing. As with carrying, there are prerequisites to this step: understanding use of tens, place value, and the principle of carrying. You can practice carrying until it is automatic, or you can introduce borrowing with the Place Value Card at the same time you introduce carrying. You can also overlap to borrowing while working to stabilize the concept. As with carrying, there is no need for cubes and the number line, unless it is to verify the concept of adding and subtracting. Since that was presented and established a few steps back on the math ladder, it shouldn't be necessary to do it now. Simply begin with the Place Value Card and discuss what it means to not have enough in the column, and have to borrow from another column.

Tory is climbing the math ladder in our sessions, but she is still behind in school because they are working on multiplication and she's not quite there yet. But we're climbing. It has only been a few weeks of daily stimulation to this point. She comes to the sessions with a little more confidence now, and a little more light in her eyes.

"Show me twenty-two on the Place Value Card with the cubes."

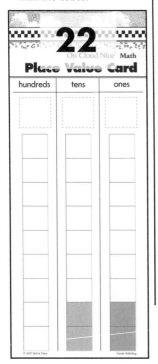

| ┌─────────── SAMPLE LESSON ───────────┐ |

Seeing the Concept of Borrowing with the Place Value Card

Kim: *"You know about adding and carrying, now let's see about subtracting and borrowing. We'll use the Place Value Card and cubes so we can SEE what it means to borrow when you subtract."*

Tory: "We do this in school, and I sort of understand it now because I know place value, but tell me anyhow. I'm ready."

Lesson

Kim: *"Show me twenty-two on the Place Value Card with the cubes."*

22-8=

"Right. You don't have enough and you'll have to borrow some from the tens."

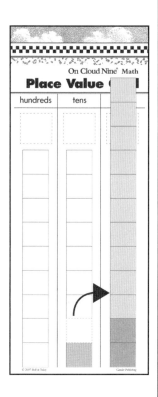

Tory: "Easy." (Placing a stack of two ones and a stack of two tens on the Place Value Card.)

Kim: *"Perfect. Now, let's take eight ones away. Do you have enough ones to take eight of them away?"*

Tory: "No. I only have two ones."

Kim: *"Right. So, you don't have enough and you'll have to borrow some from the tens. Just like if you didn't have enough sugar in your house and had to go borrow some from a neighbor. We'll borrow ten ones from the tens column. Watch. I borrow a ten from the tens column and trade it in for ten ones (placing ten cubes in the ones column). Now, do you have enough ones to subtract eight of them? Talk me through it, just like you did with carrying."*

Tory: "Yup. Now, I have twelve ones instead of two, and I can take eight cubes away. Twelve take-away eight is four. I have four ones in the ones, and one ten. The answer is fourteen. I get it."

Kim: *"When you add and the numbers won't fit you have to carry them over, when you subtract and you don't have enough you have to borrow them back. Carrying and borrowing. They're best friends. One gets bigger and has to carry over and one gets smaller and has to borrow back."*

Tory: "I get it. Let's do some more."

Lesson Summary:

Seeing the Concept of Borrowing with Place Value Card

1. Student(s) experiences the concept of borrowing with the cubes and Place Value Card.
2. Teacher sets up a number on the Place Value Card, giving the student(s) a number to subtract.
3. Student(s) uses cubes to see the concept of borrowing, with the tens, hundreds, and thousands.

Using the Place Value Card, Tory experienced borrowing, including getting into the hundreds. She saw and experienced what it was to borrow and was ready to duplicate the process on paper with the formula: *borrow, cross,* and *write.*

SAMPLE LESSON

Borrowing on Paper—Borrow, Cross, and Write

The Set

"Just like we did with carrying, we'll show our borrowing on paper."

"It's called *borrow, cross,* and *write.*"

Kim: *"Now, let's do that same thing with borrowing, but let's do it on paper. Just like we did with carrying, we'll show our borrowing so we don't forget to do it. It's called borrow, cross, and write."*

Tory: "OK. I did this before, but I really didn't know what I was doing. I just did it."

Lesson

Kim: *"I have a friend that said she did the same thing once with division. But that's another story. Here's what you do. I'll talk you through the first one and then you talk me through the next one. We'll do this problem: thirty-one minus seven."*

Tory: "OK. But I could do that by jumping down to the tens. Really. I can do that one in my head!"

Kim: *"I know. But let me show you on paper because you'll want to know how to do it on paper for when we are doing larger and larger numbers. Here's how to show our thinking on paper. Starting with the ones column, just like addition, we can't take seven away from one, so we go over and borrow a ten. We'll show that we borrowed it by crossing out the three and putting a little two over it. Then we'll put a little one in the ones so we know we gave a ten to it. (Showing the three crossed out, a little two over it, and a little one in the ones.) We borrowed, crossed, and wrote."*

Tory: "Now we can subtract the seven!"

Kim: *"Right, because now we have how many ones?"*

Tory: "Eleven ones."

Kim: *"Right. Eleven take-away seven leaves us four (writing the 4). How many do we have left in the tens?"*

Tory: "We have two tens, because we had to borrow one...and there's the little two so we can't forget that we borrowed!"

Kim: *"Right. And, we don't have anything to take-away from the two tens, so we bring that down. And our answer is twenty-four."*

Tory: "That's exactly what I knew it was from jumping down in my head. Heh. That's a good way to check my answers when I'm working on paper. My turn?"

$$\begin{array}{r} \overset{2}{\cancel{3}}\overset{1}{1} \\ -7 \\ \hline 24 \end{array}$$

"Now, we can subtract the seven!"

"Eleven take-away seven leaves us four ...How many do we have left in the tens?"

"Remember to borrow, cross, and write."

"Talk me through this problem. Always start with the ones, just like with adding."

$$\overset{3\;\;1}{4\!1}$$
$$-14$$
$$\overline{27}$$

"My number line is always with me now."

Kim: *"Your turn. Talk me through this problem. Remember to borrow, cross, and write. Do forty-one minus fourteen. (Writing the problem on paper in columns.) Always start with the ones, just like with adding."*

Tory: "I can't take four away from one, so I borrow a ten, cross, and write (crossing out the 4, lightly putting a 3 over it, and writing a little 1 next to the 1). Now, I have eleven and I subtract four, which is seven (writing the 7). That finishes the ones. In the tens, I have three instead of four, and one from three is two. My answer (writing the 2) is twenty-seven."

Kim: *"Perfect. Now, you can add those numbers back up to see that your answer is right. (Showing her how to add 27 + 14 and getting 41.) Just like when we checked your other subtraction, you can check this subtraction too. Math is easy, Tory!"*

Tory: "I know. It really is."

Kim: *"Let's do some more to be sure you have it. Talk me through it for awhile, and then you can just do them on paper by yourself and check your work. Math really is your friend. You can always count on it to be the same and once you get it, it won't leave you, especially if that visualizing is working for you."*

Tory: "It is. I especially use it to remember my facts and sort of check on my number line if that answer seems right. My number line is always with me now. Even when I'm in the classroom with all the kids, I can still see my number line and use it to help me think about numbers. (Eyes shining.) Thank you."

Blinking and clearing her throat, Kim went on.

Lesson Summary:

Borrowing on Paper—Borrow, Cross, and Write

1. Teacher sets the task as borrowing on paper rather than with cubes and cards.
2. Teacher presents a written subtraction problem well beyond the tens, in a column.
3. Student(s) always starts the computation with the ones.
4. Student(s) computes the ones, recognizing the need for borrowing when *too little in the column*.
5. Student(s) learns to *borrow*, *cross*, and *write*.
6. Student(s) always verbalizes thinking and actions.

Mixing Carrying and Borrowing for Attention to the Sign

As your students have seen and experienced the principles of carrying and borrowing, they need to do written problems with both processes mixed so they can practice more, but also attend to the sign. As in the previous work with addition and subtraction, they should first verbalize the sign, image the process, then do the problem.

Mental Math Practice

While it was important for your student to be able to do addition and subtraction on paper, it is very important to continue practicing mental math—imaged math—with them. Mental math will help them many times in their lives when paper and pencil are not available. Now is the perfect time to give them practice with mental adding and subtracting, using the principle of jumping with double and triple digits.

Practice and Pacing

Once the concept of carrying and borrowing is explored, experienced, and verbalized, students must apply the process to written computation. It is important that the application to computation be done on a daily basis, but it is also important that the process is verbalized so both teacher and students know the principles of carrying and borrowing are intact.

As with all *On Cloud Nine* steps, this step can and should be overlapped with other steps, with one exception. Do not overlap too soon to this step because the prerequisite is an understanding of the use of tens and place value. It is good to establish the concept of carrying, and then apply it to written computation prior to overlapping to borrowing.

Students who are refining their understanding of math may be moving quickly through these early steps on the math ladder, but don't *assume* any steps no matter the age or grade of the students. You really are climbing up a math ladder and you want each step to be intact as a base for higher level math. Be sure this step is experienced, visualized, and verbalized by your students. It is worth the little time it will take you.

Summary

Carrying and borrowing are taught first from a reality base with the Place Value Card, and that reality is extended to visualizing and verbalizing for written computation. With the concepts of place value, use of tens, jumping, and number line firmly in place, carrying and borrowing are learned with ease by students. Along with practice in written computation, this step includes mental math exercises for double digit addition and subtraction.

Tory is ready for multiplication—where her class is in school and the next chapter and step on the *On Cloud Nine* math ladder. You already know how she'll do. It's only addition in another form.

Summary:
Step 8

Carrying and Borrowing

> **Goal:** To teach the concept of carrying and borrowing through manipulatives, imagery, and language, and apply that knowledge to written computation and mental math.

1. *Overview:*

   a. Use the Place Value Card and cubes to teach the concept of carrying and borrowing.

   b. Verbalize and practice written addition for carrying.

   c. Verbalize and practice written subtraction, using *borrow, cross, and write.*

   d. If necessary, explore understanding and imagery of place value, jumping up/down with tens, and the concept of addition and subtraction with the cubes and the concrete number line.

2. **Seeing the Concept of Carrying with the Place Value Card**

   a. Student(s) verbalizes numbers on the Place Value Card.

   b. Student(s) experiences the concept of carrying with the cubes and Place Value Cards.

   c. Student(s) uses the dotted square for the tenth cube as an indication that a ten is carried over.

   d. Teacher sets up a number on the Place Value Card, giving the student(s) a number to add to it.

   e. Student(s) uses cubes to see the concept of carrying, from tens, hundreds, and thousands.

   f. Student(s) always verbalizes thinking and actions.

3. Carrying on Paper

a. Teacher sets the task as carrying on paper rather than with cubes and cards.

b. Student(s) represents a number above ten on paper, verbalizing the relationship of ones, tens, hundreds, etc.

c. Teacher presents a written addition problem well beyond the tens, in a column.

d. Student(s) always starts the computation with the ones.

e. Student(s) computes the ones, recognizing the need for carrying when *over nine in the column*, and places a little numeral in the tens column so as not to forget that ten was carried.

f. Student(s) adds the remaining column.

g. Student(s) repeats the process for adding larger numbers and carrying into the hundreds and thousands.

h. Student(s) repeats the process with a series of numbers in columns.

i. Student(s) always verbalizes thinking and actions.

j. Teacher always provides lots of daily practice on paper after discussing the process.

k. If necessary, student(s) may use number line and cubes to demonstrate problem and place value.

4. Seeing the Concept of Borrowing with the Place Value Card

a. Student(s) experiences the concept of borrowing with the cubes and Place Value Card.

b. Teacher sets up a number on the Place Value Card, giving the student(s) a number to subtract.

c. Student(s) uses cubes to see the concept of borrowing, with the tens, hundreds, and thousands.

5. Borrowing on Paper—Borrow, Cross, and Write

a. Teacher sets the task as borrowing on paper rather than with cubes and cards.

b. Teacher presents a written subtraction problem well beyond the tens, in a column.

   c. Student(s) always starts the computation with the ones.

   d. Student(s) computes the ones, recognizing the need for borrowing when *too little in the column*.

   e. Student(s) learns to *borrow*, *cross*, and *write*, beginning with the tens, and extending into the hundreds and thousands.

   f. Student(s) always verbalizes thinking and actions.

Group Instruction

As usual, small or large group instruction is a matter of managing the group and not changing the stimulation. Using overheads, chalkboards, teams, and the thumbs up/down approach for interaction, any size group can stay involved. Remember to use basic group management techniques, such as giving them a signal of when they can talk, when they can raise their hands, when they just think. This will help you control the group. But along with this, remember to observe your students' sensory systems. Watch for their responses, their verbalization, their attention to give you clues as to which students to call on for specific types of stimulation.

14

Multiply and Get More

Every step of the *On Cloud Nine* math ladder is dependent on the previous step, especially multiplication. *Multiplying is really a shortcut for adding. It is adding a number a given amount of times.* Since Tory has a stable base for addition, base ten, place value, and mathematical imagery for numerals and concepts, she is ready for this step.

Here is Tory's current frustration in school. Here is where she is failing tests. Prior to starting *On Cloud Nine* a few weeks ago, her parents and teacher indicated that she couldn't remember multiplication tables, her answers could sometimes be wildly off, she couldn't do two- and three-digit multiplication, and division made her tearful.

Establishing imagery and language for the concept and tables of multiplication is very much the same as establishing the concept and facts for addition and subtraction. *On Cloud Nine* repeats the process of discovery, concept understanding, reinforcement, practice, and application by (1) using manipulatives to make the concepts and multiplication tables real, (2) putting that realness into imagery for automatic use, and (3) transferring the imagery to mental and print computation. Here is a general overview of this step:

- Discover the concept of multiplication through cubes, a concrete number line, and clay.
- Discover the multiplication facts (tables) with Multiplication Family Fact Sheets.
- Reinforce with cubes to experience the relationship of the tables within the *multiplication family.*
- Use the concrete number line, with cubes, to experience specific tables.
- Use an imaged number line to image specific tables.
- Use Multiplication Family Fact Cards to place specific tables in memory.
- Discover and apply steps of multiplication to computation, through two, three, and four digits.

This is the day Tory faces an enemy and wins. Hear her sigh as this lesson gets started.

SAMPLE LESSON

Discovering the Concept of Multiplication with the Cubes and the Number Line

The Set

Kim: *"Tory, how many different number symbols do we have?"*

Tory: "We have the numbers one through nine, and we have a zero, too."

Kim: *"Right. That's all we have, just those. You've learned to add and subtract with those numbers, and you've learned to visualize the addition and subtraction facts, use the number line, use place value for the tens, and even do math in your head by jumping up and down with the tens."*

Tory: "Right. I can do all that."

Kim: *"Well, now it's time to learn to do some more things with the few numbers we have in math. Multiplication. It's the next step on your math ladder." (Checking her math ladder.)*

Tory: (Quiet. Looking down.) "I have trouble with multiplication." (Sigh.)

Kim: *"You won't have trouble any more. Multiplication is really addition. It is a way to add a number a lot of times. Let me show you. Just like we did when we were on the other steps of the math ladder, let's use the cubes and the number line first, then we'll use clay, then we'll visualize and verbalize multiplication."*

"Multiplication is really addition. It is a way to add a number a lot of times."

182

Tory: "OK…" (Looking at Kim. Hopeful. Then a puzzled look crossing her face.) "Clay?"

Lesson

"Set up the number line and make yourself some stacks of two cubes each."

Kim: *"We'll get to that later. First, set up the number line and make yourself some stacks of two cubes each. Make a whole bunch of them so we can discover what it means to multiply."*

Tory: "OK. (Getting some stacks of two in front of her.) I'm ready."

"Get eight stacks of two. Count them out and put them in front of you."

Kim: *"Get eight stacks of two. Count them out and put them in front of you."*

Tory: "Here's one stack of two, here's two, three, four, five…(getting eight stacks of two cubes in front of her)."

"Touch and count them again to make sure you have eight twos."

Kim: *"Great. Touch and count them again to make sure you have eight twos."*

Tory: "One, two, three, four…(touching and counting all eight of the stacks)."

"You have eight twos, or we could say you have a two, eight times. Now, put them on the number line to see what they add up to."

Kim: *"You have eight twos, or we could say you have two, eight times. Good. Now, put them on the number line to see what they add up to."*

Tory: "They add up to sixteen." (Placing the twos on the number line.)

Kim: *"Right. You added the two eight times and we can show that with the adding sign like this (writing 2 + 2 + 2 + 2 + 2 + 2 + 2 + 2 = 16). That's a lot of twos to write out. Imagine how many we would have to write out if we said we wanted to get a hundred twos. Imagine how many cubes we would have to*

"We can show those same eight twos (pointing to the 2 + 2 + 2 + 2 + 2 + 2 + 2 + 2 = 16 on her paper) by writing it this way with the multiplication sign: 8 x 2."

"This time show me four twos, or four times two, first put them in your hand and then put them on the number line."

"Four times two is eight." (Writing 4 x 2 = 8.)

"This time get me a two zero times. Try that! Put that on the number line!"

get and how many times we would have to write the twos."

Tory: "Wow. That would be pretty long! And it would take a long time. You're going to show me an easier way, huh."

Kim: *"Yes. And it's called multiplication. We can make adding simple by using a different sign. We can show those same eight twos (pointing to the 2 + 2 + 2 + 2 + 2 + 2 + 2 + 2 = 16 on her paper) by writing it this way with the multiplication sign: (writing 8 x 2). That sign tell us to multiply the two eight times! It says: eight times two. Much easier."*

Tory: "I get it. It seems awfully simple."

Kim: *"It really is. Let's do some more. Get those twos off the number line and back in front of you. (Tory gets the cubes back in stacks of twos.) This time show me four twos, or four times two. First put them in your hand and then put them on the number line."*

Tory: "That's eight." (Placing the cubes in her hand and then on the number line.)

Kim: *"It sure is. Let's say what we just did. Four times two is eight, and write it with the new sign that tells us what to do."*

Tory: "Four times two is eight." (Writing 4 x 2 = 8.)

Kim: *"Great. Get those off the number line, and this time get me a two zero times. Go ahead. Try that! Put that on the number line."*

Tory: "Uh…I see the two out there but I can't put a two on the number line because you said to get it zero times."

Kim: *"Right. So, if I wrote zero times two (writing), what would the answer be? How many twos can you put on the number line?"*

Tory: "Zero. I get it. Zero times two is zero." (Finishing the equation by writing a 0.)

Kim: *"Yup. It can't be anything else. Let's do another number. Let's multiply fives this time. Get stacks of five cubes each in front of you, just like you did the twos. This will be fun."*

Tory: "OK." (Getting stacks of five in front of her.)

Kim: *"Get seven fives. How would you write that in addition?"*

Tory: "It would be long." (Writing 5 + 5 + 5 + 5 + 5 + 5 + 5.)

Kim: *"Now let's write the same thing but with the multiplication sign."*

Tory: "OK. It is seven times the five. (Writing 7 x 5.) It's a lot shorter this way."

Kim: *"Right. First, put those seven fives in your hand, then put them on the number line to find the answer."*

Tory: "Thirty-five is the answer." (Placing the cubes in her hand and then on the number line.)

Kim: *"It sure is. Can you picture that without the number line? Close your eyes or look at your imaged number line and see yourself putting those fives on it."*

Tory: "That's easy. I can picture seven fives going up to the number thirty-five."

"Get seven fives. How would you write that in addition?"

5 + 5 + 5 + 5 + 5 + 5 + 5

"Now, let's write the same thing but with the multiplication sign." 7 x 5.

"Can you picture that without the number line?"

> (Finger gesturing on her imaginary number line.)
>
> Kim: *"Great. Let's do some more and then we'll do the same kind of thing with clay."*

Lesson Summary:

Discovering the Concept of Multiplication with Cubes and the Number Line

1. Student(s) uses cubes and the concrete number line to experience concept of multiplying.
2. Student(s) gets stacks of cubes for a designated number.
3. Teacher tells student(s) to get the cubes a specific number of times, such as "get eight of the twos."
4. Student(s) places the cubes in hand and then on the number line.
5. Teacher writes out the equation for adding, such as: $2 + 2 + 2 + 2 + 2 + 2 + 2 + 2 = 16$.
6. Teacher shows that multiplication is an easier way to add numbers and shows new sign and new equation, such as $8 \times 2 = 16$.
7. Student(s) experiences more numbers being multiplied rather than added, stacking and placing cubes on the number line.
8. Student(s) always verbalizes and writes the equations after experiencing the multiplication.
9. Student(s) visualizes equations on imaged number line, and verifies on concrete number line.
10. Student(s) discovers multiplying a number times one and a number times zero.
11. Teacher establishes the idea of multiplication being a simple, quick way of adding the same number.

Tory continued to experience the concept of multiplication with her cubes and number line, something she had become used to using, including imagery at the end of every discovery. Then, as an added way for her to experience the concept of multiplication, we used the cubes and clay.

S A M P L E   L E S S O N

Discovering the Concept of Multiplication with Cubes and Clay

The Set

"I'm going to show you another way to see what multiplying is, only this time we'll use some clay and the cubes."

Kim: *"Now that you have experienced multiplication with the cubes and the number line, I'm going to show you another way to see what multiplying is, only this time we'll use some clay and the cubes. This will also help you visualize it."*

Tory: *"Using clay sounds kind of fun."*

Lesson

"Laying the cubes like you would on the number line, show me your two cubes stamped into the clay one time."

Kim: *"Take this handful of clay and flatten out a large pancake. (Tory does.) Put it down on your clean paper and pick up a stack of two cubes. (Tory does.) Laying the cubes like you would on the number line, show me your two cubes stamped into the clay one time. Do this equation: one times two, and find out what it is."*

Stamp with two cubes!

1 x 2 = 2

Tory: "It's two. When I stamped once, it left a mark of two. It's an imprint of two cubes."

Kim: *"That's right, so one times two stays just two. We can write that like this: (writing 1 x 2 = 2). This time try one times four by stamping four (stacked) cubes—just one time. And write out the equation using the multiplication sign."*

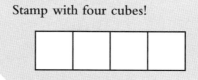

Stamp with four cubes!

$$1 \times 4 = 4$$

Tory: "One times four stays four. One times anything has to stay itself because it's just that number stamping itself one time." (Writing the equation: 1 x 4 = 4.)

Kim: *"Exactly. So, how do you picture one stamp of thirty cubes, or one times thirty?"*

Tory: "I see thirty cubes stamped one time. So... one times thirty equals thirty." (Writing out the equation 1 x 30 = 30.)

Kim: *"Great. And how about this equation? What's the answer to this: one times forty-four thousand?"*

"One times four stays four. One times anything has to stay itself because it's just that number stamping itself one time."

"So, how do you picture one stamp of thirty cubes, or one times thirty?"

"What's the answer to this: one times forty-four thousand?"

"I can only get the forty-four thousand one time, so it is still forty-four thousand…and a very, very big piece of clay!"

"First, tell me what you picture yourself doing and then check it by showing me with the clay."

Tory: "I can only get the forty-four thousand one time, so it is still forty-four thousand… and a very, very big piece of clay!"

Kim: *"Good. What about four times a zero cube, how do you picture that? Write it out for us."*

Tory: "I have to pick up a zero cube, but I can't see it or touch it because it is zero. So it doesn't matter how many times I stamp it because I'm not holding anything! The answer is zero! So, four times zero is zero." (Writing out 4 x 0 = 0.)

Kim: *"How does it change your picture to show zero times four? Tell me what you visualize and then say and write down the equation."*

Tory: "Same thing! I pick up a stack of four cubes, but I can't stamp it into the clay because it said zero times. The answer would still be zero. Zero times four is zero. (Writing 0 x 4 = 0.) Any number times zero would be zero, because either you are holding nothing or you're not stamping it any number of times."

Kim: *"That's right. Now, I'm going to give you another number to multiply. First, tell me what you picture yourself doing and then check it by showing me with the clay. Your problem is three times four."*

Tory: "I see myself picking up a stack of four and stamping it into the clay three times. I should end up with three fours." (Stamping the four linked cubes into the clay.)

Kim: *"Now, you can count your cubes to get the*

answer, but a faster way than having to count every time is to visualize these facts, just like we did for addition and subtraction. That's next."

Tory: "OK! Actually, my multiplication tables have already been getting a little better because I've been visualizing some of them. Maybe I will be able to get good in multiplication..."

Lesson Summary:

Discovering the Concept of Multiplication with Cubes and Clay

1. Student(s) uses cubes and clay to experience concept of multiplying, verifying answers on the number line.
2. Student(s) gets stacks of cubes (linked together) for a designated number and flattens out a piece of clay.
3. Teacher tells student(s) to *stamp* those cubes a specific number of times.
4. Student(s) stamps the cubes on the clay the designated number of times.
5. Student(s) experiences numbers being multiplied by stamping linked cubes into the clay.
6. Student(s) always verbalizes and writes the equations after experiencing the multiplication.
7. Student(s) visualizes equations and proves the process on the concrete number line, or with cubes and clay.
8. Student(s) discovers multiplying a number times one and a number times zero.
9. Teacher establishes the idea of multiplication being a simple, quick way of adding the same number.

With the concept establishing, your students are ready to learn some of the multiplication facts, the multiplication tables. These are taught the same way the addition and subtraction facts were taught: with imagery. As it was important that addition facts from one to twenty are memorized, it is important that the multiplication tables through ten (later twelve) are memorized. Since students have imaged and mastered the addition facts and have the ability to use mental math for jumping with the tens, addition can be a fail-safe system for the multiplication tables. When we, as adults, forget our multiplication tables, we can think our way to the answer. For example, if the problem is 6 x 7 and we can't remember the answer, but we do remember that 5 x 7 = 35, then all we have to do is talk to ourselves about adding one more seven on. "I know that five sevens are thirty-five, so six of them is seven more." Students who understand multiplication have that same mental ability available to them when their multiplication tables momentarily vanish from their head.

S A M P L E   L E S S O N

Discovering the Multiplication Family Tables

The Set

> "...Multiplication has a family also, just like addition and subtraction has a family. But these families of facts are called *tables*."

Kim: *"You're not going to believe this, but multiplication has a family also, just like addition and subtraction have families. But these families of facts are called tables. Let's discover those tables with our cubes and number line and a Multiplication Table Fact Sheet."*

Tory: "OK. I've had these multiplication tables before, but I didn't really understand them. I just tried to memorize them."

Lesson

Kim: *"I know. You will understand them and they will be as easy for you as the adding and subtracting facts. Do you think we need to worry much about the family table for zero?"*

Tory: "No, because they're all going to be zero!"

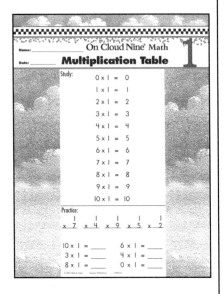

Kim: *"Right. So, let's start with the family table for one. We'll start with zero times one, and then one times one, and then two times one, etc. What would zero times one be? Here's our Multiplication Table Fact Sheet for the number one, so we know which family we are discovering. Get some single cubes and the number line, and say and write your thinking."*

Tory: "OK. (Getting a bunch of cubes in front of her.) Zero times one is zero. One times one is one." (Placing the cubes in her hand a designated number of times and then on the number line and writing the answers to the equations on the sheet: 0 x 1 = 0, 1 x 1 = 1, 2 x 1 = 2, 3 x 1 = 3, etc. until she had experienced all the ones.)

Kim: *"Good. That's the table for the multiplication family of one. Let's do the twos just like that. Get stacks of two cubes in front of you and let's experience them and then say and write. Go."*

Tory: "This is making multiplication easier for me. Am I going to learn to visualize these tables like I did the families for adding and subtracting?"

Kim: *"Yes, indeed. That's next, as soon as we get a few of these discovered."*

Lesson Summary:

Discovering the Multiplication Family Tables

1. Student(s) discovers the family *tables* up to ten with the cubes and concrete number line.
2. Student(s) gets stacks of a designated number of cubes and experiences the tables.
3. Student(s) verbalizes the equations.
4. Student(s) always starts with zero and increases to ten.
5. Student(s) sees the relationship of the tables increasing by the number multiplied.

Discovering the family tables for multiplication is so similar to discovering the family facts for addition and subtraction that students are comfortable with the process. They know where this is going and are comfortable with the thought that they may be successful. It is preferable to discover the family tables through at least a few numbers, no matter the age or level of students, because perception is aided with contrast and similarity. Therefore, Tory continued this lesson into the fives. Then we overlapped to imagery cards for multiplication facts, while we continued to discover the remaining multiplication tables a little each lesson. Too many would overwhelm her, but too little would inhibit her learning.

An important aspect of learning multiplication tables is the repetition of facts in different tables. For example, when Tory experienced the ones family table and later experienced the threes family table, she noted that the equation 3 x 1 = 3 was reversed when it was 1 x 3 = 3, but the answer had to be the same. Thus, when she learned the threes and fours there were some that she knew already from the previous family. This became a big deal as she got into the sevens and eights, because there were only a few new ones she needed to memorize within each family!

SAMPLE LESSON

Using the Family Fact Cards to Memorize the Multiplication Tables

The Set

Kim: *"How did you learn the family facts for adding and subtracting? What did you do to remember them?"*

Tory: "Hmmm. I learned to image them and practiced that imaging with cards."

Kim: *"Exactly. And, just as you thought, we're going to image the multiplication tables on these Family Fact Cards. I'll show you a Family Fact Card for you to visualize, then I'll take it away and you tell me what you saw."*

Tory: "OK. This should be pretty easy. I can visualize numbers now. Do you want me to write them in the air after you take them away?"

Kim: *"Yes, for a while, but very soon you can just tell me what you visualized."*

Lesson

Kim: *"Here we go. Let's do the family of three."* Holding up the 1 x 3 = 3 card and then taking it away.)

Tory: "One times three equals three (saying and air-writing)."

Kim: *"Great. What's the second number you saw?"*

"I'll show you a Family Fact Card for you to visualize, then I'll take it away and you tell me what you saw."

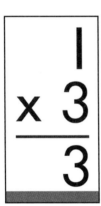

"What's the second number you saw?"

Tory: "The three." (Eyes up, hand gesturing to the spot in her imagery.)

Kim: *"Great again. What's the last number you saw?"*

Tory: "The three."

Kim: *"What was the sign you saw? Write that in the air as you say it."*

Tory: "The multiplication sign, like this…(air-writing an x)."

Kim: *"Good. Now tell me back the whole equation from your imagery. You don't have to write it in the air unless you want to."*

Tory: "One times three equals three." (Eyes up, but choosing not to air-write.)

Kim: *"Great. Here's another card, only this time I'm going to cover up the answer."* (Holding up the 2 x 4 = 8 card, covering the number 8, then taking the card away.)

Tory: "I know it. Two times four is eight." (Saying and air-writing the whole equation, including the sign, just as she had done for adding and subtracting.)

Kim: *"Perfect, Tory. Here's another one."* (Holding up the 6 x 3 = 18 card, then taking it away.)

Tory: "Six times three equals eighteen. I can easily visualize it. And when we do the sixes, that's one I'll already know because if six times three is eighteen, then three times six has to be the same. Right?"

Kim: *"Absolutely. As you get to the higher tables, you'll already know a whole bunch of them. For example, when you get to the sixes, you'll* *already know: one times six, and two times six, and three times six, and four times six, and even five times six. That means you only have to learn six times six, seven times six, eight times six, etc. And just think what it will be like when you get to the nines!"*

Tory: "There'll be hardly any left to learn!"

Lesson Summary:

Using Family Fact Cards to Memorize the Multiplication Tables

1. Teacher holds up a Family Fact Card for a few seconds, then takes it away.
2. Student(s) images and air-writes the numbers and signs.
3. Teacher questions for specific numbers or signs in the equation.
4. Discuss the relationship of 3 x 6 and 6 x 3, etc., to reduce the anxiety related to the daunting task of imaging/memorizing lots and lots of tables.

The lessons continued to overlap with Tory discovering tables up to ten, and then imaging them on cards. As with addition and subtraction, the Family Fact Cards can be practiced in two ways: with the whole equation on one side, or with the equation on one side and the answer on the back. Also, as with addition and subtraction, the tables can be sorted into fast, medium, and slow, and placed in personalized card boxes.

The tables for eleven and twelve should be established *after* students are confident with the tables up to ten. This keeps their thinking within the tens, and reduces the memory load for learning the tables. Because they know multiplication is adding, they can always add to get the answer to the elevens or twelves and later these tables can be added to their cards for memorization. Experience with teaching multiplication tables indicates that part of the difficulty is the *fear* of so much to memorize. This emotional element can interfere with the learning process; thus, establish the tables through ten before going on.

There are only a few tables that will give students difficulty. It is not the twos, fives, nines, or tens, it is primarily the sixes, sevens, and eights. And each time students learn a set of multiplication tables for a given number, there is less to learn for the next number. By the time they get to eight there are only a few new ones to memorize. It is the same with nines, but relieve their minds by letting them know that for now they will only have to learn through the tens.

Ways to Think About and Learn Some of the Tables

While you probably already know most of these, this section is just a reminder of things to help students think through, practice, or remember some of the tables.

1. Four times six is easy because students can think that 2 x 6 = 12, one of their doubles, and then they double that again to get twenty-four.

2. The twos, fives, and tens are easy to learn because they are like counting

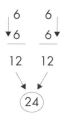

    by twos, fives, or tens, something your students can already do. They just have to count a designated number of times.

3. The nines are easy because you can think with the tens, and then take away the number you were multiplying. For example, 7 x 9 is easy if you multiply 7 x 10 = 70, and take a seven away! Since students can subtract easily by this step on the math ladder, arriving at the answer sixty-three is quick. Now, having figured out that the nines within any family are easy, when they get to the sixes, sevens, and eights, there really *are* only a few *new* tables to learn!

4. Discover the match: Students match equations that contain the same numbers. For example, 4 x 2 and 2 x 4 are a match, 3 x 5 and 5 x 3 are a match. Students form an image and verbalize for each equation in the match. Help students notice that although their image changes, the number of cubes stays the same. This is easiest to see with a grid.

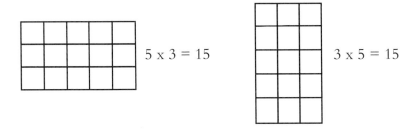

5 x 3 = 15   3 x 5 = 15

Practicing Multiplication Tables on Paper, Checking Signs, and Multiples

Because of the relationship of multiplication to addition and subtraction, it is very important to have students practice multiplication tables on paper, and then mix them with addition and subtraction to be sure they are comparing the three different processes required by the three different signs. As noted earlier, nearly every *On Cloud Nine* lesson needs to be followed by written computation.

As students multiply on paper (including problems of addition and subtraction), be sure to (1) check the sign, (2) visualize, (3) verbalize and do.

During the written computation practice you may also introduce students to the various ways to write multiplication equations: 4 x 2, 4 • 2, or even (4)(2). However, be aware of the obvious chance for overload. Know your students well enough to put parts to whole and decide if it is appropriate to throw another variation of the sign at them. The same parts-to-whole decision needs to be made by you regarding teaching the concept of *multiples*. For example, the multiples of 24 are (1, 24) (2, 12) (3, 8) (4, 6). It is important to know about multiples of a given number because they are helpful with division. Wait to give them until the tables are very strong and anxiety is reduced.

Computing Multiplication Problems: Long Multiplication

Knowing the multiplication tables and addition facts are the base needed for one, two, three, and four digit multiplication. Unless we're going to have calculators attached to our body, we need a system for our brains to multiply large numbers—or we may be back to counting hairy digits in some fashion. The following method for computing long multiplication, while tried and true, calls attention to two primary facts: *start with the ones,* and *multiply with the active bottom number.* With imagery and language as part of the base and interaction, and well-established multiplication and addition facts and concepts, Tory is ready to win this battle.

S A M P L E   L E S S O N

Written Computation: Start with the Ones and Work the Bottom Number

The Set

Kim: *"Now, it's time to apply your family facts and tables to longer multiplication problems. Two things to learn here: start with the ones column and work the bottom number. I'm going to show you first, then it will be your turn."*

Tory: "OK. This has been hard for me in school. But, once adding was hard too, and so were the multiplication tables. I had to think and think to get them right, and then sometimes my answer was way off. It's better now."

Lesson

Kim: *"I know. And this is really pretty easy. Just remember to do two things: start with the ones and work the bottom number. Watch. We'll start with twenty-four times six (writing it down). Point to the bottom number."*

"Two things to learn here: start with the ones column and work the bottom number."

24
x 6
———

"The six is going to do most of the work. It's going to multiply each number on the top starting with the ones and then going to the tens."

2
24
x 6
———
4

"We know from addition that we need to carry our tens to the tens place, so we leave the four in the ones place and carry the two..."

2
24
x 6
———
144

Tory: "The six." (Pointing to the number 6.)

Kim: *"Right. The six is going to do most of the work. It's going to multiply each number on the top starting with the ones and then going to the tens. Let's talk our way through this. Six times four is…?"*

Tory: "Twenty-four."

Kim: *"Right. Let's write that down. We know from addition that we need to carry our tens to the tens place, so we leave the four in the ones place and carry the two, and we put a little two up there so we remember to add it, not multiply it!"*

Tory: "Right."

Kim: *"Next, we multiply the six with the two in the tens column. That gives us twelve. We carried two tens from the ones column, so we add that to twelve: twelve plus two equals fourteen. Our answer is one hundred forty-four."*

Tory: "That seems pretty easy. Our bottom number does most of the work and we start with the ones. Right?"

Kim: *"Right. Remember, you only add the number you carried. Don't multiply it. Now it's your turn. Try thirty-six times seven."*

Tory: "OK. I start in the ones and my bottom number does most of the work…" (Verbalizing through the process and computing on paper.)

Lesson Summary:

Written Computation:
Start with the Ones and Work the Bottom Number

1. Teacher explains two principles to remember: *start with the ones* and *work the bottom number.*
2. Teacher demonstrates the written computation and student(s) verbalizes:
   - start with the ones
   - carry to the tens
   - multiply the tens
   - add what was carried
3. Student(s) computes and verbalizes.

Multiplying Numbers into the Hundreds and Thousands

As students practice long multiplication, the process is extended beyond the tens into the hundreds and thousands. They will need a demonstration of the system for doing that, as well as practice and reinforcement; but they also need to know that the system is only slightly, a wee bit, different than what they have previously learned. It is not a new system for multiplying numbers, only an expanded system because we are now into more columns of place value and *they have to hold their place with a zero.* Simple really. And they'll have an easy time getting it, if all their previous steps on the math ladder are intact. If not, their eyes may be glazing over.

SAMPLE LESSON

Multiplying Numbers into the Hundreds and Thousands Using a Place Holder

The Set

Kim: *"We're going to move to even greater numbers. This time we'll be multiplying two numbers into the hundreds and, pretty soon, even into the thousands. It's really the same though—*

"...start with the ones and work the bottom numbers—and then all we have to do is hold our place with a zero."

```
  2
 34
x 27
238
```

"We leave our eight in the ones and carry the two to the tens place."

"We go to the next number on the bottom. Is it in the ones or the tens place?"

```
   2
  34
 x 27
 238
 680
 918
```

---

start with the ones and work the bottom numbers—and then all we have to do is hold our place with a zero. It's thinking about place value again, and a place holder. So, this will be easy."

Tory: "OK. I'll trust you because so far I've been able to get every one of these steps. Even the last one has been pretty easy because I know my facts and tables."

Lesson

Kim: *"I'll show you first and we'll talk through it together. Our problem is: thirty-four times twenty-seven (writing it on paper). We start with the ones and the bottom number. Seven times four is..."*

Tory: "Twenty-eight."

Kim: *"We leave our eight in the ones and carry the two to the tens place. Next, we multiply seven times three and add the two tens we carried. That's..."*

Tory: "Twenty-three. This is just like what I already know."

Kim: *"Right. We go to the next number on the bottom. Is it in the ones or the tens place?"*

Tory: "It's in the tens place."

Kim: *"Right. Here's the only thing new: you need a place holder. When I multiply by a ten, what number will always be in my ones place? For example, if you multiply ten times seven. What number is in the ones place?"*

Tory: "A zero."

Kim: *"Right. Since there's a zero in my ones place*

whenever I multiply by a ten, I'm going to remind myself that I'm using the tens and place a zero in the ones place. It is holding the place: a place holder. (Writing a zero in the ones place.) And I just continue the multiplying. You talk me through it."

Tory: "So, two times four is eight, and nothing to carry. And, since I'm multiplying the tens, the number eight has to go in the tens column. Right?"

Kim: *"Exactly. Keep multiplying."*

Tory: "Two times three is six, and nothing was carried. So that must go next, and it goes in the hundreds column. Now what do I do?'"

Kim: *"Add them up and you have the answer."*

Tory: "This is pretty easy because I already know how to add and carry."

Kim: *"Now it's your turn. Talk as you work so I can hear your thinking. Tell me the thing that's new before you get going."*

Tory: "I have to think about place value and put a zero, and I also have to add them all up in the end!"

Kim: *"Exactly. Try this problem: (writing 48 x 23)."*

Tory: "Let's see, I start with the ones…"

Note: As you move to multiplying into the thousands, explain that the process is the same, only there is more place value to think about, so more place holders are needed.

"Add them up and you have the answer."

"Talk as you work so I can hear your thinking."

> ## Lesson Summary:
>
> *Multiplying Numbers into the Hundreds and Thousands Using a Place Holder*
> 1. Student(s) recognizes similarity to multiplying with tens: start with ones and the active bottom number.
> 2. Teacher explores need for *place holder* with a zero.
> 3. Teacher demonstrates the written computation and student(s) verbalizes.
> 4. Student(s) computes and verbalizes.

Estimating

It is helpful to form an estimate when multiplying two- and three-digit numbers because that estimate can help students begin to notice if their answer seems right. However, teaching students to estimate an answer first is like teaching them to guess at a word first to see if it fits context, and then go back and get the right word. It can mislead students to estimate before computing, as they can think math doesn't have to be accurate. But teaching them to estimate can help them with mental math and life situations where a quick estimate may impress someone or save a situation.

With estimating in long multiplication, students learn to round numbers to the nearest ten and then use that as the estimate. For example, if the problem is six times twenty-four, the student rounds twenty-four to the nearest ten, which is twenty. Six times twenty is one hundred twenty, and because there were four ones that didn't get multiplied, students can reason that the answer will be more than one hundred twenty, and in fact, once good in imagery and mental math, they can also learn to complete the computation by multiplying six times four and adding it to one hundred twenty. Then they have the real answer. A Cecil answer. But for now, and for estimating, just use the principle of rounding to the nearest ten and adding on.

Besides the above reasons for estimating, it can be very helpful in a world where calculators compute math. When students only have to punch in numbers, it is important they can think well enough with math to verify if an answer seems correct or not. With a world more and more dependent on calculators, estimating may become an invaluable math skill.

| SAMPLE | LESSON |

Estimating with Long Multiplication

The Set

Kim: *"Let's learn how to use the tens to estimate an answer in a long multiplication problem. Having an estimate will allow us to know whether our final answer is close or not."*

Tory: "OK."

Lesson

Kim: *"Here's the problem: six times twenty-four. First, we'll start by visualizing our number line and rounding the twenty-four to the nearest ten. Can you see what the nearest ten would be?"*

Tory: "The nearest ten is twenty."

Kim: *"Right. Since the six is less than ten we don't have to worry about rounding that. Now, I want you to picture six twenties on your number line. What do you see?"*

Tory: "Twenty, forty, sixty, eighty, one hundred, one hundred twenty."

Kim: *"Right. We can use one hundred twenty as our estimate. Since twenty-four is greater than twenty, we can reason that our answer is going to be a little more than one hundred twenty. Another way to estimate uses our knowledge of tens. Twenty is a ten and I know when I multiply a one and a ten, my answer is a ten. So if I multiply the first two digits of each number, two and six, I get twelve tens or one*

"Six times twenty-four. First, we'll start by visualizing our number line and rounding the twenty-four to the nearest ten."

hundred twenty. Let's do some more."

Tory: "OK."

Kim: *"Try estimating twenty-seven times thirty-three. You'll need to round both numbers since they are both greater than ten."*

Tory: "I round twenty-seven to thirty and thirty-three to thirty. So I have thirty times thirty. How do I do that on my number line?"

Kim: *"Well, let's think of it another way. What do you get when you multiply ten times ten?"*

Tory: "I get one hundred."

Kim: *"Right. So if you multiply the first two digits of each number, in this case three and three, what do you get?"*

Tory: "I get nine, but since my answer is one hundred, it will be nine hundred...close to nine hundred because I rounded up on one number and down on the other."

Kim: *"Good thinking. The real answer for twenty-seven times thirty-three is eight hundred ninety-one. Is that close to nine hundred?"*

Tory: "Yes! I was close, but I still need to get correct answers, don't I?"

Kim: *"Yes, indeed. Close is helpful, but not good enough. You could get in a lot of problems in life if all you could do with math was get close. So, you'll only use estimating as a way to check in your head that an answer is close. I always want you to compute first so you won't get in the habit of guessing."*

> ## Lesson Summary:
>
> ### *Estimating with Long Multiplication*
>
> 1. Student(s) rounds numbers greater than ten to the nearest ten.
> 2. Student(s) uses multiples of tens to form an estimate.
> 3. Teacher gives student(s) the answer to compare the estimate.
> 4. Teacher establishes that estimating is only a means to check if an answer is close. It is not a substitute for accurate computation.

Practice and Pacing

Practicing multiplication tables through imagery is a daily activity, both mentally and in written computation. Now that students have learned three signs (+, -, x), have them practice multiplication alone, multiplication with addition, and multiplication with addition and subtraction. Attending to the sign by verbalizing the process is still a part of your practice sessions, although eventually students need to demonstrate ownership and responsibility by doing written computation alone. If a student has visual-motor difficulties, use graph paper at first to help keep the number columns in alignment. There is no substitute for just doing lots of problems. You can make it more fun for younger students by using colored pencils—a different color for each place value.

Usually pacing students includes overlapping, but it must be done carefully here. Don't overlap into division until the multiplication tables are established through ten, and students are easily able to compute two-digit multiplication. Although the concept of division can be presented with cubes and the number line to explore very simple division, computation in division requires multiplication. Establish multiplication so it is well learned and well understood before the student moves to the division step (a step that can scare even the brightest child).

Summary

Multiplication is taught by experiencing, visualizing, verbalizing, and computing. First, students experience the concept of multiplication, then they experience the *multiplication family tables* (just as they experienced the family facts for addition and subtraction), then they image those tables with Family Fact Sheets, and finally they apply their knowledge of the concept of multiplication to written computation, including two-, three-, and four-digit multiplication with place value and place holders. Taken in chunks that build on the previous experience and imagery for each step, multiplication becomes easy. Estimating is taught to prepare students for mentally checking their work after they compute.

One more step up the *On Cloud Nine* math ladder is established. Division is next, an old fear remembered.

Summary: Step 9

Multiplication

Goal: To experience, visualize, and verbalize the concept of multiplication, memorize the multiplication tables through imagery, and compute written problems into two-, three-, and four-digit multiplication.

1. Discovering the Concept of Multiplication with Cubes and the Number Line

a. Student(s) uses cubes and concrete number line to experience concept of multiplying.

b. Student(s) gets stacks of cubes for a designated number.

c. Teacher tells student(s) to get the cubes a specific number of times, such as "get eight of the twos."

d. Student(s) places the cubes in hand and then on the number line.

e. Teacher writes out the equation for adding, such as:
$2 + 2 + 2 + 2 + 2 + 2 + 2 + 2 = 16$.

f. Teacher shows that multiplication is an easier way to add numbers and shows new sign and new equation, such as $8 \times 2 = 16$.

g. Student(s) experiences more numbers being multiplied rather than added, stacking and placing cubes on the number line.

h. Student(s) always verbalizes and writes the equations after experiencing the multiplication.

i. Student(s) visualizes equations on the imaged number line, and verifies on the concrete number line.

j. Student(s) discovers multiplying a number times one and a number times zero.

k. Teacher establishes the idea of multiplication being a simple, quick way of adding the same number.

2. **Discovering the Concept of Multiplication with Cubes and Clay**

   a. Student(s) uses cubes and clay to experience concept of multiplying, verifying answers on the number line.

   b. Student(s) gets stacks of cubes (linked together) for a designated number and flattens out a piece of clay.

   c. Teacher tells student(s) to *stamp* cubes a specific number of times.

   d. Student(s) stamps the cubes on the clay the designated number of times.

   e. Student(s) experiences numbers being multiplied by stamping stacked cubes on the clay.

   f. Student(s) always verbalizes and writes the equations after experiencing the multiplication.

   g. Student(s) visualizes equations and proves the processes on the concrete number line, or with cubes and clay.

   h. Student(s) discovers multiplying a number times one and a number times zero.

   i. Teacher establishes the idea of multiplication being a simple, quick way of adding the same number.

3. **Discovering the Multiplication Family Tables**

   a. Student(s) discovers the family *tables* up to ten with the cubes and concrete number line.

   b. Student(s) gets stacks of a designated number of cubes and experiences the tables.

   c. Student(s) verbalizes the equations.

   d. Teacher/student(s) writes the answers on the Multiplication Table Fact Sheet.

   e. Student(s) always starts with zero and increases to ten.

   f. Student(s) sees the relationship of the tables increasing by the number multiplied.

   g. The goal is for student(s) to experience, visualize, verbalize, and write each equation.

4. **Using Family Fact Cards to Memorize the Multiplication Tables**

a. Teacher holds up a Family Fact Card for a few seconds, then takes it away.

b. Student(s) images and air-writes the numbers and signs.

c. Teacher questions for specific numbers or signs in the equation.

d. Discuss the relationship of 3 x 6 and 6 x 3, etc., to reduce the anxiety related to the daunting task of imaging/memorizing lots and lots of tables.

5. **Written Computation—Start with the Ones and Work the Bottom Number**

a. Teacher explains two principles to remember: *start with the ones* and *work the bottom number.*

b. Teacher demonstrates the written computation and student(s) verbalizes:
   - start with the ones
   - carry to the tens
   - multiply the tens
   - add what was carried

c. Student(s) computes and verbalizes.

6. **Multiplying Numbers into the Hundreds and Thousands Using a Place Holder**

a. Student(s) recognizes similarity to multiplying with tens: start with ones and bottom number.

b. Teacher explores need for *place holder* with a zero.

c. Teacher demonstrates written computation and student(s) verbalizes.

d. Student(s) computes and verbalizes.

7. **Estimating with Long Multiplication**

a. Student(s) rounds numbers greater than ten to the nearest ten.

b. Student(s) uses multiples of tens to form an estimate.

c. Teacher gives student the answer to compare her estimate.

d. Teacher establishes that estimating is only a means to check if an answer is close. It is not a substitute for accurate computation.

Group Instruction

When working with small groups, or a whole classroom, have designated students verbalize answers while another verifies the answer through checking on a concrete or imaged number line. All students are to respond internally to the questions asked.

The lessons are virtually the same as presented for you in one-to-one interaction, only you must carefully interpret your students' progress and interact with them appropriately.

15

Divide and Get Less

The terror of the one-room school looms in our minds as the *On Cloud Nine* math ladder climbs into division, the last of the "big four" math functions. But the terror won't be able to strike Tory because she has a mathematical base developed at every rung on the ladder. And this new step will use the same concrete-to-imagery-to-computation plan.

Dividing is regrouping a number a given amount of times. Establishing imagery and language for the concept of division follows the same procedure used with learning multiplication. Repeat the process of discovery, concept understanding, reinforcement, practice, and application: (1) use manipulatives to make the concepts and division real, (2) put that realness into imagery for automatic use, and (3) transfer the imagery to mental and print computation. Here is a general overview of this step.

- Discover the concept of division through cubes, the concrete number line, and clay.
- Use an *imaged number line* to visualize and verbalize the concept of division.
- Discover and apply steps to compute short and long division.

Tory will understand division because she now has a mathematical mind like the best math students in her class. She understands why math does what it does, and she can demonstrate that understanding through accurate computation. She's ready to apply her knowledge of addition, subtraction, and multiplication to a part of math that only a few weeks before produced tears of frustration.

Discovering the Concept of Division with Cubes and the Number Line

The Set

Kim: *"I'm going to show you something really fun. It's called division."*

Tory: "Oh, no. I was afraid this step was next."

Kim: *"Right. Look at your math ladder. You're climbing pretty high and it's been easy. Division is also easy because it's sort of like subtracting, but it is regrouping a number a given amount of times. We'll start like we always do—get out the number line and cubes!"*

Tory: "OK. But this has been really hard for me in school."

Lesson

Kim: *"I know, but it will be so much easier for you now that you know your multiplication tables. Here we go. Put twenty-five cubes on the number line."*

Tory: "There." (Placing twenty-five cubes on the number line.)

Kim: *"Get as many fives as you can out of those twenty-five."*

Tory: "Easy. I can get five stacks of five off the number line." (Getting five fives off the number line and placing them in front of her.)

"...division is also easy because it is sort of like subtracting, but it is regrouping a number a given amount of times."

"Put twenty-five cubes on the number line."

"Get as many fives as you can out of those twenty-five."

214

Kim: *"Great. You just divided twenty-five by five. That's what this sign means. (Writing the ÷ sign for her.) This signs tells you to divide by a number: (writing 25 ÷ 5 = how much?) How many fives did you get out of the twenty-five?"*

Tory: "Five. So twenty-five divided by five equals five." (Writing out the equation: 25 ÷ 5 = 5.)

Kim: *"Exactly. You took twenty-five and divided it into fives. And there's another sign that tells you to divide: (writing 5)̄25̄). Either way tells you to divide. Now, what is five times five?"*

Tory: "Five times five is twenty-five."

Kim: *"Right. When you divide, regroup, a number you can put it back to its original group by multiplying. That's how multiplication helps you with division. Let's check that on the number line with the cubes. (They do.) Let's do another one (writing 12 ÷ 2). Say that to me first."*

Tory: "Twelve divided by two."

Kim: *"Great. So, put your twelve on the number line and get as many twos as you can. Talk to me as you think."*

Tory: "Here's the twelve cubes and I get as many twos as I can. That's six. I have six twos in front of me. Twelve divided by two is six. And six times two is twelve, so I know my answer is right. I can check myself by multiplying them back."

Kim: *"Yes! Let's do a few more. This time do: (writing 3)̄15̄). Say that equation for me."*

"You just divided twenty-five by five."

"This signs tells you to divide by a number: 25 ÷ 5 = how much?"

"And there's another sign that tells you to divide: 5)̄25̄."

215

(Checking that she can think about division with either sign.)

Tory: "That's fifteen divided by three, right? Or, I think I could say that's three divided into fifteen. Either way, right?"

Kim: *"Either way. With this sign (writing ÷) you start left to right and say the first number and then 'divided by', like twelve divided by two for this equation (writing 12 ÷ 2). There's another way to show and say this equation. When it is written like this (writing 2)12̄), you again read it left to right, but you say 'into,' like two divided into twelve."*

Tory solved 3)1̄5̄ with the cubes and the number line. While written computation would be established further in a specific lesson, at this point she put her answer on top of the fifteen, using her place value to know where the number five would go. For example, her understanding of place value easily let her know to put the five over the five in the number fifteen because she had five ones and not five tens. They did some more and then it was nearly time for her to experience the concept of *remainder*.

Using Imagery to Mentally Compute:

Kim: *"Now, use your visualized number line and tell me what you see for this problem: ten divided by five."*

Tory: "Ten divided by five is (gesturing and going down) two. And two times five is ten, so I know my answer is right!"

Kim: *"Great. Let's do a few more of those so I can be sure you are visualizing what division is."*

Tory consciously imaged and computed simple

division problems mentally. This stimulation was a means of being sure that she applied the concrete experience of the cubes and number line to imagery. Though easy for her, it was important to *not assume* the linkage to imagery.

Experiencing the Concept of Remainder:

Kim: *"Do this one with the cubes and the number line: (writing 5⟌27̅)."*

Tory: "I have twenty-seven and get as many fives as I can (snapping off five fives), but I have two left over! What do I do with them?"

Kim: *"That's what is called a remainder. Here's how…"*

Tory: "Oh, that's what a remainder means! I've had that in school and I really didn't know what it meant! Now I can see it. There is a remainder of two, because I can only get five stacks of five out of twenty-seven, and those two are the ones remaining (pointing to the two cubes left over). That's pretty easy."

Kim: *"Right."*

Tory: "I get it now. Seeing that remainder really helps me."

Kim: *"To check our division, we multiply five times five and get twenty-five, then subtract to show the remainder. (Showing the equation to her on paper.) That **R** means that we have a remainder. We're going to do more when I'm sure you understand the concept of dividing."*

"Do this one with the cubes and the number line:"

5⟌27̅

"I have twenty-seven and get as many fives as I can…but I have two left over! What do I do with them?"

"That's what is called a remainder."

"Oh, that's what a remainder means! I've had that in school and I really didn't know what it meant! Now I can see it."

Lesson Summary:

Discovering the Concept of Division with Cubes and the Number Line

1. Student(s) uses cubes and concrete number line to experience concept of dividing.
2. Student(s) places cubes on the number line for a designated number.
3. Teacher tells student(s) to get stacks of cubes a specific number of times, such as "get as many fives as you can out of twenty-five."
4. Student(s) gets the cubes, placing them in front of him/her.
5. Teacher writes out the equation for dividing with both signs: $25 \div 5$ and $5\overline{)25}$.
6. Student(s) experiences more division, always verbalizing and writing the equations.
7. Student(s) visualizes equations on an imaged number line, verifying on concrete number line if necessary.
8. Student(s) experiences the concept of a *remainder* with the cubes and the number line.

The cubes and number line give students the reality of division, including the reality of a remainder. They can see and touch the cubes as they divide a number a given number of times. They see that thirty divided by five gives them six stacks of five. They see that they can check their answer by multiplying six times five. Having used the cubes and number line at the beginning of each math process (addition, subtraction, and multiplication), they are on a familiar and concrete foundation when they use them again for division. And from the concrete number line, the stimulation can be consciously moved into imagery.

If you think your students would benefit from another way to experience the concept of division, clay balls can be helpful. If you don't have clay, any manipulative object will suffice, such as cubes, marbles, beans, wads of paper, etc. To avoid confusion, make sure your objects are all the same color and same size.

SAMPLE LESSON

Using Clay to See the Concept of Regrouping in Division

The Set

Kim: *"Now that you have experienced division with the cubes and the number line, let's use clay like we did for multiplication. This will also help you visualize what it means to divide or regroup."*

Lesson

Kim: *"Take the clay and make yourself six little balls, about the size of small marbles. Take your six balls of clay and place every other ball on either side of this line you see on the paper."*

Tory: "OK. I begin with the six. Then one of the six goes on this side, one on that side, one on this side, one on that side, one on this...now I have three on each side."

Kim: *"Good, let's talk through what you just did and then we'll write the equation. You started with six balls. You divided those six into two groups. Each group has three balls. Like we saw with the cubes and number line, division is a way of regrouping a number a given number of times. We still have six altogether, we just divided them into two groups. Now we can write the equation. (Writing 6 ÷ 2 = 3.) Six divided into two groups gives us three in each group."*

Tory: "We started with six and divided it by two. We still have the six, but now in two places.

We have three in each new group."

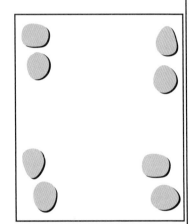

Kim: *"Yes. Try taking eight balls and divide them into four groups. Try to keep the same number of balls in each group. Use this paper."*

Tory: "This is fun. I begin with the eight balls. Each corner of the page gets a ball so that I have four groups. I end up with two in each corner."

Kim: *"Good. Write the equation and talk me through it at the same time."*

Tory: "I started with eight and divided it into four and I ended up with two in each group." (Writing $8 \div 4 = 2$).

Kim: *"Here's a way to check your answer. We know that we started with eight and didn't take any of the eight away. So, we should still have eight. We can use addition to check or we can use multiplication."*

Tory: "I can see that I still have the eight by adding up all the twos. Two plus two plus two plus two equals eight. Oh, I see I could multiply to check because four times two equals eight."

Kim: *"Like we talked about before, you can always check a division problem by multiplying."*

> ## Lesson Summary:
>
> ### *Using Clay to See the Concept of Regrouping in Division*
>
> 1. Student(s) gathers the total number of clay balls.
> 2. Student(s) moves the clay balls according to the number being divided by.
> 3. Student(s) checks how many balls are in each group.
> 4. Student(s) learns to write the equation while verbalizing.

Division and Written Equations

Calculators are probably not a fad that will go away, thank heavens, but it is still important for students to learn to compute division on paper. Reliance on calculators begs the question of what your students would do if they didn't have one? We need to teach written division.

At this juncture in division your students have (1) experienced and understood the concept of division, (2) learned two basic signs telling them to divide, (3) consciously used imagery for division, and (4) memorized their multiplication tables. Now it is time to put those concepts to paper, and learn to check their answers with multiplication.

Teach students to do three basic steps in written division:

1) *Divide* by using their multiplication tables to help get an answer,
2) *multiply*, and
3) *subtract* to see if there are any remainders.

S A M P L E   L E S S O N

Computing Simple Written Division

The Set

Kim: *"Let's do these problems on paper. Here's how you'll often see division problems: (writing 2)̄10). There are three things to do with division: (1) divide by checking your*

Three to-dos:
- Divide
- Multiply
- Subtract

$$2\overline{)10}^{\,5}$$

"Two times five is ten. I put that under the ten and then I subtract. And there are no remainders!"

"So, six times two is twelve. I put the six over the three and the twelve under the thirteen, and subtract. I have a remainder of one!"

$$2\overline{)13}^{\,6\,R1}$$
$$\underline{12}$$
$$1$$

multiplication tables to get closest to the answer, (2) multiply, and (3) subtract to see if you have any remainders."

Tory: "That sounds easy. Divide by checking multiplication tables, multiply, and subtract to see if I have any remainders."

Lesson

Kim: *"Here's what you do. How many twos will go into ten? Use your multiplication."*

Tory: "Easy. Five times two is ten."

Kim: *"Right. Place the five on top. Multiply two times five and put it under the ten. Like this (showing the multiplication). Then you subtract to see if you have any remainders. Do that and talk while you do it."*

Tory: "Two times five is ten. I put that under the ten and then I subtract. And there are no remainders. Easy, really. Especially easy because now I know why I'm doing what I'm doing. I really can see what division is all about."

Kim: *You're doing great. Let's do some more. Do this one: (writing $2\overline{)13}$)."*

Tory: "First, I divide by finding how many times two goes into thirteen. My multiplication tables let me know that it has to be six times, because six times two is twelve. If I did seven times two it would be too many. So, six times two is twelve. I put the six over the three and the twelve under the thirteen, and subtract. I have a remainder of one! I've got it! How do I write that?

222

With that **R**?"

Kim: *"Yes! Let's do some more so you can get really comfortable using those three steps. Tell me how you knew to put the six over the three and not the one?"*

"...the six has to be in the ones place, not the tens place."

Tory: "Well...the six has to be in the ones place, not the tens place."

Kim: *"Absolutely. You definitely understand math, Tory. All those steps on the ladder are in place. Good for you. Let's do some more!"*

Lesson Summary:

Computing Simple Written Division

1. Teacher establishes the frame of three things to do: *divide, multiply,* and *subtract.*
2. Student(s) visualizes and estimates the multiple.
3. Student(s) verbalizes the process of dividing, multiplying, and subtracting.
4. Student(s) checks the answer with multiplication.
5. Student(s) may use graph paper to help keep columns aligned.

Computing Long Division

Once your students know how to compute simple division, long division is a step away because it is using the same process. The only new step is how to estimate the multiple at the beginning of the dividing process. Have students check if they can divide into the first number, and if they can't then have them ask themselves if they can divide into the next number. A quick estimate gives them a starting place that will be close.

Here's the process of long division with estimating first, and then attention to the previously learned steps of divide, multiply, and subtract: *estimate* to divide, multiply, subtract, and bring down.

S A M P L E   L E S S O N

Computing Long Division

The Set

Four things to do:

- estimate to divide
- multiply
- subtract
- bring down

Kim: *"Let's divide bigger numbers, like this: (writing 6)296). Since it's not always easy to see how many times a number will go into a number, estimate first, then do the steps. They are just like the ones we did before with simpler division, only you'll estimate to divide, then multiply, subtract and bring down."*

Tory: (Sigh.) "OK. A boy sitting behind in me school has laughed at me because I had trouble with this."

Kim: *"Hmmm. That sounds familiar. You can get this. Let's start."*

Lesson

Estimating to Find the Multiple:

"Can you divide six into the first number, the two?"

Kim: *"Let's start with a quick estimate to help us know what number to put on top of the line. Can you divide six into the first number, the two?"*

Tory: "Hah! No."

Kim: *"Right. So get the next number and see if you can divide six into that."*

"Get the next number and see if you can divide six into that."

Tory: "That is twenty-nine and I can divide six into that."

Kim: *"Right. Round it up to the nearest ten to estimate, first."*

"Round up to the nearest ten to estimate, first."

Tory: "The nearest is thirty. And six will divide into thirty five times, but should I start with a five?"

Kim: *"Well, let's see. The number you are really dividing into is twenty-nine. Is that more or less than thirty?"*

Tory: "Oh. Right. That's less than thirty, so I have to start with less than five. I'll start with four. Six times four is…"

Divide, Multiply, Subtract, Bring down:

"The next step is to divide…then multiply."

$$\begin{array}{r} 4 \\ 6\overline{)296} \\ 24 \\ \hline 5 \end{array}$$

Kim: *"Right. The next step is to divide, to find out how many groups of six go into twenty-nine, then multiply. Keep going."*

Tory: "Six times four is twenty-four. I put the four over the tens place and multiply. The answer goes under the twenty-nine, and I subtract."

Kim: *"Right. That reminds you that you've used those numbers. Keep going, and keep talking to me as you go."*

Tory: Next I subtract. That leaves five. What do I do with it?"

"We have a number six in the last column that we have not dealt with yet. So bring that down next to the five, giving us fifty-six."

$$\begin{array}{r} 4 \\ 6\overline{)296} \\ 24\downarrow \\ \hline 56 \end{array}$$

Kim: *"We have a number six in the last column that we have not dealt with yet. So bring that down next to the five, giving us fifty-six. Now do just like before. We have to use all the numbers."*

Tory: "OK. We do have to use all the numbers or we'd only be dividing into the number twenty-nine. And that wouldn't give us even a close answer. So, I think that the number fifty-six is close to sixty, and six would go into sixty ten times, so since my number fifty-six is smaller than sixty, I have to try the nine."

Kim: *"Exactly. You're really getting this. Keep going."*

```
      49 R2
 6) 296
    24
    56
    54
     2
```

"It really helps to know my times tables so quickly."

Tory: "Nine times six is fifty-four. It really helps to know my times tables so quickly. Anyhow, I multiply and then subtract. That leaves me two. And I can't get any sixes out of two, so this must be the remainder!"

Kim: *"Great. Now, multiply to check your answer."*

Tory: "It's right." (Multiplying 6 x 49 accurately and adding the remainder of 2 to the ones to get 296.)

Kim: *"Great. Now, do another one and talk me through it again. Remember, estimate if you need to, then divide, multiply, and subtract. Try seven divided into five hundred thirty-eight."*

Tory: "OK. Hmmm. I can't get a seven into a five, so I'll go to fifty-three. And..." (Continuing the process, Tory visualized and verbalized her way through the written computation.)

Lesson Summary:

Computing Long Division

1. Teacher establishes the frame of four things to do: estimate to divide, multiply, subtract, and bring down.
2. Student(s) visualizes and estimates the multiple.
3. Student(s) verbalizes the process of dividing, multiplying, subtracting, and bringing down.
4. Student(s) checks the answer with multiplication.
5. Student(s) may use graph paper to help keep columns aligned.
6. The process is extended to longer division problems, and the student(s) continues to verbalize while working.

Long division with two or more digits uses the same process of thinking. And estimating the multiple becomes more and more helpful for problems such as $36\overline{)\,789}$. Rounding the number 36 to 40 and the 78 to 80 lets students try dividing with easier numbers. It is also very helpful to demonstrate what happens when you don't multiply with a large enough number. For example, you cross check with multiplication and then the subtraction tells you it is possible to get that number out again. Somewhere in the back of our minds we probably all remember those long division problems and those days when we started too high or too low on our first try. Estimating helps prevent that.

Practice and Pacing

Division needs reinforcement and daily practice, as do all steps on the math ladder. This step, however, requires that multiplication tables be imaged intact, therefore continue to have students visualize and verbalize their multiplication facts. They need to be automatic so as not to slow down the process of dividing. Our brains cannot be expected to reach a level of automaticity with a task through just quick exposure and then movement to the next task. One of the more frustrating experiences in teaching math from textbooks has been that students often didn't stay long enough on a task to have the process cemented to a level of automaticity. Thus, continue practicing long division while overlapping to the next step on the math ladder.

Practice simple multiplication and division with triangle cards where each corner of the card has a number in an equation. Cover one corner and ask students to divide or multiply. For example, "Three times what equals twenty-four?" or "Twenty-four divided by eight equals what?" The sign is not written, only verbalized.

Sample Triangle Card:

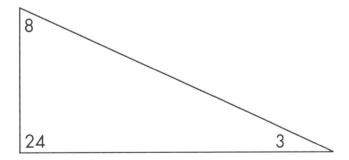

Summary

Division is a process of regrouping a number a given number of times, and students experience the reality of that through the concreteness of cubes and the number line. Students progress to written computation with the frame of: estimate the multiple, divide, multiply, subtract, and bring down. While this process has been used for many years in math instruction, *On Cloud Nine* brings an underlying sensory-cognitive processing developed through the math ladder so this step can be learned with confidence and ease.

Tory faced and won many battles up to this step, and her grades in math increased significantly. Math homework was accomplished with ease. Smiles and a sunshiny face replaced hair pulling. The next parent-teacher conference found Tory near the top of her class in math, and by year-end her achievement test scores placed her at the 80th percentile in math.

The terror was over. Now she will climb the steps of decimals and fractions with relative ease and be ahead of her class. The division chapter is done and our recollections of a one-room school and a singing swing are diminished.

Summary:

Step 10

Division

> **Goal:** To experience, visualize, and verbalize the concept of division and compute written problems into two-, three-, and four-digit division.

1. Discovering the Concept of Division with Cubes and the Number Line

a. Student(s) uses cubes and concrete number line to experience concept of dividing.

b. Student(s) places cubes on the number line for a designated number.

c. Teacher tells student(s) to get stacks of cubes a specific number of times, such as "get as many fives as you can out of twenty-five."

d. Student(s) gets the cubes, placing them in front of him/her.

e. Teacher writes out the equation for dividing with both signs: $25 \div 5$ and $5\overline{)25}$.

f. Student(s) experiences more division, always verbalizing and writing the equations.

g. Student(s) visualizes equations on an imaged number line, verifying on concrete number line if necessary.

h. Student(s) experiences the concept of a *remainder* with the cubes/number line.

2. Using Clay to See the Concept of Regrouping in Division

a. Student(s) gathers the total number of clay balls.

b. Student(s) moves the clay balls according to the number being divided by.

c. Student(s) checks how many balls are in each group.

d. Student(s) learns to write the equation while verbalizing.

3. **Computing Simple Written Division**

    a.   Teacher establishes the frame of three things to do: *divide, multiply, and subtract.*

    b.   Student(s) visualizes and estimates the multiple.

    c.   Student(s) verbalizes the process of dividing, multiplying, and subtracting.

    d.   Student(s) checks the answer with multiplication.

    e.   Student(s) may use graph paper to help keep columns aligned.

4. **Computing Long Division**

    a.   Teacher establishes the frame of four things to do: estimate, divide, multiply, subtract, bring down.

    b.   Student(s) visualizes and estimates the multiple.

    c.   Student(s) verbalizes the process of dividing, multiplying, subtracting, and bringing down.

    d.   Students(s) checks the answer with multiplication.

    e.   Student(s) may use graph paper to help keep columns aligned.

    f.   The process extends to longer and longer division, with verbalizing continuing to show thinking.

Group Instruction

All steps to develop division are applicable to group instruction. It can be helpful to have students take turns using the concrete and visualized number lines, and the steps of estimate, divide, multiply, and subtract, all the while verbalizing their thinking. For example, to divide six into thirty-four, have one student show the starting point on the number line, the next student verbalize and estimate, the next student verbalize how many groups of six can be gotten out of the estimate, the next student verbalize the multiplication, etc. Continue group management of thumbs up or down throughout the exercises.

16

Getting the Point with Decimals

Up to now, we have been learning about *whole* numbers on the *On Cloud Nine* math ladder. The next two chapters will help students take the knowledge they have about whole numbers and place value, and apply it to understanding the *parts* of a whole number.

A whole number is designated by an invisible decimal point that lives right after the number. The whole number 1 could be written with a decimal after it (1.). As long as nothing comes after the decimal point, we know the number we are looking at represents the whole. But when numbers come after the decimal we are signaled to think about parts of the whole.

The decimal point is a way of *writing* a part of the whole, and each *place* after the decimal has value and says how many parts are in the whole. The place just to the right of the decimal point designates ten parts in the whole. The next place, the hundredths, designates one hundred parts in the whole. The third place to the right of the decimal point designates one thousand parts in the whole, etc.

Understanding the parts requires understanding the whole. A while back, Becky, a ten-year-old girl, was asked what a whole number was. She said, "A whole number is located next to the decimal point and is whole." She seemed to have a very good idea of what a whole number was until she was asked to tell just a little more about the "whole" part. She said, "You know, a number that has lots of holes through it, like my shirt. The 6 and the 8 are hole numbers." Hmmm.

To avoid this kind of concept confusion, help students understand the meaning of a whole number, first. Then introduce them to the concept of parts to whole, have them visualize and verbalize, and finally have them apply that knowledge to computation.

Tory is now doing well in multiplication and division in school, but she will soon be faced with decimals and fractions, so for the next few chapters she's going to learn about parts of a one: how to visualize those parts and how to compute them. She's ready.

"They are whole numbers, not because they have holes in them, but because they stand for a whole or complete thing."

1.

$$\boxed{\text{S A M P L E} \qquad \text{L E S S O N}}$$

Discovering the Whole and the Decimal Point

The Set

Kim: *"You have climbed to the top of your math ladder (examining it together). The numbers we have worked with were called whole numbers. Do you know why?"*

Tory: "I'm not sure."

Lesson

Kim: *"They are whole numbers because they stand for a whole thing. How many whole chairs do you see in this room?"*

Tory: "Just two, yours and mine."

Kim: *"Right. If I just held up a leg of a chair, could I say I had a whole chair or part of a chair?"*

Tory: "You would have part of the chair, not the whole."

Kim: *"Exactly. How would I write the number for one chair?"*

Tory: "Just a number one." (Writing the number 1 on paper).

Kim: *"Right. All whole numbers have a decimal point after them, like this (writing 1.), but we just don't show it every time. The only time we need the decimal is when we're talking about the parts of a whole. Write the whole number four using the decimal point, and talk to me about your thinking."*

Tory: "Easy. I write the number four and put a decimal point after it." (Writing 4. on the paper.)

Kim: *"Right. Let's practice that some more. If I hold up five cubes, first visualize the number with a decimal point, write it in the air, and then write it on paper."*

Tory: "Easy. I see just the number five with a decimal after it." (Air-writing 5. and then on paper.)

Kim: *"Right. When a number is in front of the decimal it is a whole number. Let's do a few more to be sure you know where to visualize the decimal point when it is a whole number."*

"If I hold up five cubes, first visualize the number with a decimal point, write it in the air, and then write it on paper."

Lesson Summary:

Discovering the Whole and the Decimal Point

1. Student(s) discovers the whole versus parts, using objects in the room.
2. Student(s) discovers that a number coming in front of the decimal point represents a whole number.
3. Student(s) visualizes/verbalizes, air-writes, and then writes whole numbers.
4. Teacher writes whole numbers with the decimal point and student(s) verbalizes the number.

While this lesson may seem very simple, it is an important base from which your students will now experience tenths, hundredths and thousandths—without it they may be visualizing hole numbers instead of whole numbers. Tory is ready to discover tenths and she'll do that in a concrete way first, then with imagery, then through computation—the same formula.

The concrete may come with an overlay or a drawing on a familiar object such as a pizza or pie that can then be divided into parts. The picture starts plain and then has different *things* added to its parts. Here Tory is working with the Pizza Set to learn about tenths and hundredths. She will learn to write and read a decimal, using her concrete and visualized base.

> *"Place value can be for whole numbers or parts of one whole."*

SAMPLE LESSON

Discovering and Writing Tenths

The Set

Kim: *"Now that you know about whole numbers, let's learn about the parts of one whole number. A whole number can have parts!"*

Tory: "OK. But I didn't know we could have a part of a number like we have parts of chair."

Kim: *"We can. But with a chair we have language to show the parts, with numbers we can use that decimal point to show the parts."*

Tory: "Hmmm."

Lesson

Kim: *"Here is a picture of a pizza. (Showing Pizza Set picture.) If we want to show the parts of the pizza, we use a decimal point. A number in front of a decimal point is a whole number, but a number after the decimal point is a part number—and we can use what we learned about place value. Place value can be*

Pizza in ten parts:

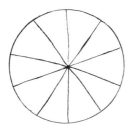

Pizza with olives:

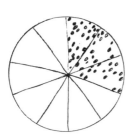

"If we want to show those three parts with a decimal point, we would show it as **.3**. The first column *after* the decimal shows tenths. "

for whole numbers or for parts of one whole. Let's use the pizza to experience this."

Tory: "I think I'd rather eat pizza…"

Kim: *"Me too, but instead let's learn about tenths with this pizza. What's the smallest whole number?"*

Tory: "One."

Kim: *"Right. And you have one plain pizza here. Let's break this one whole pizza into parts to see how to use the decimal point and place value. Place this overlay over the picture of the pizza. How many parts is the pizza broken into?"*

Tory: "Ten parts."

Kim: *"Now let's put some dots on three of the parts to show we ordered some olives on those three."*

Tory: "OK." (Putting little dots on three parts of the pizza.)

Kim: *"Great. Now, how many parts do we have olives on?"*

Tory: "Three."

Kim: *"So, if we want to show those three parts with a decimal point, we would show it as three-tenths (writing .3). The first column after the decimal shows tenths. We have three-tenths. The olives you're describing are in three of the ten pieces or three-tenths.*

"To write that as a decimal we just use the tenths column. Now, let's put some more flavoring on our pizza. Let's make two of the pieces have some pepperoni, like this."

(Adding some larger circles to two pieces.)

Tory: "Mmmm."

Kim: *"Show me with the decimal point how we would show those two tenths with numbers."*

> "Show me with the decimal point how we would show those two tenths with numbers."

Tory: "That would be like this (writing .2) because there are two-tenths."

Kim: *"Right. Now, what if we wanted to write a number that shows the pieces that contain olives and pepperoni?"*

> "Now, what if we wanted to write a number that shows the pieces that contain olives and pepperoni?"

Tory: "That would be three-tenths plus two more tenths or five-tenths."

Kim: *"Good job with your language. Now write it as a decimal too."*

Tory: "That would be...(writing .5)."

Kim: *"Great. It would be written like this: (writing .2 + .3). Add with the dots lined up. Now, write that whole equation in the air and talk me through what you are doing."*

> $$\begin{array}{r} .3 \\ +.2 \\ \hline .5 \end{array}$$

The lesson continued to cover tenths of the pizza with Tory writing the numbers Kim illustrated with tenths: picture to number. Then the stimulation was reversed: number to picture.

Kim: *"You're doing really well in writing the numbers from the picture, so let's turn it around. This time I'm going to draw a circle and divide it into ten parts or tenths. I'm going to write a number and I want you to color in the parts to show that number."* *(Drawing a circle, dividing it into tenths, and then writing the number .4.)*

> "Let's turn it around...I'm going to write a number and I want you to color in the parts to show that number."

Tory: "That's four tenths, so I color in four parts."

Kim: *"You've got it. Let's try another one."* *(Drawing another circle.)*

The lesson continued and then expanded into adding and subtracting simple numbers with decimals (carrying and borrowing were also included). First, Tory experienced the equation with a concrete picture, then she visualized and verbalized, then she wrote the equation in the air and on paper.

Lesson Summary:

Discovering and Writing Tenths

1. Teacher places a transparency over the Pizza Set picture (or draws on paper) to divide a picture (pizza) into tenths.
2. Student(s) counts parts.
3. Student(s) draws objects on designated number of tenths (olives on three tenths).
4. Student(s) discovers the first place to the right of the decimal represents the tenths place.
5. Student(s) writes the designated tenths from the picture and learns to add within the tenths, writing that number in the air and on paper.
6. Teacher writes a number and has the student(s) shade in the parts to match the written number.
7. Student(s) adds or subtracts with simple decimals and the concrete picture, air-writing the equation, and then writing on paper. Carrying and borrowing can be included, depending on the level of the student.

Once your students have a good understanding of the decimal point and the tenths column, expand into the hundredths column. Sometimes talking about only ten parts of the whole does not express enough parts, or illustrate the concept of place value and the decimal. Let your students know that you may need to talk about even smaller parts than the tens, so we will need more pieces. The stage is set for the hundredths place which gives us a hundred parts of the whole.

S A M P L E   L E S S O N

Discovering and Writing Hundredths

The Set

Kim: *"Great job with your tenths place. Do you think we can stop there or do you think there are more place values to the right of the decimal point?*

Tory: "Probably more. Just like we have ones, tens, hundreds, and thousands."

Kim: *"Exactly. Let's see what those place values are. If you want to write a number for a very small part of a whole, you need another place that will let you bring in more parts. Let's look at a new pizza and this time focus in on just one of our tenths."* (Showing a new Pizza Set picture with ten parts.)

Lesson

Kim: *"Now, let's divide one tenth into ten more parts. If each of our tenths had ten more parts, how many would we have altogether?"*

> "If you want to write a number for a very small part of a whole, you need another place that will let you bring in more parts."

> "Let's divide one tenth into ten more parts."

.04

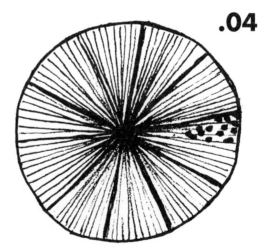

Tory: "That would be ten times a ten, or a hundred parts altogether."

Kim: *"Yes. Since we have one hundred parts we need a hundredths column so that we have a place to write that number as a decimal. The hundredths place goes one more over, like this: (writing .00)."*

"The hundredths place goes one more over, like this: **.00**."

Tory: "I get it. Just like with place value. And thousandths would be next. Right?"

Kim: *"Right. Let's show just one tenth on the pizza like this (breaking one tenth into ten more parts). Now, I'm going to put olives on only some of these (putting dots on four of the hundredths). How many hundredths contain olives?"*

"Now, I'm going to put olives on only some of these (putting dots on four of the hundredths). How many hundredths contain olives?"

Tory: "FOUR of the hundredths."

Kim: *"Yes, and this is the hundredths column to the right of the tenths column. To write four-hundredths we show no tenths in the tenths column with a zero and four hundredths in the hundredths column with the four."*

Tory: "OK. I see. I read that number as four-hundredths."

Kim: *"Good. Now, say and write that in the air."*

Tory: "Point zero four is four-hundredths." (Air-writing the .04.)

.04

Kim: *"Let's do some more (putting olives on five more hundredths). How many hundredths contain olives now?"*

Tory: "Nine-hundredths or point zero nine."

Kim: *"Great. If I put more olives on this piece (putting olives on twenty-four hundredths or two of the tenths and four hundredths), how many hundredths have olives now?"*

Tory: "I see the olives on two tenths and four hundredths. I write a number two in my tenths and a number four in my hundredths like this: (writing .24). Hmmm. How do I say that?"

"Your two tenths are equal to twenty hundredths and four more hundredths is twenty-four hundredths."

Kim: *"Your two tenths are equal to twenty hundredths and four more hundredths is twenty-four hundredths. That is how you read that number. Let's do some more. Sometimes I'll give you a picture and you'll give me the number and sometimes I'll reverse it and give you a number and you'll show it on the picture."*

Lesson Summary:

Discovering and Writing Hundredths

1. Teacher shows student how to divide tenths into hundredths, using the familiar picture (pizza).
2. Student(s) counts how many hundredths contain a certain item, writes the number as a decimal, visualizing and verbalizing.
3. Student(s) says and air-writes the decimal number, and verbalizes the concept it represents.
4. Reverse the stimulation: teacher writes number and student(s) draws concept.

Adding and Subtracting with Decimals: Lining up the Decimals

Now that your students understand the decimal point and place value to the right of the decimal point, the lessons can be extended to adding, subtracting, multiplying and dividing with decimals. This can be introduced at the time of discovering decimals or done as a separate lesson.

Once your students understand the "big four" functions and place value, the placement of the dot comes easily. For example, in adding and subtracting, Tory could use her understanding of place value and carrying/borrowing to understand that the decimal has to line up. And that is exactly what she learned.

S A M P L E   L E S S O N

Adding and Subtracting Decimals: Line up the Point

The Set

"You can add the tenths just like you would add whole numbers."

Kim: *"Now, we're going to talk about adding and subtracting the tenths and hundredths. Again, this is important because we'll be seeing a lot of decimals when we talk about money and other parts of a whole. You can add the tenths just like you would add whole numbers.*

Tory: "OK."

"...line up the decimal point."

Kim: *"When you are adding whole numbers you automatically line up your ones, tens, and hundreds columns. So, when you're adding with tenths, line up the decimal point, like this. That way you can be sure that you are adding tenths, hundredths, etc."*

Lesson

Kim: *"Let's go back to a pizza. This time count how many tenths contain olives and how many contain pepperoni."*

Tory: "Three parts contain pepperoni and five parts contain olives."

Kim: *"Add those together and show me on paper."*

Tory: "I write point three and point five, lining

.3
+.5
.8

"Now, let's add the
hundredths. Remember,
you may need to
carry numbers."

' '
1.56
+ .78
2.34

"Great. Tell me your
answer in the whole
and parts."

' ' '
2.23
- .46
1.77

up my decimals. Three plus five equals eight."

Kim: *"Right. Now, just bring your decimal down."*

Tory: "OK, I bring my decimal down. My answer is point eight or eight-tenths."

Tory practiced adding the tenths for a bit, and then extended to the hundredths.

Kim: *"Now, let's add the hundredths. Remember, you may need to carry numbers. Try this equation: one and fifty-six hundreths plus seventy-eight hundreths."*

Tory: "I write my numbers so the decimal is lined up. (Verbalizing her adding and carrying.) My answer is two point three four. Really, that is pretty easy."

Kim: *"Great. Tell me your answer in the whole and parts."*

Tory: "Two and thirty-four hundredths."

Kim: *"Great. This time subtract this problem: two and twenty-three hundreths minus forty-six hundreths."*

Tory: "On paper, I line up my decimal points. I can't take six from three so I borrow (verbalizing her subtraction and borrowing). My answer is one point seven seven. One and seventy-seven hundredths."

Multiplying and Dividing Decimals: Moving the Point

When we multiply decimals, we are computing parts of a part, essentially dividing. The decimal point is moved according to the equation and the place value represented.

For multiplication, the decimal is moved according to how many place values are to the right of the decimal: *count and move*. For division, the decimal is moved to make a whole number: *make whole and move the same*.

Teaching Tory to multiply with decimals is similar to teaching her to add and subtract decimals, only she is given the concept and language of *count and move*. In the following example, there are two places to the right of each decimal, thus the answer isn't complete until the decimal is moved the corresponding two places. We are working with tenths and we know that ten times ten is a hundred. Therefore, *a tenth times a tenth has to be in the hundredths place* and that is *why* the decimals have to move two places! If we are multiplying hundredths times hundredths, the answer will be ten thousandths, and the decimal *has* to move four places to match place value.

**Count
and
Move!**

$$\begin{array}{r} .2 \\ \underline{\times .7} \\ .14 \end{array}$$

If your students can multiply with decimals, they can also divide with them. For division, *move the decimal to the right to make a **whole number*** for the divisor (the number you are dividing by) and then move the decimal point in the dividend (the number you are dividing into) the same number of spaces to make them equivalent in place value. The formula for dividing with decimals is *make whole and move the same*.

$$.2\overline{)4.8}$$

**Make whole
and move the same!**

$$2\overline{)48}$$

Practice and Pacing

Explore tenths and hundredths with various activities and various manipulatives such as clay, drawings, tortillas, etc. Have students divide objects into various parts. For example, you might ask students to butter five-tenths or (.5) of a tortilla and sprinkle cinnamon on two hundredths or (.02). Have students create their own transparency overlays for their own drawing to explore, visualize, verbalize, and write the decimal numbers.

Introduction in computing decimals with addition, subtraction, multiplication, and division begins with adding and ends with dividing. As with all steps, the concepts should be practiced and overlapped in order to keep the lesson energy high, but there must be enough practice to establish the computation. One of the many frustrations students have with math is that a concept is often introduced and practiced a little, then left for another concept. The first concept may not be firmly cemented in the student's sensory-cognitive system and then can easily vanish or grow dim. Get these steps cemented, but extend enough to let students see application, forward movement, and the interlocking underlying concepts of math.

Be sure to do mental math activities, and always practice on paper.

Summary

When teaching decimals use the same *On Cloud Nine* formula of concrete to imagery to computation. Begin with understanding the whole and then understanding the parts. Tenths are extended to hundredths, then to the application of adding, subtracting, multiplying, and dividing on paper.

While understanding concepts behind math is wonderful, computation automaticity only comes by having a quick way to remember the computation steps:

Decimal Computation Formulas:

Adding and Subtracting:	*Line up the Points*
Multiplying:	*Count and Move*
Dividing:	*Make Whole and Move the Same*

Summary:

Decimals

> **Goal:** To discover that the decimal point represents parts of a whole, be able to visualize and verbalize that concept, write the numbers, and add, subtract, multiply, and divide with decimals.

1. **Discovering the Whole and the Decimal Point**

   a. Student(s) discovers a whole versus parts, using objects in the room.

   b. Student(s) discovers that a number coming in front of the decimal point represents a whole number.

   c. Student(s) visualizes/verbalizes, then air-writes and writes whole numbers.

   d. Teacher writes whole numbers with the decimal point and student(s) verbalizes the number.

2. **Discovering and Writing Tenths**

   a. Teacher places a transparency over the Pizza Set picture (or draws on paper) to divide a picture (pizza) into tenths.

   b. Student(s) counts parts.

   c. Student(s) draws objects on designated number of tenths.

   d. Student(s) discovers the first place to the right of the decimal represents the tenths place.

   e. Student(s) writes the designated tenths from the picture and learns to add within the tenths, writing that number in the air and on paper.

   f. Teacher writes a number and has the student(s) shade in the parts to match the written number.

   g. Student(s) adds or subtracts with simple decimals and the concrete picture, air-writing the equation, and then writing on paper. Carrying and borrowing can be included, depending on the level of the student.

3. **Discovering and Writing Hundredths**

a. Teacher shows student how to divide tenths into hundredths, using the familiar picture (pizza).

b. Student(s) counts how many hundredths contain a certain item, writes the number as a decimal, visualizing and verbalizing.

c. Student(s) says and air-writes the decimal number, and verbalizes the concept it represents.

4. **Decimal Addition, Subtraction, Multiplication, and Division Computations Have Formulas to Aid Automaticity**

Adding and Subtracting:	*Line up the Points*
Multiplying:	*Count and Move*
Dividing:	*Make Whole and Move the Same*

Discovering Fractions

Tory understands the simplicity of a decimal designating a whole or parts of a whole, and now she'll easily transition to understanding fractions—another way to represent parts of a whole. Unlike decimals, however, fractions aren't limited to multiples of ten—tenths, hundredths, thousandths, ten thousandths. Instead, fractions allow a whole to be divided into any number of parts!

Fractions have two numbers to show a part of the whole: (1) the denominator (bottom number) representing the total parts of the whole, and (2) the numerator (top number) representing specific parts in the whole (how many parts of the whole we're thinking about or using).

We wrote four chapters for the "big four" in math: addition, subtraction, multiplication, and division—and that was with whole numbers. Yet, we are going to present basic fractions in only one chapter—addition, subtraction, multiplication, division with parts of a whole! So, to make the basics of fractions as simple as possible, let's think of fractions as having five extras: *equivalent fractions, mixed numbers, common denominators, reducing to lowest terms, and improper fractions.*

It is important to understand and be able to compute with these extras. However, they create a lot of parts for working with fractions, And, therefore, they create kind of a stepladder to walk up in order to conquer the fraction step. The *fraction stepladder* is a "fraction" of the whole math ladder, just as fractions themselves are part of a whole. Here is the fraction stepladder—which includes the big four and the extras—to be given to each of your students so you and they can see the gestalt and track progress.

On Cloud Nine
Fractions Stepladder

Student Name: _____

10 **Dividing Fractions**

9 **Multiplying Fractions**

8 *Improper Fractions*

7 *Reducing Fractions*

6 *Lowest Common Denominator*

5 *Mixed Numbers*

4 **Subtracting Fractions**

3 **Adding Fractions**

2 *Equivalent Fractions*

1 **What is a Fraction?**

This step of *On Cloud Nine* has the following parts necessary for developing an understanding of basic fractions. A simple explanation of each part is provided just in case you needed to be reminded about the different functions in fractions!

- *Discover the Concept of Fractions:*
    The parts go over the whole—numerators and denominators.
- *Equivalent Fractions:*
    Fractions that can be written to equal one another, such as $\frac{1}{2}$ and $\frac{2}{4}$.
- *Adding Fractions:*
    Add the top number and the bottom number stays the same.
- *Subtracting Fractions:*
    Subtract the top numbers and the bottom number stays the same.
- *Mixed Numbers:*
    Mixed numbers are a mix (combination) of wholes and parts, such as $2\frac{1}{3}$.
- *Finding Lowest Common Denominators:*
    Adding and subtracting fractions requires the bottom number, the denominator, to be the same.
- *Improper Fractions:*
    A fraction is an improper fraction when the numerator is larger than, or equal to, the denominator such as $\frac{10}{8}$.
- *Reduce Fractions:*
    Reduce a fraction to its lowest terms, such as $\frac{2}{4}$ to $\frac{1}{2}$.
- *Multiply Fractions:*
    Multiply the numerators and denominators straight across and reduce, such as $\frac{1}{2}$ x $\frac{1}{4}$ = $\frac{1}{8}$.
- *Divide Fractions:*
    Divide fractions by inverting and multiplying, such as $\frac{1}{2} \div \frac{1}{4} = \frac{1}{2}$ x $\frac{4}{1} = \frac{4}{2}$ or 2.

As with the other steps, the first rung on the fraction stepladder begins with the concrete, then overlaps to imagery and computation. Here goes Tory. Her math abilities are astounding her teacher and parents, and math homework is one of her favorite things to do. (We think her math abilities might astound you also! She becomes a genius in a few pages.)

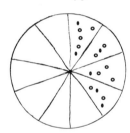

"Fractions are not all that different than decimals because they are parts of a whole."

Olives on $\frac{4}{10}$:

"The *bottom* number lets you know how many parts your whole has all together."

"The *top* number lets you know which of the parts of the total you wish to talk about. It looks like this: $\frac{4}{10}$."

SAMPLE LESSON

Transitioning from Decimals to Fractions— the Parts Go Over the Whole

The Set

Kim: *"You can think with the decimal point very easily now, but there are other ways to talk about parts of a whole. One way is with fractions, where the parts go over the whole. And fractions let us work with more than the tens. Let's learn them."*

Tory: "Fractions seem confusing, even the pictures in my school books sort of confused me."

Lesson

Kim: *"You won't be confused anymore. Fractions are not all that different than decimals because they are parts of a whole. What's your picture of this (writing .4)?"*

Tory: "It is four-tenths of something, like that picture of a pizza we used."

Kim: *"Good. Let's use the Pizza Set picture again. (Looking at the pizza again and dividing it into ten equal parts.) Now, with fractions we can do exactly the same thing, but we have a different way of writing the number."*

Tory: "Hmmm."

Kim: *"You have the whole (pizza) divided into ten equal parts and you've got four of the ten or four-tenths with olives (putting olives on four parts). When writing this number as a fraction, the bottom number lets you know how*

Olives on $\frac{2}{3}$:

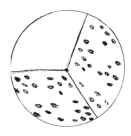

"What is the bottom number going to be?"

"How many parts of the whole do we have all together?"

many parts your whole has all together. The top number lets you know which of the parts of the total you wish to talk about. It looks like this: (writing $\frac{4}{10}$)."

Tory: "The parts go above the whole?"

Kim: *"Right. And here's what's great about fractions. With decimals, we could only do multiples of ten, but with fractions we can divide the whole into as many parts as we like. For example, we can divide our pizza into three parts. Like this."* (Using another pizza, dividing it into three parts, and putting olives on two parts.)

Tory: "I get it."

Kim: *"Right. What is the bottom number, the denominator, going to be? How many parts of the whole do we have all together?"*

Tory: "Three. So, the bottom number is three." (Writing it on paper.)

Kim: *"Right. How many of the parts, the numerator, have olives?"*

Tory: "Two. So, the top number is two." (Writing on paper: $\frac{2}{3}$.)

Kim: *"Exactly. Let's use your imagery some more. Picture all of the pieces with olives. How would you show that with a fraction? Start by telling me your mental image of the whole and then how many parts you need."*

Tory: "The whole pizza has three parts, so that's the bottom number. And all the pieces have olives, so three has to be the top number. I get it! I'd write it like this: (writing $\frac{3}{3}$)."

Kim: *"Right. Let's do another one just in your imagination and then on paper. Your pizza has eleven parts and you want to show the whole thing, visualize that and then write it."*

Tory: "Eleven of the eleven parts or eleven elevenths make up one whole pizza." (Writing $\frac{11}{11}$.)

Kim: *"Great. Now, imagine your pizza with eight parts altogether, and you have three with ham. Visualize and verbalize that. Write how many parts of the whole have ham. First air-write, then write."*

Tory: "Easy. It has eight parts for the whole and three have ham, so it's like this." (Writing $\frac{3}{8}$.)

Lesson Summary:

Transitioning from Decimals to Fractions—the Parts Go Over the Whole

1. Student(s) experiences a drawing (the Pizza Set) to see the relationship between decimals and fractions.
2. Student(s) learns that the *parts go over the whole* in the written equation.
3. Student(s) visualizes, verbalizes, and writes the relationship of numbers in a fraction.

Equivalent Fractions

With the concept of fractions established, students can be overlapped to understanding equivalent fractions, or fractions that can be written to equal one another: $\frac{2}{3}$ is equal to $\frac{4}{6}$. Using the familiar Pizza Set, this can be experienced by your students just as Tory experiences it now.

S A M P L E	**L E S S O N**

Discovering and Computing Equivalent Fractions

The Set

Kim: *"I'm going to show you how we can write the same fraction a number of different ways. They're called equivalent fractions because they are equal to one another. We'll use our good old pizza to show it."*

Tory: "OK."

Lesson

Kim: *"If I divide our pizza into three equal parts and I put olives on two pieces, what would the fraction be?"*

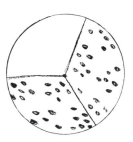

Tory: "That would be two-thirds and it would be written like this: two over three." (Writing $\frac{2}{3}$.)

Kim: *"Right. If we break that same pizza into six parts like this (breaking the same pizza into six parts by putting more lines in it), how many parts do we have for the bottom number and how many pieces have olives?"*

"They're called equivalent fractions because they are equal to one another."

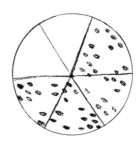

Tory: "Easy. There are six parts of the whole, so my bottom number is six, and there are four pieces with olives so my top number is four. The answer is four-sixths and it would be written like this: (Writing $\frac{4}{6}$)."

Kim: *"Exactly. But look, the same amount of pizza is used. You just discovered that two-thirds and four-sixths are the same. They are equivalent fractions because they are equal."*

Tory: "Hmmm. That seems pretty easy to understand."

Kim: *"It really is. Let's do some more. Let's draw a new pizza and we'll break it into two parts, and put olives in one part. What would the fraction be?"*

Tory: "That's like this: (writing $\frac{1}{2}$.)"

Kim: *"Right. This time you divide our same pizza into four parts."*

Tory: "Easy." (Breaking the pizza into four parts instead of two.)

Kim: *"Good. How many pieces have olives?"*

Tory: "We have two with olives, so the fraction is two-fourths (writing $\frac{2}{4}$)."

Kim: *"Great. Now, break it into six parts and tell me what you get."*

Tory: "The bottom number is six (breaking the same pizza into six parts) and now three of my six parts have olives. Wow! So one-half, two-fourths, and three-sixths are all equal!"

Kim: *"Right. You've got it!"*

Tory was later introduced to computing equivalent fractions. When we multiply a whole number by one, we always get that same whole number as the answer (3 x 1 = 3). The concept of multiplying times one applies to computing equivalent fractions. We express the whole number one in the form of a fraction $\frac{2}{2}$, $\frac{3}{3}$, $\frac{4}{4}$. When we multiply a fraction by a fraction equivalent to one, the answer will be an equivalent fraction. For example, equivalent fractions for $\frac{1}{3}$ are $\frac{2}{6}$ and $\frac{3}{9}$. Finding equivalent fractions will be very useful to students when they begin to add or subtract fractions with different denominators: $\frac{1}{3}$ x $\frac{2}{2}$ = $\frac{2}{6}$ or $\frac{1}{3}$ x $\frac{3}{3}$ = $\frac{3}{9}$.

Lesson Summary:

Discovering and Computing Equivalent Fractions

1. Student(s) uses a picture from the Pizza Set to experience equivalent fractions.
2. Student(s) writes the number one as a fraction in various ways.
3. Teacher demonstrates that multiplying a number times one, and multiplying a fraction times a fraction equivalent to one, is the same.
4. Student(s) computes equivalent fractions, visualizing, verbalizing and writing the equations.

Adding and Subtracting Fractions with Common Denominators

Adding and subtracting fractions with common denominators is very easy. It is uncommon denominators that make fractions seem complicated because more details are added to the task. For now, all we have to know is that when we add or subtract numerators, the denominators have to be the same. It is here we can also learn about mixed numbers, fractions that have a mixture of wholes and parts, such as $2\frac{1}{3}$.

SAMPLE LESSON

Adding and Subtracting Fractions with the Same Denominators

The Set

Kim: *"We're going to talk about adding and subtracting fractions that have the same denominator. Here's the plain Pizza Set picture broken into eight parts, with no extra stuff on it. Put some olives on two of the parts or two-eighths (writing $\frac{2}{8}$)."*

Lesson

Tory: "OK. There's two-eighths with olives (putting in dots for olives). Now what?"

Kim: *"I want you to put big dots to show pepperoni in one-eighth. Say and write that as a fraction. What fraction of the pizza has extra stuff?"*

Tory: "OK. There's pepperoni (putting larger dots on one part) and now I have two-eighths and one-eighth and that makes three-eighths with stuff on them."

Kim: *"Right. Let's add those on paper. First, we had two-eighths covered with olives and one-eighth with pepperoni. If I write that as an* equation, it looks like this: (writing $\frac{2}{8} + \frac{1}{8}$ $= \frac{3}{8}$)."

Tory: "I get it!"

Kim: *"Right. The denominator didn't change because we're talking about the same number of parts of the whole. When you add fractions, you add the top number—the parts—but, your denominator—the whole—has to be the same. Let's do another one to keep practicing this. Try this: (writing $\frac{1}{5} + \frac{3}{5}$)."*

Tory: "I can visualize one part added to three parts, so the answer is four parts over the whole of five. The answer is four-fifths (writing $\frac{4}{5}$)."

Kim: *"Excellent. Try this problem: (writing $\frac{6}{9}$ $- \frac{3}{9}$). Does it have the same denominator?"*

Tory: "Yes."

Kim: *"Go ahead and solve the problem. Watch that sign, just like you learned to do when you were adding and subtracting whole numbers."*

Tory: "OK. I subtract three parts from six parts, and I get three parts over the whole of nine. My answer is three-ninths (writing $\frac{3}{9}$)."

The lesson continued with written computation practice, and then extended into adding mixed numbers of wholes and parts.

Mixed Numbers:

Kim: *"Let's add some fractions where we have wholes and parts to add. Let's look at two and one-third and one and one-third (writing the fractions on paper). We call these mixed*

"When you add fractions, you add the top number (numerator), the parts—but, your total parts of the whole stays the same."

$$\begin{array}{r} \frac{2}{8} \\ + \frac{1}{8} \\ \hline \frac{3}{8} \end{array}$$

Let's look at two and one-third and one and one-third. We call these mixed numbers because they're a mix of parts and wholes."

$$2 \frac{1}{3}$$
$$+1 \frac{1}{3}$$
$$3 \frac{2}{3}$$

"Do $3 \frac{1}{4} - 1 \frac{2}{4}$."

"Hmmm. I can't take two-fourths away from one-fourth, so I have to borrow. Can I just borrow a whole?"

numbers because they're a mix of wholes and parts. We add the fraction part first and then the whole."

Tory: "I can picture and do this. One third and one third makes two-thirds and two and one make three, so the answer is three and two-thirds (writing it out as she thinks)."

Kim: *"Excellent. You could do that because the denominators were the same. It's the same when we subtract mixed numbers. We subtract the fractions and then the whole numbers. Do this equation: three and one-fourth minus one and two-fourths."*

Tory: "Hmmm. I can't take two-fourths away from one-fourth, so I have to borrow, I guess. Can I just borrow a whole?"

Kim: *"Good thinking. You need to borrow a whole in order to subtract one-fourth. Here's that on paper. We started with this equation: (writing) $3 \frac{1}{4} - 1 \frac{2}{4} = $."*

First, we try to subtract the fractions. We can't take two-fourths from one-fourth, so we have to borrow one of the whole numbers and then add it to the fraction. In three and one-fourth, I take one of the three wholes and turn it into four-fourths, an equivalent of one whole."

Tory: "Right. A whole could be four over four."

Kim: *"Exactly. I didn't want to make it three-thirds or two-halves, even though those are wholes. I need to make it four-fourths so my denominator will be the same.”*

Tory: “Right. We can’t subtract with different denominators.”

Kim: *“We add our four-fourths to the one-fourth and get five-fourths. So, we have two and five-fourths minus one and two-fourths.”*

Tory: “Now, I can subtract the fractions: (writing) $\frac{5}{4} - \frac{2}{4} = \frac{3}{4}$.”

Kim: *“Right. Don’t forget to subtract the whole.”*

Tory: “Easy: two minus one equals one. I put my whole and parts together and the answer is one and three-fourths. Not hard to understand, but I’ll need lots of practice!”

Kim: *“Yes, you will. Here’s the whole equation when worked through. It is even easier to keep track of what was borrowed when we write the problem vertically.”*

$$\begin{array}{r} {}^{2}\!\!\not{3} \quad {}^{5}\!\!\not{\frac{1}{4}} \\ -1 \quad \frac{2}{4} \\ \hline 1 \quad \frac{3}{4} \end{array}$$

Lesson Summary:

Adding and Subtracting Fractions with the Same Denominators

1. Student(s) learns *only* fractions with the same denominator can be added and subtracted.
2. Student(s) learns a *mixed number* is a whole and parts.
3. Student(s) learns the need to borrow from a whole number to create enough parts.
4. Student(s) learns mixed numbers have to have like denominators in order to compute.
5. Student(s) visualizes, verbalizes, and gets lots of practice computing!

Finding Common Denominators and Computing

If a person has two nickels, three dimes, and four pennies we do not say we have nine monies! We first have to assign the same value to each. A nickel is worth five cents, a dime is worth ten cents, and a penny is worth one cent. Since we are now dealing with a value of one cent at a time, we have established a common denominator, and can add them: forty-four ones or forty-four cents.

Fractions also need to have the whole divided into the same number of parts or have the same denominators before we can add or subtract them.

There are a lot of parts to this fraction stepladder, and one you may remember from school is "find the lowest common denominator." Oh, the chilling terror in those words for some of us. But, again, since the steps to this point have been well established, this aspect of fractions just needs exposure and practice.

Tory, dark hair full around her face, sits ready for this lesson. She's had lots of practice and success with equivalent fractions, adding and subtracting fractions with the same denominator, and she understands and computes mixed numbers. She's ready for the next step up the fraction stepladder. All her body language says she's eager to learn and not afraid. Math makes sense to her…and she can compute it quickly and easily. She has integrated math concepts with math computation. She'll learn to compute the lowest common denominator from a conceptual base to a computational level.

SAMPLE LESSON

Adding and Subtracting with the Lowest Common Denominator

The Set

Kim: *"You're going to learn to add and subtract fractions that don't have the same denominators. We're going to find out how to make the denominators the same, otherwise we won't be able to add and subtract them."*

Tory: "OK."

Lesson

Kim: *"Use this ruler to see and solve the equation one-half plus one-fourth."*

Tory: "My ruler is divided in half and that makes six inches in each half. To add one-fourth...hmmm, I see my ruler in four parts and that's three inches in each part. So, six inches and three inches make nine inches altogether. Is that what we're going to do, use a ruler all the time?"

Kim: *"No. I'm going to show you how to do it on paper, and it will be a lot easier. But you did some excellent thinking."*

Tory: "Paper will be better, especially if this gets more complicated. And somehow I think it will."

Kim: *"Hmmm. It's not too bad, though. Let's add those same two fractions on paper: (writing $\frac{1}{2}+\frac{1}{4}$). In order to make our denominators the same, we use equivalent fractions."*

$$\frac{1}{2} \ + \ \frac{1}{4} \ =$$

$$\frac{1}{2} \ \times \ \frac{2}{2} \ + \ \frac{1}{4} \ =$$

$$\frac{2}{4} \ + \ \frac{1}{4} \ = \ \frac{3}{4}$$

Tory: "I know equivalent fractions. Is that all we do?"

Kim: *"Pretty much. If we multiply one-half times two-halves, we get two-fourths. So now we can add two-fourths and one-fourth. What will the answer be?"*

Tory: "Actually, that looks pretty easy. The answer is three-fourths. But I think we'd

---

"...we're going to learn how to make the denominators the same."

"In order to make our denominators the same, we use equivalent fractions."

Find the lowest common denominator:

$$\frac{1}{2} \ \times \ \frac{2}{2} \ = \ \frac{2}{4}$$

Now add:

$$\frac{1}{4} \ + \ \frac{2}{4} \ = \ \frac{3}{4}$$

better to some more to make sure I get this. All I do is change to an equivalent fraction? I can't believe it."

Kim: *"Simple, huh? You start with equivalent fractions and then do what the sign says to do."*

Tory practiced and talked through more problems, and then it was time to climb another step.

Lowest Common Denominator:

Kim: *"As you know, we must have a common denominator before we add. We also want to have the lowest common denominator. We want our whole to be broken into the least number of parts in order to express the fraction. For example, if we want to add one-third and one-half, we need to find the lowest denominator that both fractions can have. That's called finding the lowest common denominator. The word common means they have the same denominator."* (Writing out the following.)

"Here are Equivalent Fractions for one-third:

$$\frac{1}{3} \times \frac{2}{2} = \frac{2}{6}$$
$$\frac{1}{3} \times \frac{3}{3} = \frac{3}{9}$$
$$\frac{1}{3} \times \frac{4}{4} = \frac{4}{12}$$

"Here are Equivalent Fractions for one-half:

$$\frac{1}{2} \times \frac{2}{2} = \frac{2}{4}$$
$$\frac{1}{2} \times \frac{3}{3} = \frac{3}{6}$$
$$\frac{1}{2} \times \frac{4}{4} = \frac{4}{8}$$

"What is the lowest denominator that the equivalent fractions have in common?"

Tory: "The lowest common denominator would be six."

Kim: *"Right. They also have twelve in common but that's not the lowest common denominator. We can use these equivalent fractions with the lowest common denominator in order to solve the equation. Here it is written out."*

$$\frac{1}{3} + \frac{1}{2} =$$

$$\frac{1}{3} \times \frac{2}{2} + \frac{1}{2} \times \frac{3}{3} =$$

$$\frac{2}{6} + \frac{3}{6} = \frac{5}{6}$$

Tory: "I see it. It's just a lot of steps, but it's not hard."

Kim: *"You try two-thirds plus one-fifth."*

Tory: "First, I have to find the lowest common denominator." (Tory wrote the following on paper, talking as she thought.)

$$\frac{2}{3} \times \frac{2}{2} = \frac{4}{6} \qquad \frac{1}{5} \times \frac{2}{2} = \frac{2}{10}$$

$$\frac{2}{3} \times \frac{3}{3} = \frac{6}{9} \qquad \frac{1}{5} \times \frac{3}{3} = \frac{3}{15}$$

$$\frac{2}{3} \times \frac{4}{4} = \frac{8}{12}$$

$$\frac{2}{3} \times \frac{5}{5} = \frac{10}{15}$$

"Fifteen is the lowest common denominator. I change the fractions to their equivalent fractions and add." (Writing.)

$$\frac{2}{3} + \frac{1}{5} =$$

$$\frac{2}{3} \times \frac{5}{5} + \frac{1}{5} \times \frac{3}{3} =$$

$$\frac{10}{15} + \frac{3}{15} = \frac{13}{15}$$

"My answer is thirteen-fifteenths."

(margin left)

$$\frac{1}{3} + \frac{1}{2} =$$

$$\frac{2}{6} + \frac{3}{6} = \frac{5}{6}$$

"Fifteen is the lowest common denominator. I change the fractions to their equivalent fractions and add."

$$\frac{2}{3} + \frac{1}{5} =$$

$$\frac{10}{15} + \frac{3}{15} = \frac{13}{15}$$

Kim: *"Using your times tables is a really good way to find a lowest common denominator and a quick way to use equivalent fractions. For example, to find the lowest common denominator for two-thirds and one-fifth, I can quickly run through my three times tables—three, six, nine, twelve, fifteen. Then I can compare them to my five times tables—five, ten, fifteen, twenty, twenty-five. Since five and three both go into fifteen, fifteen is my lowest common denominator."*

Lesson Summary:

Computing with the Lowest Common Denominator

1. Student(s) uses equivalent fractions to find the common denominator.
2. Student(s) reduces to the lowest terms.
3. Student(s) uses multiplication tables to find common denominator.
4. Student(s) gets lots of practice on paper!

Reducing Fractions and Discovering Improper Fractions

The basic fraction stepladder is almost complete, except for a few more important areas. Students need to know that the proper way to express a fraction is to reduce it to the lowest terms, and they need to understand what an improper fraction is as part of learning to reduce to the lowest terms. In this lesson, Tory learns to decide if a fraction needs to be reduced, as well as how to do it.

S A M P L E   L E S S O N

Reducing Fractions and Discovering Improper Fractions

The Set

Kim: *"You're going to learn how to reduce your fraction answer to the lowest terms. Rather than have an answer of two-sixths, we could have our answer be one-third, because one-third is the same as two-sixths. That would be the lowest terms for the fraction."*

Tory: "OK. One-third is easier to picture in my mind than two-sixths. I'm more familiar with what it means."

Lesson

Kim: *"Right. You know your fraction needs to be reduced when the numerator and denominator have a number that can be divided into both of them. In two-sixths, a two can be divided into both two and six. It goes into two one time and six three times, so two-sixths can be reduced to one-third."*

Tory: "OK. But I need some practice with this." (They did, then combined finding denominators with reducing fractions.)

Kim: *"Right. Solve this equation and reduce your answer to the lowest terms: two-fourths plus one-sixth."*

Tory: "OK. Both four and six can go into twelve and that's my lowest common denominator."

"Rather than have an answer of two-sixths, we could have our answer be one-third, because one-third is the same as two-sixths. That would be the lowest terms for the fraction."

"OK. One-third is easier to picture in my mind than two-sixths . I'm more familiar with what it means."

"... your fraction needs to be reduced when the numerator and denominator have a number that can be divided into both of them."

(Tory writes.)

$$\frac{2}{4} + \frac{1}{6} =$$

$$\frac{2}{4} \times \frac{3}{3} + \frac{1}{6} \times \frac{2}{2} =$$

$$\frac{6}{12} + \frac{2}{12} = \frac{8}{12}$$

"So, multiplying with equivalent fractions, my equation is six-twelfths plus two-twelfths and my answer is eight-twelfths.

"Eight can't go into twelve, but four goes into both numbers. I can get two fours out of eight and three fours out of twelve." (Writing $\frac{8}{12} = \frac{2}{3}$.) "I reduce to two-thirds."

Tory practiced more and then learned improper fractions.

Improper Fractions:

Kim: *"Try this equation: three-fourths plus four-eighths."*

Tory: "The lowest common denominator is eight because four goes into both of them. I multiply three-fourths by two-halves because I know I need to multiply four times two to get the eight."

$$\frac{3}{4} + \frac{4}{8} =$$

$$\frac{3}{4} \times \frac{2}{2} + \frac{4}{8} =$$

$$\frac{6}{8} + \frac{4}{8} = \frac{10}{8}$$

"Now, my equation is six-eighths plus four-eighths and that equals ten-eighths."

"Notice how your numerator is greater than your denominator. That is called an improper fraction."

"Picture a pizza and break it into eight pieces. How would you show ten parts?"

"I can't. I would have more than a whole. I would need another whole pizza cut into eight pieces."

Kim: *"Notice how your top number, the numerator, is greater than your denominator. That is called an improper fraction. Picture a pizza and break it into eight pieces for the whole. How would you show ten parts?"*

Tory: "I can't. I have more than a whole. I would need another whole pizza cut into eight pieces. I get it. I have one pizza, so that is eight pieces, but I have two from the pizza with ten. So, I have one pizza and two of the eight on the other pizza: one and two-eighths."

Kim: *"Exactly. You have changed your improper fraction to a mixed number and that is what you want to do. Last, you want to see if you can reduce the fraction to the lowest terms. Can you reduce two-eighths?"*

Tory: "Let's see. Two can go into both numbers so that would be one-fourth. My answer reduced is one and one-fourth."

$$\frac{10}{8} = 1\frac{2}{8} = 1\frac{8}{12}$$

Lesson Summary:

Reducing and Discovering Improper Fractions

1. Student(s) learns how to reduce fractions using knowledge of multiplication tables.
2. Student(s) visualizes an improper fraction and learns how to convert to a mixed number.
3. Student(s) gets lots of practice.

Multiplying Fractions

Tory has already had some experience with multiplying fractions during her work with equivalent fractions. You can pace your students differently by teaching them how to multiply fractions before teaching equivalent fractions (where multiplying fractions is a part of the process). Because multiplying a fraction by a whole number is very simple, we prefer to teach equivalent fractions before multiplication.

In order to conceptualize what it means to multiply a fraction, return your students to using clay. Take the equation, $3 \times \frac{1}{4}$. If we form a square with the clay and divide that square into four parts, each part represents one-fourth of the clay. $\frac{1}{4} + \frac{1}{4} + \frac{1}{4} = \frac{3}{4}$, so $3 \times \frac{1}{4} = \frac{3}{4}$. The equation $3 \times \frac{1}{4}$ means we have one-fourth three times or three-fourths. The same concept and manipulative proof works for multiplying two fractions together. For example, when one-half is multiplied by one-half, we have half of a half. Therefore, we divide a half section of the clay into a half and now that gives us one quarter of our square.

However, once that concreteness is demonstrated (if you have the courage), it is much easier to learn and work from the old formula for multiplying fractions: *Multiply the numerators and the denominators straight across, and reduce if you can.* You may remember when you learned fractions that multiplying fractions was a respite in the maze of details. It was a simple process to memorize multiplying the top and bottom numbers straight across. Because she can conceptualize multiplying fractions, let's give Tory the same relief! Automaticity in computation is the goal, and once concepts are grasped, memorization aids rapid computation.

S A M P L E   L E S S O N

Multiplying Fractions on Paper

The Set

Kim: *"Now that you understand the concept behind multiplying fractions, let's do it on paper."*

Tory: "I won't always have clay around, will I!"

"You multiply the
numerators and
the denominators
straight across."

"…to change mixed
numbers to improper
fractions, just multiply
the denominator by
the whole number and
add to the numerator.
The denominator stays
the same."

Lesson

Kim: *"Nope. Here's how you do it. Multiply the numerators and the denominators straight across."*

Tory: "That's easy!"

Kim: *"It is. For example, our equation is one-half times one-half, and we multiply across, so the answer is one-fourth."*

Tory: "That's the easiest thing we've done so far in fractions. All I have to do is multiply straight across?"

Kim: *"Right. You can just memorize that now. To multiply fractions, you multiply the numerators and the denominators straight across. Don't forget to reduce to the lowest terms, though."*

Tory: "So far this is OK. Does it get harder?"

Kim: *"Not really. Since you know how to make improper fractions, do that first, and then you are ready to multiply. To change mixed numbers to improper fractions, we multiply the denominator by the whole number and add to the numerator. The denominator stays the same. For example, let's do three and one-third times two and one-fifth. I'll talk us through it, then you can do some.*

"We can change three and one-third to an improper fraction by multiplying three by three which is nine, and then adding the numerator. Since the denominator stays the same, that gives us ten-thirds.

"We can always verify why this works because we know three is the same as three-thirds plus three-thirds plus three-thirds or nine-thirds.

"When we add the next one-third, we get ten-thirds. Here it is on paper (writing):

$$3 \frac{1}{3} \times 2 \frac{1}{5} =$$

$$\frac{10}{3} \times \frac{11}{5} =$$

"Next we multiply the numerators to get one hundred ten and the denominators to get fifteen:"

$$\frac{10}{3} \times \frac{11}{5} = \frac{110}{15}$$

"We know that five goes into both of those numbers, so we'll reduce before we change it to a mixed number. Five goes into one hundred twenty times and into ten two times so it goes into one hundred ten twenty-two times. Five goes into fifteen three times:"

$$\frac{110}{15} = \frac{22}{3}$$

"Now we change it to a mixed fraction by seeing how many wholes we get. Three goes into twenty-two seven times with one-third left over:"

$$\frac{22}{3} = 7 \frac{1}{3}$$

Tory: "Holy moly. I'd better do quite a few of these to get the hang of it. It doesn't look hard, but it has a lot of parts."

Kim: *"Right. You'll need to practice the steps, but you'll get it."*

Lesson Summary:

Multiplying Fractions on Paper

1. Teacher models and talks through computing the problem.
2. Student(s) memorizes: *multiply numerator and denominator straight across, and reduce.*
3. Student(s) discovers the need to convert mixed numbers to improper fractions in order to solve.
4. Student(s) reduces to the lowest terms and practices on paper.

Dividing Fractions

If Tory can multiply fractions she can also divide them. You can again show the concrete by using clay. Once Tory understands the process behind dividing fractions, she can do what the rest of us did: *memorize*. Memorizing is not a negative. As stated earlier, with a base of understanding, memorizing makes computation quick and easy. For dividing fractions, the formula is: *invert the last fraction and then multiply.*

The following is an example of how you can use clay to demonstrate the concept of dividing fractions. If we have the equation $\frac{1}{2} \div \frac{1}{2}$, it is asking how many halves are in one half. If we only have one half then we can only get *one* half out.

In the above example, we know we can check division by using multiplication. For example, $6 \div 3 = 2$ and $2 \times 3 = 6$. The same works when dividing fractions, the answer is achieved through multiplying the inverse.

$$\frac{1}{2} \div \frac{1}{2} = 1 \text{ and } \frac{1}{2} \times \frac{2}{1} = 1$$

The second one half is the number that has the action. If the problem reads six divided by three, we divide the six into three equal parts. In this case, the one half is divided by one-half. When we multiply the $\frac{1}{2}$ with the inverse, $\frac{2}{1}$, we get the answer one.

"When we divide fractions, we are finding out how many parts we have in another part."

SAMPLE LESSON

Dividing Fractions

The Set

Kim: *"Since you're doing well multiplying fractions, we are going to learn about dividing fractions. When we divide fractions, we are finding out how many parts we have in another part."*

Tory: "Hmmm."

Lesson

Kim: *"For example, if I have the equation one-half divided by one-fourth, I want to know how many fourths I have in one half. Using my clay, I draw a square and divide it in half. Now, I divide my square into fourths. I can see that in one half I have two fourths. So my answer is two. One-half divided by one-fourth is two."*

Tory: "OK. But, I won't have clay around all the time. How do I do it on paper?"

Kim: *"Let's think with the problem of one-half divided by one-fourth. When we divide whole numbers, how can we check our answers?"*

Tory: "We can multiply our answer by the number we divided by."

"We invert our last fraction and multiply."

Kim: *"Right. We use multiplication. That is how we divide on paper. We invert our last fraction and multiply. So, dividing fractions is the same as multiplying them, once you invert. I'll do this one for you and talk you through the process, then you'll do some and talk me through."*

"Invert:" (Writing)

$$\frac{1}{2} \div \frac{1}{4} =$$

$$\frac{1}{2} \text{ x } \frac{4}{1} =$$

"Multiply the numerators and denominators."

$$\frac{1}{2} \text{ x } \frac{1}{4} = \frac{4}{2}$$

"Reduce to the lowest terms and change the improper fraction to a mixed number. Two goes into four two times, so the answer is two."

$$\frac{1}{2} \div \frac{1}{4} = \frac{1}{2} \text{ x } \frac{4}{1} = \frac{4}{2} = 2."$$

Lesson Summary:

Dividing Fractions

1. Teacher models equation with manipulatives.
2. Teacher presents dividing on paper.
3. Student(s) memorizes: *invert and multiply* for computation process on paper.
4. Student(s) converts to mixed numbers and reduces.
5. Student(s) verbalizes his/her thinking through computation, and gets lots of practice on paper.

Pacing and Practice

Your students need lots of practice with fractions. Understanding the underlying principle of fractions is not as difficult as *remembering* how to compute them on paper. Present and practice the concepts, present and practice the formulas, mix signs within worksheets for paper practice, and encourage students to verbalize their computation. You need to know their thinking in the computation process.

Always keep in mind the lesson energy. Do some of the written practice on paper, some on a chalkboard, some on an overhead projector, *and some in the air.*

Summary

The *basic* functions of fractions are presented with the fraction stepladder, ranging from understanding the concept to dividing fractions. Using the idea of "extras," students see that fractions aren't difficult, they just have more details to learn—and the extras have to be learned in order to add, subtract, multiply, and divide. The *basic* extras are: *equivalent fractions, mixed numbers, lowest common denominators, reducing fractions, and improper fractions.*

Students understand and memorize the following functions for each part of fractions.

- Adding and subtracting fractions: *find common denominators, solve, and reduce.*
- Multiplying fractions: *multiply straight across, and reduce.*
- Dividing fractions: *invert, multiply, and reduce.*

The lessons with Tory were done over a period of weeks, and while at times it does seem that she got the concepts and solutions quickly, remember that what you are reading is not the amount of stimulation she experienced. She practiced and talked, talked and practiced. She visualized and verbalized her way through problems and when she made errors, she was questioned to get mileage from her response. The questions always responded to her response—next on our agenda for you.

Summary:
Step 12

Fractions

> **Goal:** To develop the conceptual background for fractions and computation skills for adding, subtracting, multiplying, and dividing fractions.

1. Transition from Decimals to Fractions—the Parts Go Over the Whole

   a. Student(s) experiences a picture (the Pizza Set) to see the relationship between decimals and fractions.

   b. Student(s) learns that the *parts go over the whole* in the written equation.

   c. Student(s) visualizes and verbalizes, and writes, the relationship of numbers in a fraction.

2. Discovering and Computing Equivalent Fractions

   a. Student(s) uses a picture of a pizza to experience equivalent fractions.

   b. Student(s) writes the number one as a fraction in various ways.

   c. Teacher demonstrates that multiplying a number by one, and multiplying a fraction by another fraction equivalent to one, is the same.

   d. Student(s) computes equivalent fractions, visualizing and verbalizing the equations.

3. Adding and Subtracting Fractions with the Same Denominators

   a. Student(s) discovers *only* fractions with the same denominators can be added and subtracted.

   b. Student(s) discovers a *mixed number* is a whole and parts.

   c. Student(s) discovers the need to borrow from a whole number to create enough parts.

   d. Student(s) discovers mixed numbers have to have like denominators in order to compute.

   e. Student(s) visualizes, verbalizes, and gets lots of practice computing!

4. **Computing with the Lowest Common Denominator**

   a. Student(s) uses equivalent fractions to find common denominator.

   b. Student(s) solves equations.

   c. Student(s) reduces to the lowest terms.

   d. Student(s) get lots of practice on paper!

5. **Reducing and Discovering Improper Fractions**

   a. Student(s) learns how to reduce fractions using knowledge of multiplication tables.

   b. Student(s) visualizes an improper fraction and reasons how to convert to a mixed number.

   c. Student(s) gets lots of practice.

6. **Multiplying Fractions on Paper**

   a. Teacher models computing the equation.

   b. Student(s) memorizes: *multiply numerator and denominator straight across, and reduce.*

   c. Student(s) discovers the need to convert mixed numbers to improper fractions in order to solve.

   d. Student(s) always reduces to the lowest terms.

7. **Dividing Fractions**

   a. Teacher models equation with manipulatives.

   b. Teacher presents dividing on paper.

   c. Student(s) memorizes: *invert and multiply* for computation process on paper.

   d. Student(s) converts to mixed fractions and reduces.

   e. Student(s) verbalizes his/her thinking through computation, and gets lots of practice on paper.

Group Instruction

Small or large groups, or whole classrooms can interact with you on fractions. Follow the same frame as presented above, but view each student as an individual sensory-system for your questions. You can show problems on the chalkboard or overhead projector, or you can have students take turns verbalizing through problems, or you can have students take turns air-writing problems or reciting some of the memory necessary to quickly compute with fractions.

The Summary

18

A Critical Factor

Over the years, math instruction has endured the same "religious" wars as reading instruction. Educators disputing over the "parts" of math instruction, and the "parts" of reading instruction, have often left teachers and students living with parts of those processes rather than wholes. Fortunately, however, we are currently agreeing on a gestalt approach in math, just as we are agreeing on a gestalt approach in reading. A few years ago, a cry in reading instruction began concerning a "balanced approach." Now the same cry is beginning in math instruction: "Teach concepts, but also teach computation." This is logical thinking, and thinking that matches *On Cloud Nine's* approach to math instruction, as well as Lindamood-Bell's approach to reading instruction. For many years, we at Lindamood-Bell have been drawing a Venn diagram as a way to think about the gestalt of reading—and here we are preaching the same approach in math. And more interesting than that is that we are preaching that approach with imagery and language as the foundation! Trial and error, experience with many students of all ages, has proved that bringing dual coding to a conscious level with reading, spelling and math produces significant growth in those skills. However, as important as dual coding and a gestalt approach are to the field of math, they are not the critical factor. You are.

You are the link between your students and success in math. It's not imagery and language, it's you. Your questions are the source that directs the sensory system for thinking. We could have written a summary of imagery and language as the missing link in mathematical thinking, but we feel we've flogged that horse and now its time to talk directly to you as the giver of knowledge and learning.

You are going to teach someone to think, and that means you are going to teach a sensory system to process information. The brain receives information through the five senses, and you are going to direct the sensory information of imagery. This means you will question and get a response. Then you'll respond to the response to stimulate more sensory information and your students' ability to compare their response with the stimulus.

Seem confusing? It's really not. It is very simple. Visualize a sensory system in front of you. That sensory system, like Tory's, cannot visualize numerals and concepts. You want it to, but it can't. More importantly, she wants it to, but she can't. And you can't *tell* it to visualize because telling the brain to do something doesn't provide as intensive stimulation as asking the brain to experience. So, you begin to ask questions to stimulate the sensory-cognitive processing, and questioning the brain means getting a response.

It is like this: (1) you ask a *question*, (2) the students *respond*, and (3) you help them *compare their response* to the stimulus. You respond to the response by feeding them back what they said and helping them compare it. It doesn't matter what their response is, you'll always *start with what they said and help them compare*. Meet them where they are and your instruction will always be positive. You are *valuing* them as well as teaching them to problem solve.

There are a lot of good math programs in the field of education and you can use this one alone, or you can integrate it with others. When the *On Cloud Nine* math program was completed with Tory, she was getting A's on all her homework and her tests—but more importantly, she knew she was smart and she knew she could do math. She understood it. Not only did her math improve, but also her critical thinking, language comprehension, and language expression. She was happy and bright-eyed when last seen, protected from snickers and potential wounds in academics. She was working to her potential, a potential almost obscured by a moderate weakness in sensory-cognitive processing.

You have the knowledge and skill to develop mathematical reasoning and computation for all ages of children and adults. You too can change a Tory into a Cecil. You are the critical factor. We believe in you. You can do this. You can do anything.

The Appendix

Summary:

Setting the Climate

> **Goal:** To briefly explain to the student(s) what and why.

1. *Say, "I'm going to teach you to see numbers and math in your imagination."*

2. *Say, "It will help you think about and do math."*

3. *Say, "Here's how you can picture that."*

4. *Diagram a head with student seeing and saying.*

5. *Give each student his/her own math ladder.*

6. *Keep the climate presentation succinct and relevant.*

Summary:
Step 1

Imaging Numerals

Goal: Develop the ability to visualize, verbalize, and air-write numerals, with an understanding of the reality the number represents.

1. **Numeral Imagery**

   a. Teacher shows cubes and student(s) touches them.

   b. Teacher shows the corresponding Numeral Imagery Card, then takes it away.

   c. Student(s) sees, says, and writes the number(s) in the air and on paper.

   d. Saying and air-writing should be done simultaneously.

   e. Air-writing is large enough to see a "shadow" effect.

   f. Begin with zero through ten, and then increase numbers as is appropriate for the age and level of the student(s).

   g. Occasionally image in color as a further means to stimulate numeral imagery.

2. **Developing Language Concepts**

   a. Teacher says and models movement—Student(s) says and does.

   b. Teacher says—Student(s) visualizes, verbalizes, does.

   c. Student(s) applies concepts to paper.

3. **Checkout Activities**

   a. Teacher says a number name, the student(s) shows the corresponding amount of cubes (manipulatives), says, and air-writes the numeral.

   b. Teacher says a number name, the student(s) says and air-writes the numeral.

   c. Teacher says a number name, the student(s) says, air-writes, and paper-writes the numeral.

d. Teacher points to a numeral, the student(s) shows the corresponding amount of cubes, air-writes, and paper writes.

e. Teacher shows specific amount of cubes, the student(s) says number name, air-writes and paper-writes the numeral.

4. **Pace by overlapping to the next step while continuing to develop numeral imagery**

Group Instruction

Stimulating numeral imagery for a small group or an entire classroom does not require modification of the step; but it does require group management. Have the group or the class respond as a whole, and then check specific students to be certain they are imaging. Be alert to how individuals within the group are forming numbers when they air-write, and also call on those students with difficulty in math. Have the other students in the group give thumbs up or thumbs down regarding agreement or not, thus helping them stay active rather than passive during the instruction.

Summary:
Step 2

Imaging the Number Line

> **Goal:** To establish an imaged number line for both the gestalt and parts of number relationships.

1. The Concept—Building, Exploring, and Imaging the Number Line

  a. Student(s) assembles the concrete number line from number one to one hundred.

  b. Student(s) explores the gestalt of the number line by comparing and contrasting smaller numbers with larger numbers on the concrete and imaged number line.

2. The Parts—Counting on the Concrete Number Line and Discovering Base Ten

  a. Student(s) touches and counts by ones, tens, fives, and twos (odd and even) on the concrete number line.

  b. Student(s) touches/gestures and counts by ones, tens, fives, and twos on imaged number line.

  c. Student(s) discovers base ten.

  d. Student(s) counts, varying the starting number, to discover the base ten pattern.

3. Make It Even and Up-and-Down the Number Line

  a. Student(s) uses cubes vertically to show stairs as numbers increase from one to ten.

  b. Teacher questions to help student(s) explore and verify concept of stairs increasing by one.

  c. Student(s) visualizes the stairs increasing by one.

  d. Student(s) discovers the make-it-even concept on the concrete number line.

  e. Student(s) images the make-it-even concept on the imaged number line.

f. Student(s) counts up and down the concrete and the imaged number line using finger to point to placement of numbers.

Group Instruction

An imaged number line can be established with groups of students; however, the questioning and exploring requires group management and control. Using the thumbs-up or thumbs-down response from the group while a specific child is responding is a simple method of keeping students actively involved in the questioning. If working with an entire class, numerous concrete number lines can be placed around the room with two to four students working each number line and responding to the stimulation. Each student in the class can visualize his or her own number line for that aspect of the stimulation. Be sure to spot check specific individuals for imagery.

Summary:
Step 3

Addition Family Facts

> **Goal:** To develop the dual coding of imagery and language to a conscious level for understanding and memorizing the addition facts from one through ten and twenty.

1. Discovering the Family Facts with the Family Fact Sheets

  a. Student(s) places a goal cube on the Family Fact Sheet.

  b. Student(s) discovers, with cubes in hands or on the card, the facts within the number *family*.

  c. Teacher writes the facts for each family as student(s) verbalizes.

  d. Student(s) begins and ends with the zero.

  e. Teacher and student(s) discuss numbers increasing and decreasing on either side of the sign.

  f. Teacher/student(s) dialogue and actions:

    — Teacher says, "If you have *zero*, how many more do you need to get to _____?"

    — Teacher or student(s) places one cube and teacher says, "If you have *one*, how many more do you need to get to _____?"

    — Teacher or student(s) places two cubes and says, "If you have *two*, how many more do you need to get to _____?"

2. Using Family Fact Cards to Visualize and Verbalize Addition Facts

  a. Teacher holds up a Family Fact Card for a few seconds.

  b. Student(s) images and air-writes the numbers and signs.

  c. Teacher questions for specific numbers or signs in the equation.

  d. Student(s) begins to visualize and verbalize without air-writing.

3. **Practice Activities**

   a. Imagery and Cubes Alone:

     1. Student(s) places a set of cubes on the table for a specific number.

     2. Teacher requests the student(s) to start with a specific number of cubes in hand and get remaining cubes to match a specific number.

     3. Student(s) demonstrates the facts of a specific number with cubes in hand.

     4. Student(s) verbalizes while experiencing each equation.

     5. Student(s) visualizes and verbalizes the facts, sometimes air-writing, sometimes not.

   b. Imagery and the Concrete Number Line with Cubes:

     1. Teacher gives student(s) an equation verbally.

     2. Student(s) uses the cubes on the concrete number line to experience the equation.

     3. Student(s) visualizes and verbalizes the equation, *sometimes* air-writing.

   c. Imagery and the Number Line *without* Cubes:

     1. Student(s) points to starting number designated by teacher.

     2. Teacher has student(s) add a number to the starting number.

     3. Student(s) visualizes and verbalizes the equation, sometimes air-writing, giving the answer.

   d. Addition Facts and the Imaged Number Line:

     1. Student(s) imagines own number line.

     2. Student(s) points to starting number, designated by teacher, on imaged number line.

     3. Teacher has student(s) add a number to the starting number.

     4. Student(s) visualizes and verbalizes the equation, moving finger on imaged number line.

     5. Student(s) visualizes and verbalizes the equation again, sometimes air-writing, giving the answer.

   e. Experiencing and Imaging the Doubles:

     1. Student(s) uses cubes to experience the concept of doubling

a number.

2. Student(s) verbalizes the equation.

3. Student(s) visualizes and verbalizes the equation, air-writing.

4. Student(s) sees the cubes increasing by two, one on each side.

5. Student(s) uses Doubles Cards to visualize and verbalize, committing the doubles to memory.

f. Doubles Plus One:

1. Student(s) experiences doubling with cubes.

2. Student(s) experiences doubling *plus one* with the cubes.

3. Student(s) visualizes and verbalizes the equation.

4. Student(s) computes written problems.

g. Imagery Cards and Written Computation Always!

4. Teaching Up to Twenty

a. Teach the facts from eleven through twenty with the same procedures of manipulatives, imagery, and imagery cards for memory. Use "doubles plus or minus one" and the tens for the nine combinations.

5. Math Ball Game

a. Teacher throws the math ball, saying one number in a designated number family.

b. Student(s) catches and throws/says the appropriate number back to the teacher.

c. May be played as a game with one or more students.

d. If working on the family of five, teacher says, "Here comes one," throwing the ball. Catching the ball and throwing it back, student says, "Four back to you."

e. Visualizing and verbalizing are unconsciously stimulated.

Group Instruction

As with all Lindamood-Bell programs, and all *On Cloud Nine* steps, group instruction is primarily an issue of group management and control because all of the activities can be used with large and small groups. Felt boards, chalk boards, and overhead projectors can be used to introduce number families to groups with one student setting the family, another student talking through the facts, another writing the facts, and the group or class writing in the air. The Family Fact Cards can be practiced with a group or whole class. Once the card is shown and taken away, all students can air-write, and specific students can respond to specific questions such as, "What is the second number you saw?" The Math Ball game can be played with an imaginary ball.

Summary:
Step 4

Subtraction Family Facts

> **Goal:** To develop the dual coding of imagery and language to a conscious level for understanding and memorizing the subtraction facts from one through ten.

1. **Discovering the Family Facts with the Family Fact Sheets**

   a. Student(s) explores concept and language for subtraction.

   b. Student(s) discovers with cubes, beginning with ten, the facts within the number *family.*

   c. Student(s) verbalizes and writes the equation.

   d. Student(s) discovers that adding and subtracting are twins in the same family.

   e. Student(s) discovers that adding the family facts can check subtraction.

   f. Teacher/student(s) dialogue:

      — Teacher says, "If I begin with ＿＿ and take all of them away, I have ＿＿ left."

      — Teacher says, "If I take what I have left and add it to the number I took away, I will get what I started with."

2. **Using Family Fact Cards to Visualize and Verbalize Subtraction Facts**

   a. Teacher holds up a Family Fact Card for a few seconds.

   b. Student(s) images and air-writes the numbers and signs.

   c. Teacher questions for specific numbers or signs in the equation.

   d. Student(s) begins to visualize and verbalize without air-writing.

3. **Practice Activities**

a. Imagery and Cubes Alone:

1. Student(s) places a set of cubes on the table for a specific number.

2. Student(s) demonstrates subtracting zero from the number first, then moving sequentially until subtracting the number itself.

3. Student(s) verbalizes while experiencing each equation.

4. Student(s) visualizes and verbalizes the facts, sometimes air-writing, sometimes not.

b. Imagery and the Concrete Number Line with Cubes:

1. Teacher gives student(s) an equation verbally.

2. Student(s) uses the cubes on the concrete number line to experience the equation.

3. Student(s) visualizes and verbalizes the equation, *sometimes* air-writing.

c. Imagery and the Number Line *without* Cubes:

1. Student(s) points to starting number designated by teacher.

2. Student(s) subtracts a number from the starting number, and gestures distance and direction.

3. Student(s) visualizes and verbalizes the equation, sometimes air-writing, giving the answer.

4. Student(s) notes that subtraction is going *down* the concrete number line.

d. Subtraction Facts and the Imaged Number Line:

1. Student(s) images own number line.

2. Student(s) points to starting number, designated by teacher, on imaged number line.

3. Student(s) subtracts a number from the starting number.

4. Student(s) visualizes and verbalizes the equation, moving finger to imaged number line.

5. Student(s) visualizes and verbalizes the equation again, sometimes air-writing.

e. Imagery Cards and Written Computation Always!

Group Instruction

Small or large groups can do the subtraction steps for *On Cloud Nine*, just as they did for addition. Felt boards, chalk boards, and overhead projectors enable you to present the concepts to large groups. The imagery activities can be done by all students at the same time, with specific questions asked of specific students. Again, remember that having students give thumbs up or down gives them a physical means of responding without having to speak.

Summary: Step 5

Word Problems

Goal: To be able to reason with language and math by using concept and numeral imagery to translate language into mathematical equations.

Students do the following steps to translate language to mathematical equations.

1. *Read or listen to the whole problem:*

Students read all the language, the whole problem, to know where the problem is heading. If they start solving the problem too soon, they may have an answer, but not the one the problem requests.

2. *Visualize and verbalize the gestalt:*

Students create images to match the words, then verbalize their imagery. The images are for the gestalt or the main points of the passage, and should be just enough to match without extra detail. Depending on the level of language processing of the students, the paragraph may be read in its entirety or sentence by sentence. This is the V/V program now being directly applied to word problems in math.

3. *List the math facts that are known:*

Students list the math facts that are definite on the left side of the paper under the heading, "What I Know." They need not be concerned about whether the facts are relevant—they just need to list them.

4. *List what needs to be known:*

Students list the question(s) the problem asks on the right side of the paper: "What I Need to Know."

5. *State the problem in sentence form:*

Students state the problem in their own words, orally or in writing.

6. *Convert the sentence to numbers and solve:*

Students cross out the words as they convert them to numbers. This calls attention to which words turn into which functions. For example, the words "more" and "joined" turn into addition when converted to an equation.

7. *Verify that all parts of "What I Need to Know" were answered:*

Students cross out on the right side of the paper each item they have answered.

Group Instruction

Teaching word problems to groups follows the same frame as with the one-to-one interaction presented here, but group management techniques of thumbs-up or -down are needed to keep all students involved. The concept of teams can also be helpful with groups, especially classrooms. For example, have the group begin by sharing and discussing concept images for the word problem. Perhaps begin with one student reading aloud and others describing imagery toward a shared gestalt. Have another listing the facts that are known, and another listing the facts that need to be known. Solutions can be discussed between teams and agreed upon. It is also fun to have students write word problems to match a given equation, or make a collection of word problems from events happening in their lives. This stimulates problem solving.

Summary: Step 6

Place Value

> **Goal:** To develop a concrete and imaged understanding of place value in our base-ten number system.

1. Discovering Place Value

a. Student(s) discovers the ones column using the cubes and number line, writing the numerals on paper.

b. Student(s) discovers that ten is reusing symbols, thus discovering tens column or tens place.

c. Student(s) shows on the number line various combinations of ten-stacks and cubes left over, saying and writing columns of ones/tens.

d. Student(s) uses concrete number line without cubes, saying and writing columns of ones/tens.

e. Student(s) uses imaged number line, saying and writing columns of ones/tens.

2. Discovering Hundreds, Thousands, Ten Thousands

a. Student(s) shows nine ten-stacks and nine one-cubes.

b. Teacher asks student(s) to add one more, showing how to write in columns for hundreds.

c. Student(s) writes the number and verbalizes each column.

d. Student(s) uses *imaged* number line, saying and writing columns of ones through thousands (and beyond if desired).

e. Teacher writes numbers, student verbalizes their place value.

f. Student(s) add chunks of tens, hundreds, thousands to *see* relationships.

3. Be Sure Place Value is Established in Imagery

a. Teacher calls out a number and student(s) verbalizes where it is on own imaged number line, then writes it down.

Group Instruction

As with all steps in *On Cloud Nine*, the stimulation can easily be extended to small or large groups. It is helpful to have a group or class create a running number line that is placed along one or two walls. The numbers can be shades of a single color (such as blue) and shaded in increments of ten, going as high as you choose. If the number line goes past the first one hundred, the next one hundred can be shades of a different color, in increments of ten. This way a teacher can call out a number such as one hundred forty-five and students can take turns pointing, visualizing, verbalizing, and writing.

Summary:
Step 7

Jumping

> **Goal:** To develop imagery for mental addition and subtraction using the base ten and number facts.

1. Jumping on the Number Line to the Nearest Ten with Cubes

   a. Student(s) uses the concrete number line and cubes.

   b. Teacher gives the addition or subtraction problem orally or in writing.

   c. Student(s) discovers jumping *up* to the nearest ten with the cubes and number line for addition.

   d. Student(s) verbalizes with sample dialogue while jumping *up* from one to a hundred.

   e. Student(s) begins subtraction and jumping *down* when jumping up begins to stabilize.

2. Concrete Number Line Without Cubes

   a. Student(s) uses the concrete number line and finger, without cubes.

   b. Teacher gives the addition or subtraction problem orally or in writing.

   c. Student(s) jumps *up* or *down* to the nearest ten, verbalizing action and concept of what is left over.

3. Jumping Up and Down with Imagery

   a. Student(s) uses imaged number line and imaged number facts.

   b. Teacher gives the addition or subtraction problem orally or in writing.

   c. Student(s) *mentally* jumps up or down with imagery for nearest ten and with imagery for facts, always verbalizing.

   d. Teacher introduces the use of nine as ten less one.

e. Student(s) dialogue:

Dialogue for addition:
— Student(s) says, "If I have _____, it takes _____ to get to ten. I have _____ left over to add. That gives me _____."

Dialogue for subtraction:
— Student(s) says, "If I have _____, I take _____ away to get to ten. I have _____ left over to take away. That gives me _____."

4. *Estimate:*

Student(s) estimates by checking the sign, creating an image, and comparing and computing.

5. *Use the Nine:*

Student(s) uses the number nine as one less than ten for addition or subtraction.

Group Instruction

Jumping up and down the number line can be a fun activity for a classroom or group because you can increase the size of the number line and let them actually experience jumping up and down, sort of like the Twister game from years ago. Or, you can let them see the number line on a chalkboard or an overhead projector. Call on specific students or have them work in teams to give answers using their concrete or imaged number lines.

As always, there is no change in the steps of interaction. We always look at a large or small group as one sensory system in front of us, and just adjust our language and attention to more than one person at a time. You know the students that need this the most. Call on them and help their sensory sytem image and process. Respond to their response and the lessons will be positive. Your behavior in valuing your students' responses sets the example for the rest of the class. They may begin to interact with one another in the positive, supportive manner that you modeled.

Summary: Step 8

Carrying and Borrowing

Goal: To teach the concept of carrying and borrowing through manipulatives, imagery, and language, and apply that knowledge to written computation and mental math.

1. *Overview:*

a. Use the Place Value Card and cubes to teach the concept of carrying and borrowing.

b. Verbalize and practice written addition for carrying.

c. Verbalize and practice written subtraction, using *borrow, cross, and write.*

d. If necessary, explore understanding and imagery of place value, jumping up/down with tens, and the concept of addition and subtraction with the cubes and the concrete number line.

2. Seeing the Concept of Carrying with the Place Value Card

a. Student(s) verbalizes numbers on the Place Value Card.

b. Student(s) experiences the concept of carrying with the cubes and Place Value Cards.

c. Student(s) uses the dotted square for the tenth cube as an indication that a ten is carried over.

d. Teacher sets up a number on the Place Value Card, giving the student(s) a number to add to it.

e. Student(s) uses cubes to see the concept of carrying, from tens, hundreds, and thousands.

f. Student(s) always verbalizes thinking and actions.

3. Carrying on Paper

a. Teacher sets the task as carrying on paper rather than with cubes and cards.

b. Student(s) represents a number above ten on paper, verbalizing the relationship of ones, tens, hundreds, etc.

c. Teacher presents a written addition problem well beyond the tens, in a column.

d. Student(s) always starts the computation with the ones.

e. Student(s) computes the ones, recognizing the need for carrying when *over nine in the column,* and places a little numeral in the tens column so as not to forget that ten was carried.

f. Student(s) adds the remaining column.

g. Student(s) repeats the process for adding larger numbers and carrying into the hundreds and thousands.

h. Student(s) repeats the process with a series of numbers in columns.

i. Student(s) always verbalizes thinking and actions.

j. Teacher always provides lots of daily practice on paper after discussing the process.

k. If necessary, student(s) may use number line and cubes to demonstrate problem and place value.

4. Seeing the Concept of Borrowing with the Place Value Card

a. Student(s) experiences the concept of borrowing with the cubes and Place Value Card.

b. Teacher sets up a number on the Place Value Card, giving the student(s) a number to subtract.

c. Student(s) uses cubes to see the concept of borrowing, with the tens, hundreds, and thousands.

5. Borrowing on Paper—Borrow, Cross, and Write

a. Teacher sets the task as borrowing on paper rather than with cubes and cards.

b. Teacher presents a written subtraction problem well beyond the tens, in a column.

c. Student(s) always starts the computation with the ones.

d. Student(s) computes the ones, recognizing the need for borrowing when *too little in the column.*

e. Student(s) learns to *borrow, cross,* and *write,* beginning with the tens, and extending into the hundreds and thousands.

f. Student(s) always verbalizes thinking and actions.

Group Instruction

As usual, small or large group instruction is a matter of managing the group and not changing the stimulation. Using overheads, chalkboards, teams, and the thumbs up/down approach for interaction, any size group can stay involved. Remember to use basic group management techniques, such as giving them a signal of when they can talk, when they can raise their hands, when they just think. This will help you control the group. But along with this, remember to observe your students' sensory systems. Watch for their responses, their verbalization, their attention to give you clues as to which students to call on for specific types of stimulation.

Summary: Step 9

Multiplication

Goal: To experience, visualize, and verbalize the concept of multiplication, memorize the multiplication tables through imagery, and compute written problems into two-, three-, and four-digit multiplication.

---

1. Discovering the Concept of Multiplication with Cubes and the Number Line

a. Student(s) uses cubes and concrete number line to experience concept of multiplying.

b. Student(s) gets stacks of cubes for a designated number.

c. Teacher tells student(s) to get the cubes a specific number of times, such as "get eight of the twos."

d. Student(s) places the cubes in hand and then on the number line.

e. Teacher writes out the equation for adding, such as:
$2 + 2 + 2 + 2 + 2 + 2 + 2 + 2 = 16$.

f. Teacher shows that multiplication is an easier way to add numbers and shows new sign and new equation, such as $8 \times 2 = 16$.

g. Student(s) experiences more numbers being multiplied rather than added, stacking and placing cubes on the number line.

h. Student(s) always verbalizes and writes the equations after experiencing the multiplication.

i. Student(s) visualizes equations on the imaged number line, and verifies on the concrete number line.

j. Student(s) discovers multiplying a number times one and a number times zero.

k. Teacher establishes the idea of multiplication being a simple, quick way of adding the same number.

2. **Discovering the Concept of Multiplication with Cubes and Clay**

   a. Student(s) uses cubes and clay to experience concept of multiplying, verifying answers on the number line.

   b. Student(s) gets stacks of cubes (linked together) for a designated number and flattens out a piece of clay.

   c. Teacher tells student(s) to *stamp* cubes a specific number of times.

   d. Student(s) stamps the cubes on the clay the designated number of times.

   e. Student(s) experiences numbers being multiplied by stamping stacked cubes on the clay.

   f. Student(s) always verbalizes and writes the equations after experiencing the multiplication.

   g. Student(s) visualizes equations and proves the processes on the concrete number line, or with cubes and clay.

   h. Student(s) discovers multiplying a number times one and a number times zero.

   i. Teacher establishes the idea of multiplication being a simple, quick way of adding the same number.

3. **Discovering the Multiplication Family Tables**

   a. Student(s) discovers the family *tables* up to ten with the cubes and concrete number line.

   b. Student(s) gets stacks of a designated number of cubes and experiences the tables.

   c. Student(s) verbalizes the equations.

   d. Teacher/student(s) writes the answers on the Multiplication Table Fact Sheet.

   e. Student(s) always starts with zero and increases to ten.

   f. Student(s) sees the relationship of the tables increasing by the number multiplied.

   g. The goal is for student(s) to experience, visualize, verbalize, and write each equation.

4. **Using Family Fact Cards to Memorize the Multiplication Tables**

  a. Teacher holds up a Family Fact Card for a few seconds, then takes it away.

  b. Student(s) images and air-writes the numbers and signs.

  c. Teacher questions for specific numbers or signs in the equation.

  d. Discuss the relationship of 3 x 6 and 6 x 3, etc., to reduce the anxiety related to the daunting task of imaging/memorizing lots and lots of tables.

5. **Written Computation—Start with the Ones and Work the Bottom Number**

  a. Teacher explains two principles to remember: *start with the ones* and *work the bottom number.*

  b. Teacher demonstrates the written computation and student(s) verbalizes:
  * start with the ones
  * carry to the tens
  * multiply the tens
  * add what was carried

  c. Student(s) computes and verbalizes.

6. **Multiplying Numbers into the Hundreds and Thousands Using a Place Holder**

  a. Student(s) recognizes similarity to multiplying with tens: start with ones and bottom number.

  b. Teacher explores need for *place holder* with a zero.

  c. Teacher demonstrates written computation and student(s) verbalizes.

  d. Student(s) computes and verbalizes.

7. **Estimating with Long Multiplication**

  a. Student(s) rounds numbers greater than ten to the nearest ten.

  b. Student(s) uses multiples of tens to form an estimate.

  c. Teacher gives student the answer to compare her estimate.

  d. Teacher establishes that estimating is only a means to check if an answer is close. It is not a substitute for accurate computation.

Group Instruction

When working with small groups, or a whole classroom, have designated students verbalize answers while another verifies the answer through checking on a concrete or imaged number line. All students are to respond internally to the questions asked.

The lessons are virtually the same as presented for you in one-to-one interaction, only you must carefully interpret your students' progress and interact with them appropriately.

Summary: Step 10

Division

Goal: To experience, visualize, and verbalize the concept of division and compute written problems into two-, three-, and four-digit division.

---

1. **Discovering the Concept of Division with Cubes and the Number Line**

a. Student(s) uses cubes and concrete number line to experience concept of dividing.

b. Student(s) places cubes on the number line for a designated number.

c. Teacher tells student(s) to get stacks of cubes a specific number of times, such as "get as many fives as you can out of twenty-five."

d. Student(s) gets the cubes, placing them in front of him/her.

e. Teacher writes out the equation for dividing with both signs: $25 \div 5$ and $5\overline{)25}$.

f. Student(s) experiences more division, always verbalizing and writing the equations.

g. Student(s) visualizes equations on an imaged number line, verifying on concrete number line if necessary.

h. Student(s) experiences the concept of a *remainder* with the cubes/number line.

2. **Using Clay to See the Concept of Regrouping in Division**

a. Student(s) gathers the total number of clay balls.

b. Student(s) moves the clay balls according to the number being divided by.

c. Student(s) checks how many balls are in each group.

d. Student(s) learns to write the equation while verbalizing.

3. **Computing Simple Written Division**

    a.   Teacher establishes the frame of three things to do: *divide, multiply, and subtract.*

    b.   Student(s) visualizes and estimates the multiple.

    c.   Student(s) verbalizes the process of dividing, multiplying, and subtracting.

    d.   Student(s) checks the answer with multiplication.

    e.   Student(s) may use graph paper to help keep columns aligned.

4. **Computing Long Division**

    a.   Teacher establishes the frame of four things to do: estimate, divide, multiply, subtract, bring down.

    b.   Student(s) visualizes and estimates the multiple.

    c.   Student(s) verbalizes the process of dividing, multiplying, subtracting, and bringing down.

    d.   Students(s) checks the answer with multiplication.

    e.   Student(s) may use graph paper to help keep columns aligned.

    f.   The process extends to longer and longer division, with verbalizing continuing to show thinking.

Group Instruction

All steps to develop division are applicable to group instruction. It can be helpful to have students take turns using the concrete and visualized number lines, and the steps of estimate, divide, multiply, and subtract, all the while verbalizing their thinking. For example, to divide six into thirty-four, have one student show the starting point on the number line, the next student verbalize and estimate, the next student verbalize how many groups of six can be gotten out of the estimate, the next student verbalize the multiplication, etc. Continue group management of thumbs up or down throughout the exercises.

Summary: Step 11

Decimals

Goal: To discover that the decimal point represents parts of a whole, be able to visualize and verbalize that concept, write the numbers, and add, subtract, multiply, and divide with decimals.

1. Discovering the Whole and the Decimal Point

a. Student(s) discovers a whole versus parts, using objects in the room.

b. Student(s) discovers that a number coming in front of the decimal point represents a whole number.

c. Student(s) visualizes/verbalizes, then air-writes and writes whole numbers.

d. Teacher writes whole numbers with the decimal point and student(s) verbalizes the number.

2. Discovering and Writing Tenths

a. Teacher places a transparency over the Pizza Set picture (or draws on paper) to divide a picture (pizza) into tenths.

b. Student(s) counts parts.

c. Student(s) draws objects on designated number of tenths.

d. Student(s) discovers the first place to the right of the decimal represents the tenths place.

e. Student(s) writes the designated tenths from the picture and learns to add within the tenths, writing that number in the air and on paper.

f. Teacher writes a number and has the student(s) shade in the parts to match the written number.

g. Student(s) adds or subtracts with simple decimals and the concrete picture, air-writing the equation, and then writing on paper. Carrying and borrowing can be included, depending on the level of the student.

313

3. **Discovering and Writing Hundredths**

    a. Teacher shows student how to divide tenths into hundredths, using the familiar picture (pizza).

    b. Student(s) counts how many hundredths contain a certain item, writes the number as a decimal, visualizing and verbalizing.

    c. Student(s) says and air-writes the decimal number, and verbalizes the concept it represents.

4. **Decimal Addition, Subtraction, Multiplication, and Division Computations Have Formulas to Aid Automaticity**

Adding and Subtracting:	*Line up the Points*
Multiplying:	*Count and Move*
Dividing:	*Make Whole and Move the Same*

Summary:

Step 12

Fractions

> **Goal:** To develop the conceptual background for fractions and computation skills for adding, subtracting, multiplying, and dividing fractions.

1. **Transition from Decimals to Fractions—the Parts Go Over the Whole**

   a. Student(s) experiences a picture (the Pizza Set) to see the relationship between decimals and fractions.

   b. Student(s) learns that the *parts go over the whole* in the written equation.

   c. Student(s) visualizes and verbalizes, and writes, the relationship of numbers in a fraction.

2. **Discovering and Computing Equivalent Fractions**

   a. Student(s) uses a picture of a pizza to experience equivalent fractions.

   b. Student(s) writes the number one as a fraction in various ways.

   c. Teacher demonstrates that multiplying a number by one, and multiplying a fraction by another fraction equivalent to one, is the same.

   d. Student(s) computes equivalent fractions, visualizing and verbalizing the equations.

3. **Adding and Subtracting Fractions with the Same Denominators**

   a. Student(s) discovers *only* fractions with the same denominators can be added and subtracted.

   b. Student(s) discovers a *mixed number* is a whole and parts.

   c. Student(s) discovers the need to borrow from a whole number to create enough parts.

   d. Student(s) discovers mixed numbers have to have like denominators in order to compute.

   e. Student(s) visualizes, verbalizes, and gets lots of practice computing!

4. **Computing with the Lowest Common Denominator**

  a. Student(s) uses equivalent fractions to find common denominator.

  b. Student(s) solves equations.

  c. Student(s) reduces to the lowest terms.

  d. Student(s) get lots of practice on paper!

5. **Reducing and Discovering Improper Fractions**

  a. Student(s) learns how to reduce fractions using knowledge of multiplication tables.

  b. Student(s) visualizes an improper fraction and reasons how to convert to a mixed number.

  c. Student(s) gets lots of practice.

6. **Multiplying Fractions on Paper**

  a. Teacher models computing the equation.

  b. Student(s) memorizes: *multiply numerator and denominator straight across, and reduce.*

  c. Student(s) discovers the need to convert mixed numbers to improper fractions in order to solve.

  d. Student(s) always reduces to the lowest terms.

7. **Dividing Fractions**

  a. Teacher models equation with manipulatives.

  b. Teacher presents dividing on paper.

  c. Student(s) memorizes: *invert and multiply* for computation process on paper.

  d. Student(s) converts to mixed fractions and reduces.

  e. Student(s) verbalizes his/her thinking through computation, and gets lots of practice on paper.

Group Instruction

Small or large groups, or whole classrooms can interact with you on fractions. Follow the same frame as presented above, but view each student as an individual sensory-system for your questions. You can show problems on the chalkboard or overhead projector, or you can have students take turns verbalizing through problems, or you can have students take turns air-writing problems or reciting some of the memory necessary to quickly compute with fractions.

On Cloud Nine Math Ladder

Student Name: _____

12	Fractions
11	Decimals
10	Division
9	Multiplication
8	Carrying and Borrowing
7	Jumping
6	Place Value
5	Word Problems
4	Subtraction Family Facts
3	Addition Family Facts
2	Imaging the Number Line
1	Imaging Numerals

On Cloud Nine
Fractions Stepladder

Student Name: _____

10 **Dividing Fractions**

9 **Multiplying Fractions**

8 *Improper Fractions*

7 *Reducing Fractions*

6 *Lowest Common Denominator*

5 *Mixed Numbers*

4 **Subtracting Fractions**

3 **Adding Fractions**

2 *Equivalent Fractions*

1 **What is a Fraction?**

The Bibliography

Arnheim, R. (1966). Image and thought. In Kepes, G. (Ed.). *Sign, image, symbol.* New York: George Braziller, Inc.

Bell, N. (1991). Gestalt imagery: a critical factor in language comprehension. *Annals of Dyslexia, 41,* 246-260.

Bell, N. (1991). *Visualizing and verbalizing for language comprehension and thinking.* San Luis Obispo, CA: Gander Publishing.

Bell, N. (1997). *Seeing stars.* San Luis Obispo, CA: Gander Publishing.

Dehaen, S. Ecole des hautes etudes en scences socials, Paris (Doctoral dissertation).

Galton, F. (1880). *Nature,* 1880.

Kline, M. (1967). *Mathematics for the nonmathematician.* Reading, MA: Addison-Wesley.

Kosslyn, S. M. (1983). *Ghosts in the mind's machine.* New York: W.W. Norton.

Kunzig, R. (1997). A head for numbers. *Discover the World of Science.* July 1997, Vol. 18 No. 7: 108-115.

Levin, J.R. (1973). Inducing comprehension in poor readers. *Journal of Educational Psychology.* 65: 19-24.

Levin, J.R. (1981). On functions of pictures in prose. F. Pirozzolo & M. Wittrock (Ed.). *Neuropsychological and Cognitive Processes in Reading.* New York: Academic Press.

National Council of Teachers of Mathematics. (1989). *Curriculum and Evaluation of Standards of School Mathematics.* Reston: National Council of Teachers of Mathematics.

Marks, D.F. (1972). Vividness of visual imagery and effect on function. P. Sheehan (Ed.). *The Function and Nature of Imagery.* New York: Academ Press.

Moore, D. S. (1990). On the shoulders of giants: New approaches to numeracy. L. Steen (Ed.), *Uncertainty* (pp. 95-137). Washington, DC: National Academy Press.

Moyer, R., & Landauer, T. *Nature*, 1967.

Paivio, A. (1971). *Imagery and verbal processes*. New York: Holt, Rinehart, and Winston. Reprinted (1979). Hillsdale, NJ: Lawrence Erlbaum Associates.

Paivio, A. (1986). *Mental representations: A dual coding approach*. New York: Oxford University Press.

Papert, S. (1993). *The children's machine: Rethinking school in the age of the computer*. New York: Basic Books.

Peters, E.E., and Levin, J.R. (1986). Effects of a mnemonic imagery strategy on good and poor readers' prose recall. *Reading Research Quarterly*, 21: 179-192.

Pressley, G.M. (1976). Mental imagery helps eight-year-olds remember what they read. *Journal of Educational Psychology*, 69: 355-359.

Pribram, K. (1971). *Languages of the brain: Experimental paradoxes and principles in neuropsychology*. New York: Brandon House, Inc.

Richardson, A. (1969). *Mental imagery*. London: Routledge & Kegan, P.

Sadoski, M. (1983). An exploratory study of relationships between reported imagery and the comprehension and recall of a story. *Reading Research Quarterly*. 19 (1), 110-123.

Sheehan, P.W. (Ed.). (1972). *The function of nature of imagery*. New York: Academic Press.

Sorabji, R. (1972). *Aristotle on memory*. Providence, RI: Brown University Press.

Stemmler, A. (1969). Reading of highly creative versus highly intelligent secondary students. *Reading and Realism.* 13: 821-831.

Stern, C. and Stern, M. B. (1971). *Children discover arithmetic.* New York: Harper & Row, Publishers, Inc.

Tierney, R.J. and Cunningham, J.W. (1984). Research on teaching reading comprehension. In Pearson, P.D. (Ed.). *Handbook of Reading Research* (pp. 565-609). New York: Longman.